The Digital Money Reader 2008

Other books in the Reader series:

Digital Money Reader, 2006

Digital Identity Reader, 2007

Other books by David Birch:

Digital Identity Management

The Digital Money Reader 2008

A selection of posts from the Digital Money Forum Blog from 2007/2008

By David G.W. Birch

www.mastodonpress.com

Published in the United Kingdom in 2008 by:

Mastodon Press

Unit 9, 68 Shepherds Hill

London, N6 5RL.

© 2008 David G.W. Birch.

David G.W. Birch has asserted his right under the Copyright, Designs and Patents Act 1988, to be identified as the author of this work.

All rights reserved. No part of this book may be reprinted or reproduced or utilised in any form or by any electronic, mechanical or other means, now known or hereafter invented without permission in writing from the publishers.

Paperback

ISBN: 978-0-9557390-1-9

Printed in the UK by CPI William Clowes Ltd, Beccles, NR34 7TL.

Preface

It is a year since the experiment of the first Digital Money Forum "blook". I could not possibly have known how popular it would be! This is not simply because the subject has continued to evolve and fascinate -- the world of retail electronic payments is becoming more complicated as time goes by, with more players, technologies and opportunities -- but also because it looks as if the blook is the perfect business book form for public transport:. With no narrative structure, people enjoy dipping in and out when they have a few minutes and the blogging style that I happened across seems to work well in that environment. Bringing the subject and form together has definitely delivered more than the sum of the parts.

The constructive criticism that I received for the first Digital Money Reader was most welcome and in this year's Reader you will find a much more detailed index, a glossary and a tighter layout. The Reader is also bigger, and includes considerably more posts than before because of the good feedback we received on the similarly-sized Digital Identity Reader.

This Reader collects together blog posts to the end of February 2008. All posts are mine unless otherwise stated. I hope that once you've read the blook, you'll want to get involved in the discussion, so please drop by the blog at http://www.digitalmoneyforum.com/blog/ to read the latest posts (often with erudite and fascinating comments) and to listen to our series of podcasts (available on the Consult Hyperion website at http://www.chyp.com/podcasts/).

Dave Birch, March 2008.

You can contact Consult Hyperion at:

Consult Hyperion
Tweed House,
12 The Mount,
Guildford,
Surrey,
GU2 4HN,
England.

Telephone: +44 (0) 1483 301 793
Fax: +44 (0) 1483 561 657

info@chyp.com
http://www.chyp.com

All trademarks and registered marks used within this book are duly acknowledged to their owners.

Contents

PREFACE 5

CONTENTS 7

ABOUT THE AUTHOR: 9

PART 1 – THE TECHNOLOGY AXIS 11
    CHAPTER 1: MOBILE 12
    CHAPTER 2: CONTACTLESS 32
    CHAPTER 3: OTHER TECHNOLOGIES 48

PART 2 – THE BUSINESS AXIS 59
    CHAPTER 4: BANKING AND CREDIT 60
    CHAPTER 5: RETAIL AND WHOLESALE 81
    CHAPTER 6: REAL AND VIRTUAL 93
    CHAPTER 7: DEVELOPING MARKETS 108

PART 3 – THE SOCIAL AXIS 126
    CHAPTER 8: THE WAR ON CASH 127
    CHAPTER 9: LEGAL AND REGULATORY 152
    CHAPTER 10: FRAUD 171
    CHAPTER 11: HISTORY AND PERSPECTIVES 191

GLOSSARY 205

INDEX 214

About the author:

David Birch is a director of Consult Hyperion, which he helped to found in 1986. Prior to this he spent several years working as a consultant in Europe, the Far East and North America. He graduated from the University of Southampton with a B.Sc. (Hons.) in Physics. Described by *The Independent* newspaper as a 'grade-A geek', by the Centre for the Study of Financial Innovation as 'one of the most user-friendly of the UK's über-techies' and by *Financial World* as "mad" (but also "an expert, engaging and witty writer"), Dave is well-known as a writer and speaker.

He is a member of the editorial board of the *E-Finance & Payments Law and Policy Journal*, a columnist for *SPEED* and UK correspondent to the *Journal of Internet Banking and Commerce*. He has lectured to MBA level on the impact of new information and communications technologies, contributed to publications ranging from the *Parliamentary IT Review* to *Prospect* and wrote more than 100 *Second Sight* columns for *The Guardian*. He is a media commentator on electronic business issues and has appeared on BBC television and radio, Sky and other channels around the world.

He edited *Digital Identity Management* (Gower: May 2007).

Acknowledgements

This blook was only made possible by the hard work of Katie Facey and James Sellwood at Consult Hyperion. All I did was to suggest the posts to be included: everything else is down to those guys and I can't thank them enough.

Part 1 – The Technology Axis

Chapter 1: Mobile

Mobile phones offer things that cards do not: keyboards, screens, power and above all connectivity. With mobile payment schemes up and running around the world and near-field communication entering the market, there's plenty to discuss. This collection of posts looks at mobile payments and covers topics like whether they really are the future and what lessons can be learned from services already in place.

Party like its 1999, part 2 [29/01/2007]

Ah, mobile payments. What could be simpler than a system like *Feed Tribes*? Consumers sign up through the company's website, establishing an account that's linked to a bank account. When customers are ready to pay at a participating retailer, they punch a PIN number into a text message and send it to the Feed Tribes SMS short code. They get back a code that's good for 15 minutes. Then the customer gives that code to the cashier, who enters it into a machine at the point-of-sale (POS) terminal. This sounds (to me) remarkably similar to all the other pay-by-text services that didn't work in Europe a decade ago. I'm sure that Feed Tribes really believe that their payment method is not only convenient for consumers, but also allows merchants to have a closer marketing relationship with their customers. But it isn't convenient, and there are better ways to build a relationship with customers.

Look at what our good friends at Eagle Eye are doing with ITV in the UK. Here's how it works:

- The consumer views a commercial on ITV that contains a promotional offer.
- The consumer texts in to advertised number to receive a promotional coupon.
- The consumer receives an SMS mobile coupon from the ITV/EES system that contains a message and an 8 digit unique code.
- The consumer takes mobile phone into retailer and makes purchase.
- When prompted, the consumer types an 8 digit code into the EPOS or chip and PIN terminal to redeem the offer.
- The promotional data is provided instantly to brands/retailers for tracking/CRM.

Isn't this a more worthwhile attempt to harness SMS at retail?

I wonder if mobile phones will really catch on? [11/04/2007]

Yet more mobile money launches. *KushCash* is one, another is AT&T. They are planning a "single front door" format for full service mobile banking. Apparently this means that banking will work the same way as e-mail and instant-messaging services, where AT&T provides a user interface that offers access to a number of different Internet service providers. So instead of a number of applications from different banks having to be tested, configured and so on, there will just be one AT&T banking application and it can connect to multiple banks. An AT&T person said that although banks might be reluctant to put their brand and services up next to those of competitors, the single interface would help prevent market fragmentation. I'm still not sure if I would want to use this kind of application, but then I'm probably not the target market because I'm happy banking on the web. What's important is, as Hannes van Rensburg says, that mobile banking is enabling people who never had access to electronic banking before. Internet banking enabled people to access their banking electronically only if they had been banked before, whereas mobile banking is leading to a revolution where people are being banked who never had a banking relationship in the past. This is largely because of the utility and functionality that is now being made available to people with mobile phones (a much greater number than those with access to the Internet).

I was looking for an old paper for reasons not germane to this particular subject and I came across the proceedings of "Mobile Phones and Electronic Commerce" organised by IBC in September 1997. It was mildly interesting to flick through the presentations ten years on, particularly the stuff about the Cellnet / Barclaycard phone. There were some quotes about it selling 20,000 handsets in 6 weeks. I believe the figures because they came from Tom Alexander. We were working for Tom at the time, doing some feasibility work on electronic payments. I don't recall the ins and outs, but I do remember that the Mondex e-purse was a focus of particular interest, but it came up against a brick wall: you couldn't just put Mondex purses into the SIMs; you had to get a bank to issue them. And none of them would: I expect they were waiting see whether this mobile phone thing would catch on or not. Tom was always very forward-looking: he eventually left Cellnet to set up Virgin Mobile, the first UK mobile virtual network operator (MVNO). Needless to say, he doesn't have to work anymore.

The Cellnet "blue button" Barclaycard phone later morphed into the two-slot phone (a Motorola Startac) that you could put your chip (UKIS) Barclaycard into and, much more importantly, worked with *VisaCash*. I always loved the logical purity of the two-slot phones and I was very disappointed when they faded away. But now they're back! Instead of a slot, they have NFC (near-field communication), but the ideas (and the benefits) are the same: let the telco do telco stuff, let the bank do card stuff. Of course, the card is going to disappear inside the phone soon, but it will still be the banks' application.

I wonder if the first contactless prepaid debit product will be launched on commercially-available NFC handsets in the UK by 22nd September 2007 (hint: no). If it is, then it will only be 10 years after the delegates at this conference were discussing such a thing. A nice piece from Kevin Duffey, then at Logica, about a vision of a phone with all of the functionality of an ATM (including e-cash withdrawal) being launched within 18 months. In the end, it's taken nearly a decade to get the UK banks on board with this -- *MoniLink* started in 2006 -- and we still don't have e-cash but it is, at last, in sight.

Japanese lessons [25/04/2007]

I'm back looking at Japan again, but this time thinking about the non-bank entrants to the payment space, other than DoCoMo of course. There was a detailed story in *Card Technology* covering the transit side of things. Mobile *Suica*, the mobile version of the JR East Suica transit card, has got off to a slow start. There are 19 million of the contactless transit cards in circulation but after its first year only 350,000 people signed up for the mobile version. In addition to the mobile implementation, JR East has started to extend the e-purse usage to retailer, but there are only 10,000 POS locations in Tokyo where it can be used. Not for long, though, because JR East, DoCoMo, JCB and bitWallet have announced that they have agreed to share a common platform so that all of the payment brands (Suica, *iD*, *QUICPay* and *Edy*) will work in the same POS. There are currently about 100,000 contactless POS terminals in Japan.

Why the slow take up? Akio Shiibashi, director of the Suica Systems Department at JR East is quoted saying that the registration process has been "difficult" for many prospective users. Sounds like a common problem for "traditional" business moving into the mobile space: a generation accustomed to instant messaging and interactivity colliding with multi-page application forms and postal services.

According to the Card Technology article, DoCoMo now has 2.6 million contactless credit customers, although transaction rates are still low, plus some 4 or 5 million contactless e-purse users (i.e., people who have activated the purse). In total, DoCoMo has sold some 30 million phones with contactless interfaces so far and are on target for 40 million by March 2008. They've just introduced their new premium *DCMX GOLD* credit card. Like the regular card, it is compatible with iD mobile platform and customers will be issued a standard Visa or MasterCard stripe card for use overseas or at shops in Japan that do not have contactless terminals. And it has a reward programme as well.

If there has been a slow start (and 2.6 million customers in such a short time doesn't sound particularly slow) it isn't putting other people off: the Seven & I Holdings Co. have just started electronic payment services called *nanaco* at some 1,500 Seven-Eleven convenience stores in Tokyo. This is more interesting than "yet another e-purse", because they're the first Japanese retailer to issue e-money. The company will gradually expand the number of stores where the e-money can be used. At the end of May, the electronic payment services will be available at all 11,800 Seven-Eleven stores in Japan

So now there are banks, mobile operators, a transit operator and a retailer competing to provide e-money. No wonder we're fascinated by developments there.

Phones are better than cards [01/05/2007]

The Visa USA President John Philip Coghlan has said that wallet phones are "inevitable". And he's right, as I have consistently insisted. As a mechanism for retail payment, mobile phones have it over plastic cards: a card is merely a receptacle for the consumer's data, whereas a phone can initiate a payment or accept one, can act as a channel for the customer and can manage payment-related data. Bob Egan, Research Director for Emerging Technologies at TowerGroup (which is owned by MasterCard Worldwide) says that m-payments "will do for debit and credit card transactions what the iPod did for music": I think he means that they will make credit and debit card transactions available to all and easy to use rather than they will make credit and debit cards proprietary, under the distribution control of a third-party and unusable by older persons.

There's still a lot to be done. For a start, a mass-market payment product must be managed across its entire lifecycle: installation and personalisation; updates such as account expiry; deletion of the application from the phone; and moving the payment application to a new mobile phone. The operator vision -- whereby the application management is SIM-centric -- appears to have won for the time being.

The card brands are moving ahead now. In the US Visa, MasterCard and Discover have launched trials. Visa is encouraging banks and telecoms to start trials by debuting a mobile payment platform created just for launching pilots. Pam Zuercher, Visa's Vice President of Product Innovation, says that consumers want a single device "that can get them through their day". That's not a plastic card: it's a mobile phone, which customers prefer for accessing e-mail, text messaging, listening to music, surfing the Internet and just about everything else. A mobile phone enabled with NFC will have the capability to enhance all of these complementary uses, like card account management, coupon delivery, authentication and ticketing.

Ticketing is one of the most important applications from a payments perspective, because of the critical role of ticketing in driving "top of wallet". Now, Deutsche Bahn and Vodafone plan to launch one of the new services, called *Touch & Travel* in Germany. Passengers touch tags, called "touchpoints", when they board or leave the train or bus stops. The locations are registered and the phone sends the data over the network. The system then calculates the fare and bills the passenger at the end of the month. The application is, naturally, stored on the SIM card.

Wallet phones are, indeed, inevitable. But is the SIM the inevitable pivot? Bouygues says it is not essential for the payment or other applications to be stored on the SIM, at least not for the foreseeable future. Separate secure chips embedded in the handsets or in flash memory cards inserted into the phones could store the applications. So a new open approach to NFC? No. What Bouygues are saying is basically that the SIM could store code that grants rights for those applications to be downloaded to the phone or authorization to run the applications while the applications need not be stored on the SIM. As we've been saying in a number of workshops with our clients recently, this is the rather obvious architecture for the next phase of the mobile payment evolution until the "Release 7" SIMs with high-speed USB interfaces arrive.

Phone alone [23/05/2007]

Well, it finally happened. After sitting through literally innumerable conference presentations where someone from a telco refers to some spurious statistic about the typical person being more likely to forget their wallet than their phone, I forgot my wallet **again**. Perhaps this is an age related disorder. I filled the car up with petrol and when I wandered in to pay I realised that I'd left my wallet at home. Aargh! I did have my phone, but sadly the UK is one of those backward countries where you can't use your phone at point-of-sale.

As it happens, it didn't really matter. I filled out a form -- this being modern Britain, me and the car (and more particularly its registration) had already been captured on CCTV -- so I just had to sign a form to promise to pay and then I drove home and got my credit cards. As a testament to the inherent goodness of mankind (at least in Weybridge), I was looking so embarrassed that the guy behind me even offered to pay for me: he saw I had some business cards that I'd taken out of my pocket while searching for money and said that if I gave him a card then I could just post him a cheque.

This incident has had me thinking since the weekend, because it links identity, authentication and payment in such interesting ways.

Now this is what I call mobile payment strategy [28/05/2007]

Who can't help be fascinated by Japan. DoCoMo started bringing mobile and contactless together sometime ago -- they've sold 30 million or so phones with Sony's *FeliCa* chip in them -- and use them to provide a mobile purse (Edy). Then they wanted to offer a credit product, but you have to be a bank to offer credit. So they bought a bank and began offering the *DCMX* credit "card" alongside the purse. Now they apparently want to accelerate retail acceptance of mobile payments, so they're buying into a retail chain, FamilyMart. Currently, only 140 out of their 7,000 stores accept mobile payments. But from July 10, FamilyMart convenience stores nationwide will begin accepting mobile credit via DoCoMo's iD platform, thereby enabling users to make payments simply by waving their phones over a reader/writer. So instead of whining about retailers, arguing about fees or trying advertising or whatever, DoCoMo have decided to spend their money in a more effective way to get all 7,000 on board: invest in the retailer.

This is not the only retail e-money fun in Japan right now. A few days ago, Seven-Eleven there launched their nanaco e-money service. It started rather well: an estimated 100,000 applications were filed on the first day for nanaco cards. The service is currently available at about 1,500 Seven-Eleven convenience stores in Tokyo, with plans to expand to 11,700 stores around the country in May and 1,800 Ito-Yokado supermarkets and 586 Denny's restaurants starting in autumn. It is available in two form factors, a smart card and a mobile phone. They're hoping to do a deal with JCB to introduce e-money payment with nanaco cards by the spring of 2009, expecting that more than 60,000 stores will accept the card. I'm sure they'll make it. In Japan, e-money is not in the least futuristic. Look at some of the results from this April 2007 survey in Tokyo and surrounding prefectures...

Q2: Which of the following electronic cash services do you know about? (Sample size=1,030, multiple answer)

- Suica, Mobile Suica 92.9%
- Edy 85.8%
- *PASMO* 84.8%
- iD/DCMX 31.1%

- QUICPay 21.4%
- *Smartplus* 7.7%
- *Visa Touch* 7.5%
- Other 0.4%
- Don't know any electronic money services 3.3%

Less than 1 in 30 people don't know about e-money.

Only 8% of people surveyed use e-money less than once a month. Check it out on *What Japan Thinks*[1] for more details.

Is mobile the new smartcard? [29/06/2007]

The Chicago Federal Reserve published an interesting letter asking whether mobile is the new smart card by which they mean, in an American context, will mobile payments flare and then die away. They agree with me (!) that mobile holds a significant advantage over contactless cards in the area of paperless two-way communication. Cards just do not allow for the sending, receiving, and presenting of information, as mobile devices do. These are clearly factors that point to mobile beginning to encroach on cards territory. They are already are in some places. France, for example, where Orange has announced that it will launch the first mobile contactless services, based on NFC technology, in Bordeaux in early 2008. And in the US, where Wells Fargo and Visa are to conduct a public mobile payments trial with up to 500 customers in the fourth quarter of the year. So is mobile the new smart card: i.e., a new payment technology that starts in France and then spreads worldwide except for the US, finally sneaking in to the US under the guise of contactless? Well, I guess, the answer must be yes!

Note that Orange have said that they are preparing similar launches in its other European markets. But retailers still have some questions despite being enthusiastic. Marina O'Rourke, the director of retail technology at the Subway restaurant chain, says that as the mobile phone becomes more ubiquitous, there are many opportunities for retailers to use the technology to market products to customers. She means things like using a phone's GPS to locate a Subway shop, send

---

[1] http://whatjapanthinks.com/2007/05/20/electronic-cash-usage-part-1-of-2/

an order via text message to the store and then going to pick it up, paying (of course) with the phone. She also says that Subway is in the early stages of piloting some different options for mobile. This kind of vision will, I think, become commonplace more quickly than many anticipate. Many other observers (i.e., not just people like me who are obsessed with mobile NFC) think that ultimately may drive acceptance of contactless technology with consumers and retailers is its integration with mobile phones.

Javelin have just come out with a similar perspective, saying that adding contactless to consumer mobile devices will replace payments cards and will spur 30 million additional users over the next 5 years. The numbers are starting get pretty serious.

Stickers are the future, I'm telling you [09/07/2007]

Well, that's what someone said to me in Portugal a couple of weeks ago. I'd mentioned the story about how a bank and operator in China are launching something which Card Technology oddly called the first commercial project putting contactless stickers on the back of mobile phones but sounds rather like -- in fact, exactly like -- the *Dexit* scheme in Toronto. Anyway, Chongqing Commercial Bank began issuing cards with the contactless *Pay Ease* e-purse onboard earlier this month. Chongqing Mobile, a branch of China Mobile, will distribute the contactless stickers with the same Pay Ease purse on them for sticking to the back of the subscribers' handsets. Several hundred merchant locations in Chongqing are already accepting the scheme: coffee shops, restaurants, beauty shops and cinemas. Cardholders will be able to reload the purse -- using either the bank card or the telco sticker -- at bank branches, putting up to 1,000 yuan (US$131) on it. Predictably, and rather confirming last week's comments about contactless as a step on a mobile roadmap, Chongqing Mobile is considering moving to NFC phones when the handsets hit the market, probably next year sometime.

We've been playing around with some plastic, self-adhesive, branded stickers on a couple of the projects we're involved in and I have to say I'm enthusiastic about the possibilities in general, but I've been think about them in this particular context of delivering limited services to consumers via phone-mounted stickers as a way on engaging consumers, and trialling consumer services, in advance of full NFC deployment or mass market rollout. The advantages are obvious, and with a little intelligent back-end integration -- so that someone, somewhere can (with informed consent) associate the sticker with a phone number or person -- can deliver some great services. Low-value payment, yes, but also loyalty and so forth. Most importantly, it's a simple and inexpensive way of piggybacking on the mobile without have to actually integrate anything into the phone, which I predict will bring some new and innovative solutions into the space.

Turkish delights [20/10/2007]

I've been in Istanbul working for a customer in the telecommunications field. As always, I've really enjoyed it. I love coming to Istanbul because it's a dynamic place. There's a lot going on and people are always trying to launch new products and services. Right now, it's a really great living case study of the co-evolution of banks and telecommunications operators because of the early adoption of contactless payment technology in Turkey.

Garanti Bank began issuing *PayPass* cards last year. They issued the US version of PayPass rather than the non-US (i.e., EMV) version because they wanted to get it off the ground quickly, I imagine. This means that all the transactions have to be online, which has (I would have thought) limited its uptake in some applications. Nonetheless, they've already issued 40,000 cards and have already signed up 1,600 merchants (primarily in and around Istanbul). I was looking for one of the terminals so that I could try it out using my new UK-issued Visa contactless card and post an encouraging message about standards and interoperability, but I couldn't find one.

I did, as an aside, conduct just such an interoperability test at RBS HQ the other day: I am pleased to report that my Barclays Visa *OnePulse* worked flawlessly in the RBS terminals. More interestingly, so did a phone that I'd loaded a payment card into as well: I didn't say anything to the guy serving me at the Starbucks, I just waved the phone over the terminal. The terminal beeped and the guy immediately said "That's really smart. Where can I get one?".

Anyway, Garanti then moved on to issue a few thousand self-adhesive stickers, a quarter the size of regular PayPass cards, that customers can stick on their phones and then they can make contactless payments using their handsets but without having to wait for the NFC phones that we're always going on about. Now, I know from our experience with a sticker-payment pilot here in the UK that you have to choose the stickers very carefully. In particular, you need stickers that have electromagnetic shielding so that the phone doesn't stop them from working. Garanti found (as we have, and so have others) that with the right stickers it all works rather well and (despite the fact that the sticker antenna is much smaller than a regular card antenna) there's no need to change the POS terminals.

Why did they do this? Well, Mehmet Seazgin, the head of payment systems at Garanti Bank sets the tactic in context:

"Since we came up with this sticker idea, which works with all operators and brands of handsets, that gave us a whole new negotiation power with the network operators."

The negotiation that he is referring to is about NFC. In essence, Garanti didn't want to cave into the mobile operators and put the application on the SIM. But in the end they knew that they would have to cave, so they wanted the best hand possible before they sat down with the operators. Stickers gave it to them.

Now they are going to take part in an NFC pilot with mobile operator Turkcell under the auspices of the GSM Association's *Pay-Buy Mobile* initiative announced last February. Since the GSMA represents hundreds of operators worldwide, the architecture that they are developing -- which is SIM-based -- is something that banks will have to learn to live with.

Pride in battle [05/11/2007]

Excellent, another excuse to mention the brightest star in the heavens that is the world of association football. Manchester City "might" extend their farsighted experiment with NFC phones from simple entry through turnstiles to enabling fans to buy food and other goods at half time, as well as making it easy to offer loyalty discounts to regular match-goers. Fans will be able to swipe their mobile phone at dedicated terminals or readers to make payments, in the same way that contactless cards are already being used for payments and in other contexts, like travel. Forum friend Duncan Martin, head of retail for The Blues, highlights one of the key advantages retailers get by persuading customers to use contactless payment technology instead of cash:

"By linking this technology to our customer database, we will use this trial data to analyse customer demand, create more targeted campaigns for our most loyal fans

and tackle wider issues such as ticket touting and crowd security. The net result will be a much richer matchday experience."

This illustrates a general point: shifting from cash to "cards" ought to provide merchants with valuable information. Incidentally, I read today that revised forecasts from Juniper Research now predict 52 million consumers will adopt new mobile technologies such as NFC and other physical mobile payment methods to pay for everyday goods and services by 2011. They also estimate that by 2011, around 12% of the total mobile phones in circulation will offer support for NFC payments (nearly half-a-billion handsets worldwide).

These revised forecasts also serve to remind us that the battle between banks and mobile operators is far from over. They'd been out playing football between the trenches recently, but the operators came out all guns blazing at a US event about mobile marketing. Chris Black, a director at AT&T Mobility, said with admirable clarity:

"I think as a carrier we have always taken the approach that we add a significant portion of value to the whole [mobile marketing] process... We are going to do whatever it takes to hold onto that value when it comes to things like mobile banking and mobile marketing."

I can understand that point of view, because the alternative is to accept that you are basically just a pipe, a utility carrier of bits. Now this may well actually be true in the long run, but if I were an operator I'd do my best to stave the day off as long as possible, perhaps by reconstituting myself as a utility provider of services rather than raw bits. By services, in this case, I naturally mean component digital money and digital identity services rather than the branded payment and authentication services that will be used by consumers and businesses. So, the operator provides the PKI, the brands provide the virtual identities.

The title of the post, by the way? Manchester City's Latin motto: superbia in proelio.

Mobile, business cases, that sort of thing [04/12/2007]

In the last few days, two of the UK's biggest banks have announced mobile payment projects. Barclays Bank, O2 and Transport for London have announced a combined payment/transit pilot in London and RBS and MasterCard have announced a mobile debit card trial in

London and Edinburgh. Still, just because lots of people are going nuts about a new payment technology doesn't make them right. Payments is a notoriously conservative "marketplace", where custom, practice and network externalities act to constrain innovation. Therefore, we must be very careful about predicting success. After all, who was the savant quoted in *Wired magazine* in December 1994 in this paragraph:

> "[Mondex] creators envision the system spreading worldwide, as people slip their smart cards into special phones and wallets to conduct cash-like, tamper-proof transactions, even across borders. 'It will become ubiquitous - it's the cheapest way of moving money around.'"

Me, of course. I'd become very excited by the link between electronic money, smart cards and phones and a few back-of-the-envelope calculations had convinced me that since people all had phones and since smart cards were very cheap, the fact that telecommunications costs were going to fall would mean that no-one in their right mind would use any other technology for payments. Still, there's no harm in making mistakes, provided that you learn from them.

It is obviously difficult to construct worthwhile business models and ROI (return-on-investments) calculations around disruptive technology and part of the problem is that people tend to look forward in terms of the existing business. This is why it's easy to dip into any book on the history of technology and find no end of quotes underestimating the potential of a new technology (which is what I did when writing this post).

> *"There will never be a mass market for motor cars -- about 1,000 in Europe -- because that is the limit on the number of chauffeurs available!"* -- Gottlieb Daimler, inventor of the gasoline-powered automobile, 1889"

I was recently quoted by Deloitte, in a report on mobile payments called "Reversing the Charges", as agreeing with the head of Visa USA. He had said that mobile payments were inevitable and I thought (and still think) he was right. But Deloitte are not so sure. Louise Brett, their head of UK Customer and Channel Strategy, writes that

> "...our research suggests that the substantial and growing investment in mobile POS payments is misjudged, at least in the United Kingdom."

I thought it would be interesting to both air and play with these different perspectives. Barclays and RBS presumably do not see their investment as misjudged. Perhaps the apparent disconnect between the Deloitte and banks' perspectives are in some way linked to the way that innovation is accounted for. As has often been discussed here, it is very difficult for incumbents to invest in anything other than core business: this is why BT didn't invent Skype, Wells Fargo didn't invent *PayPal* and Sears didn't invent eBay. And, more relevantly I suppose, it's why banks didn't invent payment cards or ATMs. What banks did do is waited until someone else had invented them and then drew the technology into mass market financial services. Why would NFC-equipped mobiles follow any different trajectory?

More to the point, what trajectory might they follow if banks don't get involved? Perhaps mobile phones are so different from previous technology waves eventually embraced by banks (e.g., the web) that not being involved is a dangerous strategy, akin to record companies deciding not to support music downloading because they (genuinely) couldn't see how to make money from it. But they had made the mistake of trying to do the spreadsheet on their existing business model, with only the distribution technology changing. Other people (e.g., Prince and Madonna) were meanwhile looking at new business models, and they've turned out to be on the right track.

"Remote shopping, while entirely feasible, will flop - because women like to get out of the house, like to handle merchandise, like to be able to change their minds. TIME magazine (1966)."

It's not just me and the head of Visa USA who are on this particular bandwagon. The GSM Association has announced that, over the next several months, 12 mobile operators will run trials of contactless mobile payment services in Australia, France, Ireland, Korea, Malaysia, Norway, The Philippines, Singapore, Taiwan, Turkey and the US as a precursor to commercial launches. They seem confident that the services will gain traction. Two-thirds of the 2,574 consumers in 17 countries that they surveyed said they expect to begin using their mobile phone to pay at point of sale within two years of the service becoming available. It's not all about what is convenient for the customers, though, and half of the 240 merchants from 10 countries surveyed said that they see "promotional opportunities" in using the mobile phone as a payment device. So it's not all about payments, either. Simply taking the contactless payment applications and putting them in phones instead of in cards is not enough. We need to use the phone environment as a means to add significant value around the phone at POS.

"The Americans have need of the telephone, but we do not. We have plenty of messenger boys. Sir William Preece, Chief Engineer, British Post Office (1878)."

Now, naturally, Deloitte are entirely right to point out that the money to pay for the new infrastructure must come from somewhere and they are equally right to point out that for technologists to expect banks to pay simply to "impress" their customers is crazy. It's the operators who select, order and subsidise the mobile handsets, so they must be persuaded that they will gain revenue from creating (a quite complex) NFC infrastructure for application management and use. That revenue is unlikely to come from:

- Retailers volunteering to pay higher fees. Or, at least, higher fees for the same service (more on this later).

- Banks volunteering to hand over a slice of transaction fees (the margins are too thin, as we very accurately predicted back in the days of *Simpay*).

- Processors volunteering to forego a portion of their fee. We work for a processor in this field at the moment and I can assure you that nothing is further from their mind (or business plan).

- Customers paying a premium to use the mobile wallet. Again, I hate to agree with Deloitte so publicly, but there's no chance of charging customers for a payment mechanism when all the other mechanisms are free. That's not to say, however, that you may not be able to charge customers for some new services around the mobile wallet.

So in the digital money corner, we think mobile payments are cool, we want operators to get the phones out there, but we know that banks don't want to pay more for payment infrastructure. And Deloitte show clearly in their report that there's not enough margin in card transactions to provide a living for another player: their figures indicate that in a typical credit card transaction there might be a penny available to pay for the mobile operator, handset subsidy and so on. That's not enough.

"The wireless music box has no imaginable commercial value. Who would pay for a message sent to no one in particular? Associates of David Sarnoff responding to the latter's call for investment in the radio in 1921"

But this kind of analysis assumes that a mobile phone is a substitute for a payment card and that bank-issued payment "cards" are the only reason why mobile operators would sell phones with NFC and that transactions are the only source of income. This combination seems unlikely. A consumer is not terribly likely to go into a shop and buy an NFC phone because they can put their Visa card in it (although they might because they can put their *Oyster* card in it). Consumers will want NFC because of service discovery (the whole smart poster/tag thing is going to be huge), zero-configuration data exchange (no more sodding about pairing your Bluetooth headset: just touch it to your mobile and hey presto!) and as-yet-un-invented person-to-person (P2P) services (we touch our phones together in the nightclub -- romantically, of course -- and thereby swap contact details)

The service discovery aspect is probably the one to generate the short term revenue for the operator. A great many consumers don't use data services (other than text) on their phones. It's just too much hassle to figure out how to type in URLs and then it's too much hassle to actually type them in once they've figured out how. But if you could simply hold your phone against the timetable in the bus stop to bookmark the bus timetable in your phone browser, you might well open it up and take a look sometime.

So who is right? Are the investments misjudged or is Paul Geedes (Chief Executive of Consumer Banking at RBS) right to say that RBS:

"...therefore believe that mobile phones will be the next step in the payments evolution."

One of our clients asked me about this a few days ago and I said that I thought that both views are accurate: the answer depends on the question (if you see what I mean). Deloitte are posing a particular question: given that the business model remains the same as it has been for decades, what is the ROI on this particular payment technology? Answer: not that great. Other people are asking an innovation question: given the possibilities opened up by the new technology, what new business models will emerge? Answer: no-one knows, but for a relatively small expenditure it is worth it for banks not to take the chance of getting outflanked and gain the opportunity to (as Deloittes note inside their report) explore new value-creating opportunities around the payment itself. And if a few more people choose RBS or Barclays' cards because they can have them on their phones, and if mobile operators can charge a quid for letting the banks put the application in the SIM, then that's great too.

More mobile business models [07/12/2007]

Mobile payments aren't all about NFC and proximity. As you may recall, some time before RBS and Barclays announced their NFC pilots, the UK mobile operators launched a payment scheme allowing customers to pay through their mobile phone accounts for items such as train tickets, and parking fees. The new *Payforit* technology scheme allows mobile phone customers to credit small purchases up to £10 to their mobile phone accounts, a scheme likened (not by me) to turning mobile phones into 'digital wallets'. The reason why I don't like this terminology is because in my distorted world view, a wallet is something that you can put cash in, and cash is something you can use to pay other people, not just merchants. Real m-cash can be transferred from person to person.

Meanwhile, there's at least one mobile payment system that is already providing real m-cash, using secure SIM toolkit applications and encrypted and signed text messages in a mass market. And before anyone comments to point out the connection, let me say up front that my employer, Consult Hyperion, provides paid professional services to Vodafone in connection with this project. *M-PESA* has gone from having 140,000 customers back in June to having a million customers today. That's a million customers in its first nine months of operation, a seventh of the Safaricom customer base. In October alone, £7.5m was transferred, mostly in small sums of about £10. (According to that *Times* article, the mobile operator takes some 5% commission, worth £375,000 of October's dealings.) Good for them.

The old business model for m-payments [11/12/2007]

I didn't want to bore people with more stuff about mobile payments so soon, but judging from the comments and e-mails that I've been getting, it's a topic that plenty of people want to discuss more. In particular, the issue of business models around mobile payments seems to be a live one. I can't help noticing that the division between those who think that existing business models can be re-applied to the new technology environment and those who expect new business models to emerge is still wide. As an example of this, I note that a recent survey by Aite Group found that mobile network operators say they will derive POS payment revenue chiefly from consumer transaction fees. This seems hard to believe, frankly, especially given the discussion we had here about the lack of margin in the transaction. Yet four-fifths of the carriers who responded to the Aite survey said that per-transaction fees charged to users are the most likely way they will get revenues from mobile-payment services. Aite's Nick Holland points out the contradiction here:

Mobile operators are confident that they will be able to generate revenues from fees per end-user transaction for all forms of mobile transaction services... However, banks and card networks have expressed that they are unlikely to allow this to happen.

As he goes on to point out (and I agree with him)

Operators are much more likely to generate revenues from end-user subscription fees for mobile data access, as well as from mobile advertising and from handset upgrades to support contactless technology.

Decoupling the small print [21/02/2008]

I went to Germany for a couple of days. Amongst other things, I saw a presentation from Vodafone Germany, talking about the new retail payment scheme that they are launching in partnership with O2...

"The new payment system combines the direct debiting system (German: Lastschriftverfahren) with SMS payment confirmation through mobile phones. That means:

1. You order a product on a mobile portal or web shop

2. Then you type in your mobile phone number and password

3. Following you will receive a text message (SMS), which you have to confirm in order to debit the amount from your bank account via direct debiting system."[2]

The system is open to all mobile phone users and anyone can register of course the registration is much simplified for Vodafone and O2 subscribers who already have bank details filed with their operators ready for direct debiting (because there existing phone subscription works that way). I spoke to Vodafone about it and they said that they

---

[2] O2 and Vodafone starting new payment system, *PavingWays*.com - web applications on (mobile) devices

anticipated two revenue streams: additional text messaging for one, a merchant service charge for the other. I got the impression that the Merchant Service Charge (MSC) would be pitched around the same as for credit card acceptance. As for the future, they said that

"We hope to have more NFC-enabled POS-Systems in the future to combine both technologies."

and furthermore

"Security is the key requirement in Germany"

This might well be the way in for mobile phones: yes, they are more functional than cards but they are potentially far more secure as well. Look at Japan again: remote application locking, 24/7 shutdown, location services. These are all security capabilities that come with the mobile environment to deliver a level of security far above the card platform. It's 9am; do you know where your cards are?

Thinking about the phone as a secure token opens up other possibilities as well. Might it be possible that decoupled debit could spread but without debit cards, if you see what I mean? In other words, with some form of token (such as a mobile phone) instead of traditional debit card. It could be that the single euro payment area (SEPA) zone sees just this kind of experimentation. In the US as well. There was an excellent post by Carol Coye Benson over at *Payments News* the other day. She highlights the new rules interpretation around decoupled debit in the US. The three key points are:

"First, the transactions must be classified as "POS" transactions, rather than using other ACH transaction codes.

Second, the transactions cannot represent an aggregation of underlying consumer purchases - e.g. three separate purchases at one (or more) merchants on a given day cannot be combined into a single ACH debit transaction.

Third, the "payee" in the ACH transaction, which is carried through to the consumer's bank (and therefore appears on the consumer's statement or online transaction listing) must be the underlying merchant, and not the card issuer: in other words, "Capital One" could not be the payee shown on the consumer's statement."[3]

---

[3] ACH@POS, Glenbrook Partners

I'll leave you to look at the article, but I wanted to highlight another angle on the second golden rule. One of the reasons why merchants might want to do this is because they are authenticating the customer themselves and want to minimise payment costs. An example of how this might happen is through REAL ID in the US and through identity cards in the UK. You go to the supermarket and buy something, you use your identity card to authenticate, and off you go. The retailer doesn't even bother authorising the transaction -- why would you cheat them when they have your identity card details and you are already a member of their loyalty programme etc -- but simply saves the transactions up for an overnight ACH (Automated Clearing House) run. They would obviously want to combine multiple payments into one transfer. If a retailer issues their own decoupled debit loyalty-cum-payment card or uses some other 2FA token to front-end such a service (e.g., a mobile phone), surely they would want flexibility on how to structure the relationship between the transactions and the payments, so rule no.2 might cause some friction if I've understood it properly.

Chapter 2: Contactless

Contactless payment technologies evoke all kinds of thoughts and emotions in people. These posts explore the evolution of the contactless payments market but also the changing public perception of the technology and the products.

The devil is in the details [02/02/2007]

I'm still thinking about the coverage of contactless technology. One of our favourite anti-contactless payments groups, CASPIAN, made some comments on the topic last month. Liz McIntyre, CASPIAN's communications director and "a former federal bank examiner" says that contactless technology "not only poses a threat to customers, but to the financial institutions that have issued millions of contactless cards". She goes on to say "What excuse will organizations like JP Morgan Chase make if consumers are harmed financially because they have their personal information siphoned by identity thieves? These issuers stand to lose millions of dollars." Gee, I bet they've never thought of that.

As in the case of the publicity following the *Wall Street Journal* article, I can't help but find it faintly amusing that reporters, commentators and observers think that no-one in banks or amongst their advisers (e.g., us) have the faintest idea about security or risk analysis. The question that they should be asking the US issuers is: is contactless more or less secure than the magnetic stripe cards being issued today? The answer is unequivocal.

Contactless charge [18/05/2007]

The outlook for contactless cards continues to look pretty bright, with 109 million contactless card users expected in the US by 2011. Some recent figures put 2006 spending on contactless cards at $15 billion (which looks like around $7-8K per card to me, which seems a little high) with the percentage of retailers having contactless payment systems expected to nearly triple within two years, so the transaction volume will continue to climb healthily. I don't say card volume, of course, because they may not be cards. Our friends at *Glenbrook* have being doing a survey at their payment boot camps asking people how they would like to pay for small purchases (e.g., coffee) given the choice between a contactless card, a keyfob, their mobile phone or their fingerprint. The winner? The mobile phone with 46% of votes, followed by cards without signature (27%), finger print (15%) and fob (12%). I think you'd get an even stronger preference for phones outside the US, frankly.

A key reason why transaction volumes will continue to climb is that contactless payments are very attractive in a vending environment. Even for cans of well-known soft drinks, the convenience of contactless begins to dominate the argument about transaction costs. Since nearly a fifth of US cards are now contactless, vending is going to start going contactless in a big way. The obvious question, given that you'd think it costs more to pay the merchant service charge on a card transaction than to take cash, is why? Well, Rob Balgley, CEO at SkyTek, says "The increase in revenue is substantial where smart cards can be used for incidental purchases, less than $5. Revenue goes up 30 percent to 40 percent," Why? He says it's because the vendor now has a lot of information about you and can offer you all kinds of promotional incentives to buy more. He may well be right, but I think it's because of simple convenience in the first instance.

Mind you, some observers say that a barrier to the take up of digital money in general is that it doesn't implement the anonymity of cash. So if you buy a Coke (all trademarks acknowledged, naturally) from a machine and the machine says "Thank you, Dave" (or, more worryingly, in a nightmare future Britain) "I'm sorry Dave, I'm afraid I can't do that" then it might well put me off! For the general public, I suspect, it isn't a matter of principle about collecting the data (look at the number of loyalty cards out there) but what is done with it.

Contactless in the marketplace [04/06/2007]

Looking at figures coming from various markets, it looks as if a bullish position on contactless is reasonable. Statistics from a MasterCard research study on how PayPass is being used show an increased spending of 19 percent per PayPass account, as compared with accounts for which consumers have only been issued magnetic-stripe cards. The study also shows that consumers with PayPass cards or fobs are using them 29 percent more often than those with non-PayPass cards, and that the average transaction size of a PayPass payment is smaller than for transactions made with magnetic stripe cards which confirms their position as a cash replacement: almost 80 percent of PayPass transactions are for purchases of $25 or less. In the US, $25 is the "no signature" boundary, so retailers do not have to require signatures for the transactions anyway and contactless fits in neatly. But I am starting to wonder if the same dynamic will work in the EMV environment. In the UK, the transaction limit is 10 pounds and contactless is predicted to do well: Datamonitor rate the UK as the biggest European market for low-value cash transactions. One of the key subsectors is service stations, but only around 18% of service station transactions are suitable for contactless payment (Datamonitor research shows that this would increase to around 40% if the ceiling was increased to 20 pounds). This leads me to suspect that the limit will be raised sooner rather than later.

For the US as a whole, a Synergistics Research survey found that 9% of 1,000 shoppers polled said they had used a contactless card or fob to make purchases, which represents a more than doubling of the 4% of the respondents who answered yes to similar polls conducted at the ends of 2004 and 2005. Another survey, by Report Buyer, says that there were about 27 million contactless payment cards (and keyfobs) in use and that there were about 777 million contactless payment transactions in 2006, around 3% of all credit and debit card transactions. These figures are projected at 2.2 billion transactions on 109 million devices by 2010.

So, does the growing use of contactless and the focus on low-value transactions threaten cash? I rather think it will, but meanwhile, in a "Turkey's view of Christmas" YouGov survey, Bank Machine Limited, the UK's leading independent ATM operator, has revealed 75% of today's consumers still prefer to use cash for smaller transactions and 81% believe financial institutions are pushing them to use their credit and debits cards more. I hope the latter claim is true, or a lot of the investment in contactless is going to be wasted. Nearly two-thirds of transactions under £5 are still paid for in cash and this is not in the interest of the banks, says Bank Machine, as cards encourage consumers to splash their cash more. Ron Delnevo, managing director of Bank Machine, says that:

"At a time when consumer debt in this country is at an all time high, it is completely irresponsible of card issuers to suggest that cash transactions are somehow old fashioned. It is an increasing worry that big institutions and retailers are continually attempting to manipulate the ways in which we spend our money, and subsequently what it is spent on."

Now, it has to be said that Ron has a point -- one of the key retailer drivers for contactless low-value payments is that consumers spend more than they do with cash -- but is that a reason to continue the hidden subsidies to cash? I imagine that consumers spend more using notes and coins than they would do if they had to barter livestock, but that's hardly a moral justification for a return to ancient Babylonian economic order.

As it happens, some e-barter people popped in to see us last year, which led to some discussions about whether barter can work well in a networked economy and thus bypass some other digital money developments. One line of thinking is that the whole reason that money was invented was that bartering isn't a particularly efficient means of paying for goods and services and therefore bartering has no role. As *Techdirt* said,

"In the last decade, over and over and over again, we've seen companies keep trying to bring back the concept of bartering, as if it were something new and wonderful. In the early days of the web there were a bunch of online bartering sites, and they all died out pretty quickly. A couple years back, the new set showed up, and they seemed just as pointless. One of the higher profile ones was Peerflix, where it didn't take long for people to realize that when you have to trade DVDs straight up, there are going to be a lot of crappy DVDs available, and not many good ones."

Interestingly, they call this economic phenomenon "the ghost of Gresham's Law", although I think the "precursor to Gresham's Law" might be a more accurate homage to our hero Sir Thomas. On balance, I think I predict that I am more likely to be using a contactless card, with a limit of more than 10 pounds, next year than I am to be bartering home made yoghurt for Volvo parts.

Contactless update [17/08/2007]

The arrival of contactless cards in the mass market continues to attract attention. As the first flush of enthusiasm passes, however, the coverage is beginning to fracture into two rather predictable perspectives. On the one hand, speed and convenience. This is particularly attractive to certain merchant categories (e.g., fast food) and customers. So, for merchants like Arby's, where speed is important; the faster transaction time is the dominant factor. American Express say that *ExpressPay*-enabled transactions can be completed in about one-third the time of a cash transaction and about half the time of a swipe-card transaction, and figures from Visa and MasterCard show similar gains. If anything, the merchants in the USA are upset that the contactless roll-out is too slow. Less than 2 percent of Visa's cardholders in the US currently have the technology. MasterCard has distributed 13 million PayPass cards and claims that 46,000 merchants now accept them. The pharmacy chain CVS/Caremark, which has had contactless readers in operation since 2005, says that less than 1 percent of its card transactions are contactless. McDonald's has been prepared for contactless payment for two years. David Grooms, vice president of IT at McDonald's USA says

"We're deployed in all of our restaurants in the US"

The installation of contactless terminals by merchants is clearly going to grow -- and is one of the reasons that the forecasts for mobile payments are so bullish, with Juniper Research predicting that P2P fund transfers and mobile payments in the developing world, together with the commercialisation of NFC based m-payments will generate transactions worth approximately $22bn in 2011 -- even in the UK, where merchants have just been through the process of replacing all of their terminals for chip and PIN. Now, chip and PIN was of course extremely costly to card issuing companies, merchant companies and retail outlets. Indeed, some observers think that the USA will simply bypass it, moving via contactless to NFC and the next generation of retail payment devices. But even in the UK, where the roll-out of the first contactless cards is imminent, merchant terminals are appearing. Barclaycard has signed its first 1,000 retail outlets for contactless and will launch its OnePulse combo chip, contactless and Oyster card next month. Elizabeth Chambers, chief marketing officer for Barclaycard, says

"Cashless payments are starting to become a reality."

The retail outlets signed for contactless already include Coffee Republic, Threshers, Books Etc, YO! Sushi, Eat and Krispy Kreme. Once again the quick-serve retail (QSR) category is predictably dominant. In the US, Arby's won't discuss actual numbers, although they do say that the trend is positive, but rather interestingly say that they put the technology in because it was a convenient time to do so, not because it expected to see an immediate benefit. In other words, they were upgrading the company's in-store point-of-sale system and decided to add contactless as part of the process. I'm sure this will be the general picture in the mass market outside certain very special cases. UK merchants won't upgrade because of contactless, but when they do upgrade then contactless will be part of the new specification.

Yes speed and convenience, but on the other hand, contactless cards will be the end of civilization as we know it because of fraud. They will lead to increased street crime, according to the ATM operator Cash Machine, because thieves can use the cards without PINs for transactions under ten pounds. They go on to say that the cardholder "is likely to be asked only every 10-15 transactions to enter their PIN" to verify they are the lawful user of the card. Actually, the cards can only be used nine times without a PIN: the tenth time, the card must be used in a contact mode and the PIN entered. I'm not saying that this is a good idea, or that it won't annoy the hell out of consumers, but the issuers' assumption is that a dual interface contact/contactless debit card will be used by consumers in contact mode as well as contactless mode, so the number of times that a contactless transaction will be refused and a contact transaction will be required is statistically only gong to be in 1 in every 150 transactions or something like that. My assumption is that consumers may well stick a contactless card in a pocket or the bottom of a handbag because they want to use it to buy coffee the same way they use an Oyster card to get on the Tube. In which case, they will get annoyed quite quickly.

There's a different context to all of this in the US, where there is no chip and PIN and since all transactions are online the risk analysis around contactless payments is quite different. There's no need to sign for every tenth transaction or whatever. There are still security concerns, of course. Javelin Strategy & Research conducted an online nationally-representative survey of some 2200+ consumers in the spring and found that

- A bit more than half were neutral or positive on the concept of contactless.

- Among the neutrals-to-positives, the group's security worries graphs like a perfect bell curve, with about half neutral on contactless as a security threat and the remaining two quarters being evenly split between those that expect contactless to be either "safe" or "unsafe".

- Among those that are not yet ready to use contactless, security appears to be the dominant consideration. This means, of course, that whatever we might think about the actual security situation we must get better at communicating it.

They end up by speculating that since consumers prefer the safety of PIN, the perceived advantages of PIN will become more significant on eventual increases in contactless transactions, which is a fair point. On balance, though, I think that despite the worries (remember, there were similar predictions of chaos when chip and PIN was introduced) people will as always opt for convenience over security. Anyway, only a month to go and we'll see if the *Evening Standard* front page will be about disgruntled customers, street robberies or nothing much happening!

Fight the contactless menace [04/09/2007]

Yesterday morning I heard the first story on the BBC concerning contactless cards in the UK because MasterCard officially launched its contactless 'tap and go' payments system, PayPass in London. The BBC coverage wasn't bad -- I particularly liked Forum friend (and head of Strategy at MasterCard) Oliver Steeley's firm comment:

"You can't stand in the way of progress."

but the radio report I heard spent a lot of the coverage on the security issue. Now, I'm not aware of any figures from either the US or Asia-Pacific that show fraud on 'tap and go' payment schemes to be any more or any less than on other schemes (if anyone has such figures, please do share them) but that's not the point: the point is the focus on what could go wrong -- despite the explicit statement by MasterCard that customers will not be liable -- rather than an exploration of new opportunities.

The security question is a reasonable one: why would anyone want one of these cards when anyone else can use it without a signature or PIN? So you can see why 70% of the public believe that contactless cards will increase the likelihood of fraud, with only 15% stating that they were "very likely" to use their card for transactions under £10 (i.e., without cardholder authentication). Ron Delnevo, MD of Bank Machine Limited says

"So far they have run tests in places like bank staff canteens, very sanitised and safe environments... In the real world, there are a number of serious issues"

I think that's a little unfair on places like the USA, which despite some evidence to the contrary are generally considered to be in the real world. People using the 30 million contactless cards already in circulation there seem to like them. Yet the industry does have to answer his central point: surely people will get beaten up and the cards will get stolen, since each one represents somewhere between £0 and £89.91 of easy money to a thief. Or at least a thief that shops at McDonalds, Eat, Coffee Republic, Yo!Sushi and Krispy Kreme (e.g., me). Ron detects a hidden agenda:

"There can therefore be only one motive behind this new "wheeze" – rather than being about customer service, it's simply another manoeuvre by the banks to get rid of the cash that they so hate. I find it ironic that so many people fought to keep our British Pound when it was threatened by the introduction of the Euro, yet we have yet to wake up to this obvious ploy to deprive our citizens of the right to use the cash – and £s - that they prefer."

I won't comment about the British Pound -- since I'm with the Monster Raving Loony Party on this one, in that I think we should invite other European countries to leave the euro and adopt Sterling -- but I have to say that the agenda is not particularly hidden. Why else would banks introduce a new card product if not to get more usage and in the sub-£10 band, that means attracting customers away from cash by providing a better service than cash. In other words, if contactless cards weren't going to replace cash, why bother with them? The noted strategic thinker Clayton Christensen understood this the first time he saw the technology demonstrated and agrees with me completely :)

"For the consumer, PayPass is replacing cash, not credit and debit card purchases."

Where next for UK cards? [09/10/2007]

In an article about the immediate future of credit cards in the UK, which I found via the *Sun* newspaper I think (it's a key source of financial insight...), the commentator focuses on dull subjects such as the continuing popularity of balance transfer deals -- though these seem to me to encourage, rather than, "stop rate tarts". For foreign viewers, I should explain that a rate tart (e.g., me) is someone who takes a zero-interest balance transfer deal from a card issuer, never uses the card, and then switches to another zero-interest balance transfer deal at the end of the term. And why not? If a bank sends me a letter saying "please have some free money", then of course I'll tick the box marked "yes". Anyway, what caught my eye was the comment that the only thing likely to change the market will be some genuine innovation (a topic of some discussion previously). The article goes on to say that

"Perhaps Barclaycard's upcoming Oyster/contactless payment/credit-card combo [he means the OnePulse card] will do that, at least for the London market. I expect it to significantly increase people's spending, just as credit and debit cards did. Other providers will see its impact and will want to work on similar technology and infrastructure as fast as they can -- if they can."

I think it's fair to observe that in the case of Oyster, they can't (because the deal with Barclays is exclusive for an initial period). But perhaps the author is right that contactless will spark off some new products -- as it has in the US, where Visa USA has just announced the *Micro Tag*, a contactless key ring (like the PayPass fob and the American Express companion fob) instead of cards to pay for purchases under $25 by waving the device in front of a contactless payment terminal. Sadly, we can't use these in the UK -- for technical reasons to do with transactions being online, PINs, EMV scripts and such like -- but we don't especially need to worry about this, because there's no doubt in my mind that the preferred contactless doo-dah (sorry for the technical argot) for most consumers, in most of the world, is their own phone.

Another prediction that could have been made by the Sun pundit -- especially had they listened to some of the first customer and merchant responses in a recent BBC report -- might well have been the import of contactless panic from the US, where people are destroying the contactless chips in their cards:

> "I was out at dinner with a friend in the States earlier this year and I noticed that his credit card had a hole in it, approximately hole-punch size. I wanted to know -- was this some new card feature? Turns out that, when he received his new MasterCard in the mail and found that it had a PayPass RFID chip on it, he took a hole punch to it and punched it out. Why? Because, as widely reported and summarized here, there are very legitimate privacy concerns associated with RFID technologies."

My pet hate. Equating contactless payment technology with the (in the US market anyway, scary mark-of-the-beast) RFID technology. It's fair enough to raise security concerns for discussion, but confusing the technology used in contactless payment cards with the technology used for tracking pallets of baked beans gets us (i.e., the industry, consumers and activists) into the wrong conversation.

A subset of Americans really do not like contactless, for whatever reason, and we're not going to change their minds with pie charts. But plenty do like it, and they are encountering different problems. Such as: never mind a hole punch in a card, what do you use to render a keyfob harmless? Especially if you are someone who takes identity theft so seriously that you cut up old credit cards and gradually mixes the pieces into the garbage over several days to make it difficult for even a dedicated attacker to get information from the cards. Citibank apparently sent this concerned citizen a new credit card and a new PayPass key fob. As usual, she cut up the old credit card. But she couldn't figure out how to destroy the thick, durable key fob. Of course, if both the card and the keyfob gave up a per-device alias PAN through the contactless interface (as we have consistently advised: this isn't dreary hindsight dressed up as consultancy!) then there wouldn't be a problem, because the keyfob and card chips can't be counterfeited.

But back to the point. Are these security concerns really affecting the roll-out of contactless cards? Someone whose opinions I always take seriously, Steve Mott, says that they are and points the finger specifically at the *New York Times* story as a turning point in the story of contactless in the US. As you will recall, researchers who built a contactless reader and used it to obtain track 2 data from credit cards inside envelopes. This data could be used to make counterfeit magnetic stripe cards. I think Steve may be wrong when he says that all brands were exposed, because if memory serves the American Express cards gave up alias PANs and not card PANs (although the researchers wouldn't have known that, because they just see them as

PANs, if you see what I mean) but nonetheless the damage was done. Although other researchers, the banks, the suppliers and others already knew all about this issue, once it made the Grey Lady there was, as Steve says, hell to pay.

The report was soon followed by a Wall Street Journal story about consumers putting their cards in microwave ovens and so forth. But is Steve right to attribute the subsequent downward revision of contactless card forecasts to these stories? Were consumers really more worried about using cards with contactless interfaces than using cards without them, even though both types have the cardholder name, PAN, expiration date and CVV clearly written on them for anyone who can read to steal? Well, no-one has the right to demand rationality from consumers, who have (as I've said above) perfectly reasonable security concerns. Consumer education has to be part of the rollout plan: certainly, consumers in London (where the roll-out began last month) are raising the obvious issue: what happens if someone steals my card? The banks are dealing with this by being admirably clear and specific, telling consumers: it's not your problem, don't worry about it. But when Steve asks whether the perception of going light on security early on might have rendered a "serious body blow" to contactless, I think I'd answer that a big part of the scare doesn't come from genuine worries about the security of contactless transactions but from emotional responses to that labelling of contactless transactions as "RFID". For an expert view, let's see what the Charles Bronson, Florida State Commissioner of Agriculture and Consumer Services has to say:

"with the right technology, a hacker could walk into a crowded room and get ID information from dozens of people if they were carrying RFID-type cards... the cards should be carried in special mesh-type paper sleeves that block radio transmissions... Another way, he added, is to use a wallet that's been rated as scanner-proof."

Wise counsel indeed. But if this actually happened (it hasn't -- you can't light up the chips in the cards from more than a few centimetres away) then it's simple to fix. Just change the cards so that all this readable "ID information" consists of are alias PANs. You can't use them to create counterfeit cards and you can't submit them to contactless terminals (because you can't forge the digital signature that is needed). Please, let's keep some perspective.

The Digital Money Reader 2008

Which planet? [31/10/2007]

I had a fun time in London the other day. I took my son to the Forbidden Planet London Megastore and when I got to the cash register I was genuinely shocked to see a Barclays Business contactless terminal there. I couldn't use it, of course, because my purchase was over ten quid, as I imagine most of their purchases are. Yet when we went to the Cafe Nero down the road, and our coffee and hot chocolate came to less than a fiver, they didn't take cards at all, let alone contactless ones. So we couldn't buy the pastries we wanted (I only had a five pound note in cash on me). Their ridiculous cash-only restriction meant that I didn't get the goods that I wanted and they didn't get the money that they wanted. Afterwards, I was still consumed with curiosity -- a genetic flaw, I imagine -- so we went back to Forbidden Planet and I bought a Pirates pack for my son just so I could use my OnePulse card: it worked great, and I estimate that it was about thirty times quicker than using my chip and PIN card.

I hope this isn't going to be Mondex all over again, where the shops that take cards take contactless but the shops (and vending machines and buses etc) that take cash carry on taking cash. I'm sure the lessons have been learned from the last decade, from the days when you could buy a coat in Bloomingdale's using VisaCash but had to use cash in the parking meter outside. The rather odd distribution of points of use came down to banks driving a new product through their existing channels into the marketplace. Please let's not let this happen again: I think I'll pop into Cafe Nero again and ask the boss why they don't take contactless cards. I strongly suspect that it will be because he'd be happy to take contactless cards but doesn't want to take contact cards and at the moment (as I understand scheme rules) that's not allowed.

At the very least, we should hope that the industry can get to a degree of penetration (on the acquiring side) to give consumers a real choice between cards and cash in different environment. I wonder how the statistics might evolve? There was a fascinating take on this in a Working Paper (no.212, September 2007) from the Swedish Central Bank. They were trying to estimate the probability that different groups will pay with a card. They found that for "typical" consumers, once a transaction reached about 17 euros then consumers were 50 per cent likely to use a card rather than cash. For older consumers, the limit goes up to around 50 euros. But guess what: a 20 year-old male is more than 50 per cent likely to use a card no matter how small the purchase value. They also discovered that people who are University-educated are more likely to pay with cards whereas people with "little formal schooling" are more likely to pay with cash. Their detailed model (you can read it for yourself here[4]) seemed to show that gender, income and household size are, by comparison, insignificant.

I cannot highlight one of their other conclusions strongly enough, so I will quote it in full:

"Our study shows that even when not paying explicit fees for payments, consumers do incur substantial costs and that these costs are higher for cash than for card payments."

The lack of proper price information is one of the key reasons why the market for payment instruments is broken. In particular, variable costs are poorly reflected in transaction fees and cash gets a big subsidy (primarily from cards). But I guess we all knew that anyway. So am I right to use the word "broken"? Well, as the very careful study of the Swedish economy shows, the consumer's choice of payment instrument is based on their private cost, not the total social cost (i.e., people choose what's best for them, not what's best for society as a whole). The fix is simple: price cash correctly so that consumers can make informed choices about payment instruments. How should this be achieved? The authors tell us that as well:

"Consumers pay too little for cash... merchants, on the other hand, pay too much for credit card payments... Swedish banks use their profit from card payments to cross-subsidise cash handling. This situation could be improved if ATM withdrawal fees were introduced and interchange fees were lowered."

Sensible policies for a better Sweden.

Slow penetration [18/02/2008]

The roll-out of contactless payments is proceeding, but it's still slow, because it takes a long time for merchants to change or upgrade their POS technology, even when they want to. But they may not want to, because they don't perceive enough value for them, or because they anticipate incentives from other players in the market.

"An absence of incentives -- particularly for merchants -- is handicapping contactless payments in the US, and by extension mobile payment at the point of

---

[4] http://www.riksbank.com/templates/Page.aspx?id=25848

sale could suffer, according to a new report by Aite. About 40,000 US merchants now accept contactless cards and fobs, or 0.5% of all merchant locations. That number will grow to 271,000 over the next six years, but the penetration rate after that time will still be only 2.5%. If these projections prove accurate, it will mean rough going at best for near-field communication (NFC). To make NFC work, cashiers must be equipped with contactless readers. The painfully slow merchant penetration by contactless "kills NFC", according to the report author Nick Holland."[5]

Nick is, of course, right to highlight the feedback loop that is operating here. There are some banks and retailers who are investing in contactless for its own sake, but there are many who are investing in contactless because they see it as a stepping stone to the greater value-added possibilities around mobile. Now, I certainly see myself in the mobile camp, but that doesn't mean that contactless can't be successful in its own right as well, as I was reminded yesterday when driven insane by a Woking Borough Council parking machine that purported to accept cash (credit cards, having been invented less than fifty years ago, are not yet on the menu) but refused my tenner and my 5p pieces, rendering me unable to pay until I found some more coins on the floor in my car. How can it be more cost-effective to operate an antiquated system than to accept cards? Anyway, the point is that converting unattended points of sale to contactless must be a good idea if you want to drive acceptance:

"MasterCard Worldwide and USA Technologies announced the expansion of ePort cashless payment terminals to 17,500 vending machines nationwide, adding more than 4,000 new locations that accept MasterCard PayPass contactless payments."[6]

I wonder if the roll-out will naturally accelerate as merchants replace their POS terminals and systems or whether specific incentives (as noted above) will be required to tilt the balance? If I was a merchant, I'd think it worthwhile holding out and even though I know that it makes commercial sense, I'd still want to try and get a better interchange rate out of the bank if I could. In theory, if the benefits are distributed between banks, consumers and merchants then the costs should be distributed similarly, but in practice in the short term

---

[5] *Digital Transactions News*

[6] MasterCard Expands PayPass Acceptance to Over 17,000 Vending Machines, *FinanceTech*

it means banks spending money issuing contactless cards and the acquiring side catching up later (this, incidentally, is one of the lessons from the DoCoMo "curves" in Japan). Therefore, so long as the merchant benefits are sufficient, the infrastructure will sort itself out.

But what are the merchant benefits? I've just been reading a report from Deloitte -- the audit, tax, consulting and corporate finance company -- called "Contactless Payments Technology, Catching the new wave", which says that their research with leading merchants has identified six main benefits to the transition to contactless:

1. Improved speed of throughput.
2. Increase in average transaction value.
3. Competitive differentiation.
4. Reduction in cost.
5. Better customer insight.
6. Improved service delivery.

Point 4 is in my mind because of something else I'm working on at the moment: if the merchants are underestimating the cost of cash, then charts and spreadsheets will eventually convert them, so it's not a real blocker, but if the cost of cash really is much lower than the banks think (I don't believe this, by the way) then there's going to be more of a problem. Anyway, I wouldn't disagree with any of these benefits, but reading them reminded me that I have some (albeit anecdotal, but) recent evidence that things may not be going as smoothly as may have been hoped so far as the London rollout of contactless technology is going. A couple of days ago, I found myself at a Tube station in North London. As I was wandering out, I saw a small newsagent kiosk and I went over to buy a paper and some gum. It came to about a pound. I was just about to unzip a pocket in my backpack and rummage around for change, when I noticed that the kiosk had a contactless reader. Since I had my OnePulse card in my pocket, as I'd just used it to get off the Tube, I waved it over the reader.

This is precisely the circumstance for which nature intended contactless cards in general and the OnePulse card in particular: the low-value cash-replacement transaction coupled to transit. In my fevered imagination, I could already picture myself turning smartly on my heels after less than 500 milliseconds and going about my day with a spring in my step. But, unfortunately, nothing could have been further from the reality.

When I waved my card at the reader, nothing happened. The woman serving me asked if I really wanted to use the "terminal". I said yes. She said: "It will be an extra five pence". I said that I still wanted to use it -- I am nothing if not dedicated to gathering practical experience -- and so she rekeyed the amount into a separate POS and indicated for me to wave again. Which I did, and it worked. Nevertheless, something that should have been fast and convenient was in practice slow and inconvenient (and expensive). Uh oh. I missed out on a pleasant experience, the merchant may well have missed out on a sale while I was messing around at the kiosk and neither of us was left feeling positive about the exciting new technology.

Whether it's the lack of suitable terminals for the kinds of merchants, miscommunication between acquirers and merchants about benefits, simple unfamiliarity or whatever, I hope someone on the business side has a handle on this.

Chapter 3: Other Technologies

Although many people interact with payment systems in fairly regular and nowadays more and more common ways there are still technologies and services being developed which provide that little something different.

It's the PayStation 3! [24/01/2007]

Leo van Hove was the first to point to a super story coming from Japan. If you needed a reminder just how far Europe (and for that the matter, the US) is behind Japan when it comes to digital money, Sony is rolling out a USB contactless interface for the PlayStation 3 so that Japanese consumers can pay for online games with their Edy cards and, of course, their FeliCa-equipped mobile phones.

I think I noted somewhere previously that more than 1.5% of Edy transactions are already online. It's only a matter of time -- probably a very short time -- before the new generation of Japanese consumers find themselves loading their e-purse using their PlayStation rather than mucking around on the Internet or walking around to an ATM.

I am literally green with envy. Not because of my deep-seated nerdism, but because this sort of development should be -- assuming that banks and operators learn to get along together -- a vision of what's to come with NFC-equipped mobile phones in Europe. This is digital money for the masses, an instantiation of the Mondex dream using disruptive technology. Mind you, my new phone did come with a mini-golf game, so you can't say that UK operators, banks and content providers aren't pushing the envelope of innovation to breaking point.

Me and Britney [04/04/2007]

I loved my Britney Spears card. Younger readers may not remember the time when Ms. Spears was the biggest pop star in the world and, astonishing as it may seem, her fan club launched a smart card kit. Fearing that I would end up on some police database, I bullied my sister-in-law into joining the fan club on my behalf and ordering one for me. That's how dull my life was: I wasn't interested in Ms. Spears big hits, I wanted the card reader. The kits, which had been developed by Internet PLC, a UK-based company. The company developed the SmartFlash content and sold the kits via the web and at her concerts. The Britney smart card provided access to a secure web site with video clips, e-cards to mail to friends and a preview of her upcoming video game. They sold more than 25,000 kits at $29.95 before they were discontinued. But they worked.

This is the experiment we carried out in the office...

- We plugged in a financial services company's smart card reader. It didn't work. We downloaded some drivers, reloaded the software, rebooted. The card reader was visible to the software, but nothing happened when we put the card in, so we gave up.

- We plugged in the Britney smart card reader (actually, as I recall, a rebadged GCR 400) and it worked first time. We inserted the Britney card and it launched Explorer and took us straight to the members-only section of the Britney website.

- Somewhat surprisingly, we discovered that the financial services card that we were testing worked perfectly in the Britney reader. In other words, having installed the Britney reader we could now carry out secure financial transactions on line.

The point is, it worked. And it was designed for 9-year old girls to use. I always wondered why banks couldn't learn from Britney's trailblazing smart card expertise. It would seem relatively trivial to use a $5 smart card reader, an EMV card and a few bytes of application code to create a Britney-like home banking experience. Plug in the reader, insert your debit card, your default web browser takes you to your bank home page. You enter your password and you are away, provided that the card is present. No card, no log in. The software to do this (standard SSL client-side certificates) is present in almost all web servers and web browsers but it's not used because the average person has no idea what a certificate is. This way, they don't need to know: all the customer needs to understand is no card, no log in.

If you're wondering why I was thinking about this, it's not because I've been looking at pictures of Britney in *Heat magazine*, but because I came across another female pop singer while searching for something else to do with smart cards (honestly). Lebanese-Columbian songstress Shakira has been touring in the UAE and a 'smart chip payment concert card' was one of the attractions. The card issuer, Vice Versa International said guests would be able to purchase the card prior to the concert for use as an e-purse and as an access card for the VIP area. The credit on the card can be topped up at reloading stations within the VIP area by using cash or a credit card. I couldn't see if it can be used on line, but where Britney has blazed a trail, others will surely follow. To borrow David Edgerton's phrase, it's the shock of the old.

Back to biometrics [23/04/2007]

I was surprised that the first item on the BBC news yesterday was again about card fraud (which they insist on calling chip and PIN fraud when it is only the PIN that is compromised). The main part of the report was entirely about petrol stations -- and even claimed, I think somewhat imaginatively -- that motorists are starting to use cash instead of cards. I wonder if the extent of the reporting of the fraud, if not the fraud itself, will genuinely cause a backlash against card use for fuel? And if it does, will people really go back to cash or will they instead prefer to move to a biometric solution such as the Pay By Touch system installed at the Stop 'n Save gas and convenience stores in Colorado, some of the 2,000 US retailers that use the technology. Of these, Piggly Wiggly has the best name, in my opinion.

To use the biometric payment and loyalty scheme, Stop 'n Save customers register by scanning their fingerprints and providing a cancelled cheque. They can then pay for purchases by scanning their fingers and entering a 10-digit PIN number (I think this is generally their phone number) to verify their identities. A case study of Pay By Touch deployment at a grocery store named Green Hills seems very positive. Nine months after the introduction of the technology, 25% of Green Hills' sales are made via biometric payments, and 28% of those are processed over the Automated Clearing House network (i.e., swerving round payment card networks). Now, I'm up front about being a smart card and mobile phone fan, but if people like using biometrics and they are fast enough at POS, then I can see why they will gain ground.

As we have discussed before at Digital Identity, however, I think the main mass market thrust for biometrics will be about convenience, not security, as in the case of the biometric ATMs that Citibank has launched in India for microfinance customers. The ATMs authorise transactions by scanning customers' thumbprints instead of a PIN code. Citibank plans to establish a network of 25 to 35 such ATMs within a year, specifically targeted at its Citibank *Pragati* savings account holders. Citibank Pragati is a no-frills savings account with nil minimum balance and is offered directly or through a microfinance institution (MFI). I'm not sure why using a thumbprint is quicker or easier than using a PIN, but perhaps in a largely illiterate target group it could make a big difference.

I could imagine using this [22/06/2007]

There's been a rash of announcements of new payment schemes recently, many of them centred on mobiles. I find myself reading some of these announcements and thinking "well, that sounds neat" but then saying to myself "I couldn't see me using it". There's a disconnect. But some of them I could see myself using. For example, Pay By Touch have developed a Reward and Gift Card Kiosk. The Internet-enabled kiosk lets shoppers create customized store-branded and third-party gift cards with personalized "to" and "from" names and single or multiple design full-colour graphics. Gift cards can be purchased and dispensed directly from the self-serve kiosk, eliminating the current requirement of purchasing gift cards at the check-out lane or customer service counter. The kiosks store an unlimited number of graphics, so multiple merchants or brands can be supported on a single kiosk. Here's how it works:

1. Using a touch-screen, the shopper chooses from multiple designs to match the gift-giving occasion, and chooses the denomination he or she prefers.

2. The shopper then types in both the recipient's and the gift giver's name (likely her own) into the "to" and "from" fields.

3. Using a credit card, the shopper purchases the gift card directly through the kiosk. The shopper presses "print" and a

personalized, activated gift card is printed in seconds, along with a receipt.

Now that is a kiosk I could imagine using. The kids want to play *World of Warcraft* or whatever, so I get them a card with a WoW character on and money loaded on to it to keep them going for a while. Assuming that these are Visa or MasterCard gift cards (i.e., "open" gift cards), then I'm in.

I could also imagine using the following. According to Transaction Directory, Citibank is introducing a new electronic deposit service for its commercial business clients. The service, Citibank *Remote Check Deposit*, will allow clients to deposit checks into their bank accounts without taking them to a branch or mailing in the items. CitiBusiness clients will now be able to digitize checks from remote locations, such as their business offices, and transmit them electronically to the bank in real time. Business customers will be offered a comprehensive solution including scanning equipment with a full replacement warranty. Now scanners are cheap -- and I'm sure most offices have them anyway -- so the idea of simply scanning a cheque that arrives in the mail and then e-mailing the image to bank is very attractive.

But why is this just for business customers? I find it really annoying when people send me cheques: why can't they just PayPal me for small amounts or send the money via home banking for larger amounts? When someone sends you a cheque, it's like being set homework: you have to find your chequebook (always a hassle in our house), get a paying-in slip out of the back, fill it in, put both the cheque and the paying-in slip into your bag and hope that you remember it next time you go past a bank. Never mind the UK's impending "2-4-6" change to the cheque clearing system, it's time to start pricing cheques out of existence just as our Scandinavian cousins have done.

Fingering suspects [08/11/2007]

Biometrics continue to advance in Japan with the news that Hitachi is teaming with Japanese issuer JCB to develop a biometric payment system based on its finger vein authentication technology that can be used as an alternative to cards and cash at the point of sale. Hitachi is set to begin testing the system with 200 employees in September to determine whether the technology is commercially viable for introduction in banks and shops. The system identifies the veins on a person's finger when it is held over a scanner and matches the image with customer data already stored in the application. The vein authentication system has been available in the Japanese market since October 2006 and has already been deployed by Sumitomo Mitsui Banking Corporation as the user ID system for ATMs located in am/pm convenience stores throughout Japan, which is why I thought the technology deserved its own podcast. Japan isn't the only place where biometrics are being rolled out in this way. Banks in India are looking at deploying biometric ATMs targeted to reach the unbanked population in rural India. Using thumbprint and voice guidance in ATMs reduces literacy requirements to a considerable extent. Thus, establishing the identity of a rural depositor through biometrics makes it possible for illiterate or barely literate people to become part of the banking user community.

So is the triumph of biometrics around the corner and is the end of cards assured? Well, not really. Biometrics work well in controlled environments such as ATMs, it's true. But it's not clear -- despite a number of roll-outs -- whether they offer a realistic alternative to cards at POS because, as we have consistently advised our clients, biometrics at POS are driven by convenience, not by security. Therefore, developments in mobile and contactless payments will stunt the growth of retail biometrics. A few years ago, biometrics at POS had what seemed to be a bright future. By registering a card or bank account against a fingerprint, customers could pay without plastic, and it has to be admitted that this does have its attractions. Biometrics offered things to the retailers as well: security and a permanent CRM association. If the customer changed accounts, address, names or mobile operator, the retailer wasn't affected and the fingerprint would still allow all purchases to be associated with an individual customer. But, as that article highlights, vendors -- particularly market leader Pay By Touch (which had the distinction of having purchased the infamous CardSystems, of data breach fame) -- focused on queue-busting and convenience. But this wasn't that smooth a path and retail deployments -- such as the Piggly Wiggly grocery chain -- began to feel the pain of consumer resistance.

But the biggest problem turned out to be technology innovation. The rapid acceptance of contactless payment cards by the incumbents essentially usurped the speed/convenience argument away. When I last used my Barclays OnePulse contactless Visa card in London (a couple of days ago), it took a couple of seconds at most to take the wallet out of my pocket and hold it to the POS terminal, hear the "beep" and then put it away again. And as contactless merges with mobile, the convenience/functionality curve moves further away from fingerprints.

Biometrics still has a very robust future in many verticals outside of retail payments right now (e.g., ATMs), and will undoubtedly come to retail payments in time. I don't even think it will be that long (five years?) before biometric PIN augmentation for higher-value transactions enters the UK mass market. So, were the biometrics guys deluded to think that they had a place in retail payments already? Maybe not. Maybe there was another dynamic behind stakeholder actions. It's not really a conspiracy theory, but let's just say for sake of argument that retailers were playing around with biometrics because they wanted something on their side of the table for future discussions with the cards business and now that interchange looks to be on the way down (and the principal of lower interchange rates for below-the-threshold contactless transactions is established), they don't really need them anymore. Perhaps that's why Pay By Touch is backing off the retail payment at POS, according to The Nilson Report (issue 890), which says that

"Pay By Touch has shifted its focus away from being a company that provides biometric-based payments at the point of sale to becoming one that provides target marketing services... As a result, its payment processing assets are no longer part of the company's core business and are being considered for sale. Those assets include Pay By Touch Payment Solutions and Pay By Touch Processing, which handle merchant card processing contracts and a proprietary card-not-present gateway."

I wrote on the Digital Identity blog that cards plus biometrics offer a much better solution than either cards or biometrics alone, and I'm sure that when biometrics do return to retail, mass-market POS it will be in that mode.

Zig zag [15/11/2007]

Contactless and RFID aren't the only new local wireless interfaces out there that should be of interest to payment innovators. There's *ZigBee*, for example. The ZigBee Alliance, a global collection of companies creating wireless solutions for use in energy, residential, commercial and industrial applications, has already announced its expansion into the telecommunications market with an initiative extending mobile networks while providing new capabilities for phone users. The new ZigBee Telecom Profile will feature secure mobile payment, information delivery, health care monitoring, peer-to-peer small data sharing and other location-based services and features. If you're not familiar with it, ZigBee is a suite of communication protocols that use small, low-power digital radios based on the IEEE 802.15.4 standard for wireless personal area networks (WPANs). The technology is intended to be simpler and cheaper than other WPANs, such as Bluetooth. ZigBee is targeted at contactless applications that require a low data rate, long battery life, and secure networking: sensors in the home, for example.

Some time ago, I saw a fascinating presentation from Telecom Italia Mobile concerning their experiment adding a ZigBee interface to a SIM card. This means that otherwise unmodified handsets can be integrated into their physical environment without waiting for NFC. They are using a SIM Toolkit application to access the ZigBee interface -- which has been working up to five metres -- to carry out payment and other transactions. Now, five meters might seem rather a long range for an EMV transaction, but for vicinity payment applications such as road tolling or bus riding it might work rather well: no actual transaction takes place over the air interface; it's just the presence of the device that triggers a transaction in the back end somewhere.

Future imperfect [23/11/2007]

I went to Dublin for a client of ours to give a talk about the future of payments. One of my favourite sites for helping me to think about such things is *Paleo Future*. It's a super blog all about past views of the future, if you see what I mean. Not only is it fun, but it contains some tremendously relevant information that ought to help us (by which I mean people trying to understand the relationship between technology and business) improve and refine our own views of the future A great example was the recent posting about a New York Times Magazine advertisement from 24th May 1964 about the "credit card ring". It's actually an advertisement for Sheaffer Pens, but it features a ring that projects an American Express card. The gist of the advertisement is that your credit card of the future may not actually be a physical card any more, but you will still need to sign for it. It's fascinating to reflect on how wrong this is: my credit card still looks like a credit card, but I haven't signed for it in a couple of years (except in, if I remember correctly, Tunisia and the USA: no, wait, the hotel in Tunisia had an EMV terminal).

I think I ought to take the time to look this up, but from memory it was the science fiction author Brian Aldiss who pointed out that classic SF novels rarely dealt with money, because their target audience is teenage boys, and money is the one resource they don't have (or at least didn't during the Golden Age of Science Fiction). It may be an outdated analysis now, I suppose, but I mention it because I wanted to point out that where money does appear in depictions of the future, it appears in somewhat unimaginative ways. There tends to be a passing reference to a universal credit or Galatic Guinea: "Captain Narg here. Please send a pizza-droid with a pepperoni and double-cheese thick crust"... "Certainly. That will be 7 GGs, please. We will charge it to your account". There's never a section on the complexities of managing the same bank rate across the entire galaxy. Given the complexity of managing interest rates across Europe or, for that matter, the United Kingdom, you'd think it might show up from time to time. I once took my sons to a Star Wars film -- I've never liked Star Wars -- and fell asleep in the first few minutes during some interminable dialogue about trade negotiations and alliances. I might have perked up if the characters had been discussing the tightening of Galactic Central Bank rates and its impact on the housing market on Pluto (sub-prime and sub-zero).

When people are asked to imagine the future of payments they tend to think of novel implementations of existing payment instruments rather than new payment instruments, electronic versions of existing institutions rather than new institutions and further centralisation rather than decentralisation, experiment and diversity. I'm not saying that I have any more idea of where things are going than anyone else, but I think I can at least see that there's going to be more change than taking a MasterCard and putting it inside a personal communications device (let's call it a phone for argument's sake). Although that's not a bad place to begin experimenting.

3D Secure, give it your best shot [08/02/2008]

How pathetic is it that when I want to buy something on the Internet using my bank card I have do mess around typing in endless details, numbers, codes, passwords and the like. It's all so 1994. In a modern economy, that sort of thing is seen as being on a par with Babylonian clay tablets or filling out paper forms to make a SEPA Credit Transfer. But in advanced countries, there is another way:

"According to Sony Japan, the company has just sold its five millionth USB RFID dongle for home computers... the USB gadgets can be used in multiple ways. The most common involves swiping an IC-chipped phone or credit card to pay for purchases made online. The advantage lies in encryption applied to the card number before it is transmitted - a valuable safety net in these days of endless data breaches.

Other uses for the technology - terminals are already built into all Japanese Sony Vaios, by the way - include encrypting files on the PC, authenticating users for access to secure parts of a network and even acting as a screensaver lock. The most prosaic FeliCa application is, however, considerably more useful than any of those. Instead of using a ticket machine in a train station, travellers with IC passes can add cash to or renew their validity from the comfort of their desk using the PaSoRi, something we can expect to see in the West soon."[7]

So when you want to buy something online with your DoCoMo phone, you just touch the phone to your dongle. That's it. Since I have a brand-spanking new Barclaycard with *Visa PayWave* on board, what's the barrier to a dongle to go with it? I've got my calculator-thingy from Barclays, and that works really well for using my bank account, but it doesn't help me with payments at all. There are millions of these things being issued in the UK...

"Nationwide Building Society has contracted with French vendor Xiring for the provision of over one million handheld authentication devices which it will begin rolling out to its online retail banking customers this spring."[8]

You'd think we'd at least be able to use them in 3D Secure, if nowhere else. I hate to be a big whinger, but isn't this just another example of the silo mentality at work, where the guys in charge of home banking are nothing to do with the payment guys.

Both MasterCard and Visa have programmes to use the handheld readers for 2FA in 3D Secure transactions (the CAP and DPA programmes) but as far as I know none of my bank issuers offer them as services. Perhaps it's too late now? The natural way forward would seem, to me, to integrate the mobile phone into the transaction loop rather than require special-purpose hardware. In the not-too-distant future I will have a phone that can interface to my Barclays OnePulse card, so I won't need another dongle. Since the Card Authentication

---

[7] Personal RFID terminals go big in Japan, *TechRadar.com*

[8] Nationwide to dish out Xiring smart card readers, *Finextra*

Programme (CAP) and Dynamic Passcode Authentication (DPA) implementations depend on the cryptography in the secure chip on the EMV card and do not need any security in the device, it should be easy to implement the software in the mobile handset.

Except that you're not supposed to enter PINs into a mobile phone keypad because it's not seen as being a secure PED (PIN entry device). However, since Monetise have managed to persuade VocaLink to let them enter ATM PINs into the phone (hence the Monilink joint venture), there ought to be a way of making this all work for payment transactions as well.

Part 2 – The Business Axis

Chapter 4: Banking and Credit

The visible (and not-so-visible) costs of banking are an important dynamic and these posts explore them, using real-life examples as well as informed speculation to wonder where the industry is heading.

Where next for ATMs? [27/03/2007]

According to The Guardian (Friday 9th March, page 29), ATMs are about to change. As a way of making ATMs even more expensive, Tesco and RBS are about to begin trials of ATMs that dispense euros. As a way of making ATMs even more annoying, the good people at Bank Machine Limited are planning to offer ATMs that allow customers to download ringtones and print photographs as well as dispense cash. They say that these new ATMs are perfect for, amongst other places, pubs. I find this very hard to believe: imagine a Newcastle pub at midnight on a Friday, when someone goes to draw some cash out to go clubbing only to find that the person in front of them at the ATM is going through their camera album and printing out a few snaps.

It makes you wonder where ATMs might actually go next. Here's an idea for the marketing guys to work with. As everyone knows, it's the cost of getting cash into virtual environments that puts a floor under the transaction costs in those environment. But what if you want to attract young people (who don't have payment cards) into a virtual environment (where notes and coins don't work)? Simple -- let them pay in blood! The Chinese virtual world ("Cabal") is offering free accounts to players who donate half a litre of blood. Now, if you could make your deposit at an ATM instead of having go all the way across town to a hospital...

Credit, debit, prepaid [16/04/2007]

I often find myself using "credit card" as a generic term for payment card. It's a reflection of my age, I suppose, and a deep-seated response to the first payment card I ever had: a Barclaycard that I rather unwisely obtained as a student. But credit cards are in retreat online and shunned elsewhere, mostly in favour of debit cards. Visa says that about 55% of its e-commerce transactions are now debit cards rather than credit cards. This is more than double the proportion of just two or three years ago! Now, I don't get this. I use my credit card for absolutely everything, but clearly I'm in the minority. In the US, debit card transactions grew nearly a fifth last year and issuers expect continued strong growth this year. Bizarrely (to Europeans), signature debit grew 20%, PIN debit only 16% and active cardholders performed about 11 signature debit transactions and 5 PIN debit transactions. Anyway, I was wondering if in a decade or so, we might be seeing debit cards becoming the minority as prepaid products come to dominate globally.

I'm focusing on "open" prepaid at the moment. Both MasterCard and Visa have been active expanding prepaid product ranges and cutting deals to extend the load networks. Visa, for example, has announced *Visa ReadyLink*, which will rapidly expand the accessibility of Visa's prepaid load network service. They recently announced an agreement with Blackhawk Network's alliance partner stores, making Safeway the first in Blackhawk Network's alliance of 60,000 stores in North America to implement Visa ReadyLink. (ReadyLink lets consumers easily add funds to eligible Visa reloadable prepaid cards at participating retail locations.)

"Open" doesn't mean universal and there are plenty of niches to be exploited within the open prepaid umbrella. Government and benefit cards are an obvious case. In the UK, Alliance & Leicester has launched a prepaid Visa card designed for public sector organisations that can be used to deliver welfare payments. Being in the UK, it is a chip and PIN card of course. Importantly, the card does not require the recipient to have a bank account. This doesn't necessarily mean that it will be easy or convenient to get: for all I know you will still have to turn up with a passport, gas bill and a note from your mother.

Nevertheless, as has been discussed before, products like these are critical for social inclusion. A typical target for such a product is migrant workers, of whom there are a great many in the UK -- an estimated 600,000 Polish workers have arrived in the UK since accession, and they sent an estimated 1.6 billion pounds back to Poland in 2006 -- with more arriving every day. That's why there's a *Maestro* card being marketed at major migrant arrival points, such as Victoria bus station in central London which can also be used to send money abroad. This should become even more convenient now that MasterCard are tying up with the GSM Association. Note that the *Daily Mail*-based article says that this is "inevitably raising fears that criminals and illegal immigrants in[to] Britain could use the card to send cash to foreign accomplices financing terrorism" as if they haven't figured out how to put 500 euro notes in an envelope. The Maestro card has a maximum balance of £2,500, with a £1,500 daily load limit. And only £200 can be sent abroad daily, which seems entirely reasonable to me.

The reason I'm looking at prepaid a lot at the moment is because we have clients who want to focus on this growth area. One of our clients has been carrying out a survey of the existing products in the UK and they are, frankly, rather poor, so there is plenty of opportunity to come in with better products. I've been thinking about how existing business processes need to be modified to really capture market share. Putting prepaid card products, in particular, on top of existing credit card infrastructure can result in situations that actively drive customers away. Here are a couple of examples.

The first concerns a guy who used his prepaid card at a hotel in San Francisco, then a few weeks later got a letter from the issuer asking for payment because his prepaid card was overdrawn by a significant amount. As the customer notes, "I was mystified how this was possible". The issuer customer services agent told him that it is possible for a merchant to overcharge the card if they force the transaction, and do not abide by the rejection. You can see how a customer who thought that prepaid meant prepaid would find this strange: one of the reasons I want my kids to have anonymous prepaid cards to use on the Internet is precisely so that they cannot be overcharged if they stupidly give their card number to someone dodgy.

The second concerns a girl who bought a $1 bag of popcorn and found her card debited $50. She used her $50 Visa gift card to buy the popcorn but when she tried to use the card next day at Walgreens, it was declined. Why? Because she used the card at a gas station, so her popcorn purchase showed up as a "gas" purchase at the issuer, causing them to deduct $50 automatically, as a safeguard. To prevent customers from swiping their card and pumping more gas than they have money for in their accounts the issuer deducts $50 and then waits for the merchant to report how much the customer actually spent, and refunds the rest, a process that takes about three days. So the girls card was declined, then the money was refunded a couple of days later. But the girl would never find this out: if you've been told the card balance is zero, why would you check it again three days later?

I'm not making a point about the specific issuers or schemes here, I'm just pointing out that there are tremendous opportunities to for people to design and deliver prepaid programmes that work better. How about a card that sends you a free text message following every debit or credit, a bit like the Visa debit card linked to a phone in the *Faithfone* service?

Extending debit [29/04/2007]

Our good friends at Edgar Dunn have produced a study showing that more consumers prefer debit cards than any other type of payment for point of sale purchases, for the first time. So it looks as if the march of debit at POS continues. It may well continue beyond POS as well now that the Star EFT network plans to start testing PIN-less online debit payments. The test will run about four months and involves Solana Corp., which will act as an aggregator of $25-and-under transactions generated by the online merchants. The idea is that customers can buy digital junk like ring tones or cartoon subscriptions from PCs. Through Solana, participating merchants will be required to register and authenticate consumers for the payments and bear the risk in disputed transactions. If they are happy to do this, then presumably the consumer preference for debit will begin to extend into cyberspace. It looks as if debit cards are set to displace cash even further, with PIN-less transactions to eat into virtual cash transactions and contactless interfaces to eat into real world cash transactions.

On which topic, replacing cash is environmentally friendly, I've decided, after reading in the newspaper (The Daily Mail, 24th April 2007, p27) that the Royal Mint estimates that 6.5 BILLION one penny coins are missing presumed down the back of the sofa in the

UK. The penny was introduced with decimalisation in 1971, as was the halfpenny that was scrapped in 1984. Now, it transpires, 38% of the all the pennies ever issued are unaccounted for. This is not too surprising, given another UK poll result: 60% of people wouldn't bother to bend over and pick up a penny in the street. What a waste.

Given that one penny coins actually use up 1.65 pence worth of metal, they are (as in America) not only pointless but value-destroying. No-one is going to go to the trouble of melting them down (which is, of course, illegal as well as impractical) but its still time to either scrap the penny and stop wasting copper (well, copper-plated steel) or, as one of the most popular suggestions for a referendum put forward on the Prime Minister's website points out, introduce a more useful 99p coin. (I'm not sure I would have voted for this, but I definitely would have voted to make police car sirens play the Benny Hill music.) Introducing a 99p coin used to be one of the Official Monster Raving Loony Party manifesto commitments, but I can't find it on their website at the moment. I wouldn't sneer. When the Monster Raving Loony Party was first launched (as the National Teenage Party) in 1964, two of its policies were votes for 18 year-olds and all day opening for pubs (both of which are now law). The other one was putting Parliament on wheels and taking it round the country. Give them time.

"Bank" "accounts" [26/07/2007]

A couple of months ago, the British Department for International Development (DFID) set out an "action plan" to try and find a way to get one billion of the poorest people in the world to open their own bank account for the first time. Having just helped my thirteen year-old son to open his first bank account, I estimate that this will take about 700 years: let's hope Tuareg tribesmen have their electricity bills and passports out and ready for inspection, otherwise the queues will stretch all the way round the Sahara. Anyway, we have a connection with this effort because mobile phones are seen as the only viable way to achieve anything like this goal and it was DFID's Financial Deepening Challenge Fund (FDCF) that in 2003 provided a one-off grant to Safaricom to pilot and launch the M-PESA mobile banking solution in Kenya. So I wholeheartedly support the drive to provide payment services to the poorest people using the mobile handset. But bank accounts?

The cost of maintaining bank accounts, compared to the cost of maintaining a prepaid balance, especially when the potentially reduced regulatory burden is taken into account, surely mitigates against trying to provide full service banking to some of the poorest people in the world. By contrast, using the mobile phone to provide enhanced payment services looks better and better. The possession of a mobile integrates people into the economy but without a payment service their participation is constrained. Put the two together and surely we get 90% of the way forward. Even in developed countries, there are a great many people who don't need any kind of full-service banking or even a current account (e.g., my son). But here's what I don't get: my son's new current account provides a debit card, free ATM withdrawals and pays interest on the balance. And it's free. By comparison, a basic prepaid "debit" card has an initiation fee, monthly fees, load fees and ATM fees. Why? And why, when I looked into getting a basic prepaid card, did it involve sending photocopies of passports and various other things I couldn't be bothered with. (Rhetorical question: Know Your Customer (KYC) and anti-money laundering (AML) legislation).

Prepaid growth [02/08/2007]

The forecasts for the prepaid market have been bullish for a while. One recent survey put prepaid card spending at $64 billion in 2004, $113 billion this year and predicts $178 billion by 2010, although the rate of growth that is predicted is lower. But it's a big business. As previously discussed, it's steadily shifting to the big networks. Aite's survey says that Visa/MasterCard/etc cards will have 44% of the prepaid market by 2010 compared with only 20% in 2004. About two-thirds of their volume comes through cards issued on behalf of government agencies and corporate clients. This is in contrast with private-label cards (e.g., the *iTunes* card I gave to my son last week) which are predominantly issued by retailers. Note that while the survey predicts the total number of prepaid cards in the US will be 7 billion in 2010 (compared with 4.3 billion this year) they will still account for only 1.6% of personal consumption expenditures (PCE).

Europe is seeing plenty of activity as well. We've looked at the Italian prepaid market before as it is the home of the widely-used Poste Italiane prepaid (*Visa Electron*) card. Now it's going to be home of a contactless prepaid MasterCard, as BancoPosta, the financial services arm of Poste Italiane, will launch a trial by the end of the year, offering prepaid cards to new cardholders with the PayPass application onboard. Cardholders will be able to tap to pay at a relatively small number of merchant locations in Rome and Milan during the six- to eight-month trial but it will still be interesting to see how the usage patterns develop. I'm particularly curious about this because cash accounts for 93% of transactions in Italy, the highest in Europe, so it will be a real litmus test of contactless' ability to displace cash in retail transactions.

There have been a number of new prepaid products entering the UK market as well. Barclays have just announced another re-loadable, PIN-protected travel money card that has been designed to replace paper travellers' cheques and cash. It can be loaded with British Pounds, US dollars and euros at Barclays branches, or over the telephone, using a debit or credit card. Customers can put the equivalent of between £100 and £2,500 on the card and the funds are available instantly. Balances can be checked at ATMs or over the phone. Lloyds TSB, Virgin Money and the Post Office have similar products. Lloyds TSB have also launched a money transfer card. Basically, you give the card to someone (e.g., a child away at college) and tell them the PIN. Then you top it up from your bank account whenever. The card is charged £1.50 per ATM withdrawal and there's a 3% currency conversion charge on foreign exchange transactions.

I was thinking of getting a couple of these to try them out and report back on them in more detail, but it's frankly too much hassle. I have to go to a branch with the usual passport and gas bill combination and fill out a load of forms, and I'm not dedicated enough to the cause to do this. Sorry.

Online payments [07/08/2007]

I was involved in a discussion yesterday about young persons' use of financial services. Thinking about payments, I remembered that our good friends at Payments News ran a *Facebook* poll on online payment choices amongst young persons. It basically came down to around a third credit card, a third debit card and a third PayPal (within the bounds of statistical error). They point out that it's no surprise that the debit card is most favoured among this age group, but also remark on how PayPal's showing is also especially strong. New entrant *Google Checkout* barely moves the needle in this particular survey and almost no one likes to pay by providing their checking account details (also known as *eCheck*).

I'm sure this supports Javelin's conclusions that younger persons think differently about payments and because more profits will be coming from their purses, wallets, Internet connections and even mobile devices, payments and financial services companies need to understand where the crucial differences are and what to do about them. One crucial difference that might be apparent in the Facebook case is that these consumers don't distinguish between banks, non-banks and third-party offerings. They go by convenience, utility and brand. And brand is so, so important.

Sub-prime [21/08/2007]

Credit card issuers aren't very popular in the US and they're getting a torrid time from some quarters, including Congressional hearings this spring held by Senator Carl Levin. According to testimony, one witness exceeded his charge card's $3,000 limit by $200 -- triggering what eventually amounted to $7,500 in penalties and interest. After paying an average of $1,000 a year for six years, the man still owed $4,400. That experience has become all too common as the credit card industry has stealthily adopted methods designed to maximize burdensome penalties and fees, while ratcheting up interest rates as high as 30 percent. Companies bombard unwary consumers with teaser packages that promise very low interest rates to start, while reserving for themselves the right to raise rates whenever they choose. The details are buried in deliberately arcane contracts that run 30 pages long and that even lawyers have trouble understanding. What this means in practice, as with all payment systems, is that the costs fall on the people least able to afford them. One-third of US cardholders are paying interest rates in excess of 20 percent. About a third of credit card accounts with balances pay little or no interest each month, which essentially amounts to a free or very low- cost loan. More than a third (36 percent) of accounts pay the regular interest rate. The final third of accounts -- which are presumably the "sub prime" customers -- pay interest rates that range from more than 20 percent to as high as 41 percent. What this kinds of press reports seem to show is that neither credit cards nor debit cards (i.e., bank accounts) are good solutions for people with little or no money. What they need is cheap, simple, prepaid solutions.

Last year, we started some interesting discussions by asking "Where's the Wal-Mart?" Well, talking of Wal-Mart, it is following other retailers who hope to tap into a large pool of consumers who deal mostly in cash, but want the convenience of plastic. Alfredo Padilla, a Wal-Mart spokesman, says

"We want to help the underserved -- the people without a traditional banking relationship."

The Wal-Mart *MoneyCard*, a prepaid Visa card that allows customers to pay bills, sign up for direct deposit and shop online. There is a $4.94 monthly fee, which is waived when $1,000 or more is loaded in one calendar month or the cardholder takes advantage of direct deposit. It requires no credit check or checking account, eliminating some of the barriers non-bankers shy away from. According to a Federal Reserve study, while 22.6 percent of non-banking families reported that they didn't like dealing with banks, the top reason for not having a bank account was that 27.9 percent simply don't write enough checks. To help alleviate some of these deterrents, Wal-Mart has added already extensive financial services with this MoneyCard. Before the prepaid card was the ability to cash checks, make money orders and transfers, pay bills, apply for a credit cards and request credit reports. There are already 2,600 MoneyCenters in Wal-Mart stores.

A survey of US consumers by the Network Branded Prepaid Card Association provides further support for the prepaid push into the sub-prime market. They found that satisfaction among consumers who have already used a reloadable prepaid card is extremely high: 88 percent had a positive experience with the cards and found them useful. There are differences, however, in the details. Although cash-based consumers are more likely to have used a reloadable prepaid card (25 percent compared to 14 percent of all respondents), as a group they are less likely to have heard of the card (48 percent compared to 60 percent of all respondents), presumably because they don't pay attention to card advertising of any kind. Anyway, interest in getting a prepaid card is high amongst cash-based consumers:

- 74 percent of those who pay their bills using money orders,
- 73 percent of those without a checking account,
- 63 percent of those who use cash to pay a bill or ask friends to write checks,
- 63 percent of those who are paid in cash or use a check cashing store.

But note that -- as Consult Hyperion found in some previous studies for clients looking to enter the prepaid card business -- in addition to the obvious need for reloadable prepaid cards among cash-based consumers, consumers with traditional banking relationships also find them valuable: 54 percent of consumers who are paid through bank accounts still say that reloadable prepaid cards would be useful. So it's wrong to see prepaid cards as a sub-prime only opportunity. Consumer like the idea of having different "jam jars" (as we used to call them back in the Mondex days) for different spending purposes, and there's no reason not to help them to do this with cards rather than cash.

More on banks and payment futures [18/09/2007]

Gartner have published a report agreeing with Aneace Haddad that payment schemes need to offer merchants new promotional marketing capabilities at the POS to reduce pressure on interchange. They tend to be thinking about loyalty, receipting and that kind of thing. But I also wonder if one of the most obvious value-added services around payments isn't, after all, a bank account? Perhaps a way to bring down costs is to provide limited functionality payment accounts rather than full-blown bank accounts that overshoot the needs of a substantial fraction of the customer base and don't address the needs of the population of non-consumers of bank services, thereby matching the value offered more closely to the customer needs.

Talking about non-consumers being converted consumers, here we are on the appointed "day to open eldest son's first bank account". He doesn't really need a bank account, of course. What he needs is a "payment account". A Visa or MasterCard that he can use in shops on the web and at ATMs, that I can transfer money to. The bizarre thing is that the bank will give him an account with a debit card for free and pay him interest on the balance, but will charge him (through the nose) for a prepaid card with no account and no interest on the balance. Odd. Anyway, he has some birthday money that he no longer wants to keep in cash under his pillow, he's now a teenager and it's time to enter the financial system...

Me: *Have you got a letter or something with your address on it?*

No.1 Son: *No, who sends me letters?*

Me: *I don't know; the school or someone...*

[five minutes later]

No.1 Son: *I've looked everywhere, I don't have anything. Anyway, why do I need it, I can just tell the bank what my address is.*

Me: *It doesn't work like that. Now go away and find something.*

[several minutes later]

No.1 Son: *I found this Lego magazine.*

Me: *Great. Let's go.*

No.1 Son: *This is boring. Why can't we do it on the Internet?*

Me (in head): *Good question.*

Me (out loud): *Get off the phone, shut down the computer, get your coat on and get in the car.*

Where will the innovation come from? [20/09/2007]

Having been reading some of James Gardeners insightful reflections on innovation banking, and in particular having been thinking about some of the questions he posed when talking about Xerox and Microsoft, I am forced to ask a tough question: where is the innovation in payments going to come from? Bank's IT budgets are going to be sucked up by SEPA initiatives for the foreseeable future and those initiatives mean downward pressure on payment income. Insofar as I understand the strategy of banks that we work for, in recent times it has been to change the cost/income ratio by both increasing income (perhaps by making riskier investments!!) and becoming more operationally efficient: factories for money. But I wonder how this works in the longer term?

There's an undeniable tension between operational efficiency and innovation. There was a good case study in the Inside Innovation section of *Business Week* a while ago. When 3M (a company noted for innovation) switched to "six sigma", cost-cutting and process improvement, things looked good at first. Now, though, the picture is less rosy. The company used to earn a third of its revenue from products introduced in the previous five years: that is now down to one quarter. The issue of where the next innovation is going to come from has meant undoing the "improvements". In an innovation economy, process-based approaches are not a cure-all. This may be one of the reasons why management consultants, who are experts in process, don't always come up with the optimal strategies for new technology and the innovation it facilitates.

You hear a similar story in the banking sector: a focus on operations means the short term is terrific but there's nothing in the pipeline for the longer term. Now, in the case of banking as a sector, it doesn't really seem to matter because the income from the core business is so much larger than the income from payments -- as one head of innovation in retail payments (I hope you don't mind me stealing your quote!) said to me when he left the job, "there is no innovation my team can deliver that will ever generate more profit next quarter than lending a bit more money to a few more people". The core business is not payments, but if innovation in payments is choked off -- by SEPA, by R&D cutbacks, by IT priorities, by lack of interest -- then surely the core business is reduced to a back office utility (I don't mean this in a bad way) because payments are actually the connection to customers.

More than just a connection, it might be argued that it's clear that in some ways, payments can be seen as being a "portal" into the financial services world. Thus, despite the fact that a bank might make little or no real income from its payments business, it has to keep the payments business not only up-and-running but evolving in a competitive market. This is because the loss of payments businesses means the loss of a significant channel for bringing new customers into the bank. Banks in some regions have to be prepared to give up a fair amount of payment revenue from transactions in order to achieve other goals. For example, ICICI Bank waives transaction fees for customers who transfer more than $1,000 as they recognise that the long-term value of these customers lies not in the remittance fees the bank can earn twelve times a year. Rather, these customers who remit more money each month than the average Indian earns each year are likely to be consumers of credit cards, insurance and other financial services as well. For organisations hoping to compete with banks in providing payments, this means that the game isn't simply about collecting transactions fees: strategically, banks will fight much harder to retain a share of the payments business than the share of net income directly attributable to payments indicates. But can they do this without innovating?

The six main trends in European payments [02/11/2007]

In this month's excellent SPEED magazine, there is an article by Harry Leinonen. I know Harry from the conference circuit, where we occasionally fetch up together, but you probably know him as an advisor to the Bank of Finland and the Finnish representative on the Payment and Settlement System Committee with the Eurosystem. I always pay attention to his well-informed and well-thought out points. In the article he looks over the last decade's worth of statistics to highlight six main trends in European payments. I'll get on to those in a moment, but what I wanted to first draw attention to was this paragraph in Harry's piece:

"Payment developments seem to be quite slow. Major changes in payment habits need five to ten years to be implemented. One reasons for the slow pace is probably the lack of transparent price and cost information."

I realise that I sound like a ~~broken record~~ scratched CD on this topic, but it seems to me to be a question of rudimentary economics: no price information, no working market. If the European Commission wants to make the European payment market work better, they could do worse than start by actually turning it into a market in the first place by insisting on better price signalling. One inevitable consequence: the cost of cash will go up; the cost of cards will go down.

The six key trends that Harry outlines are

1. Non-cash payments are steadily replacing cash payments. A few days ago I was working with a bank in Iceland where more than nine in ten retail payments are non-cash (in the UK its one in four).

2. Electronic payments are taking over from paper payments. One particular form of paper payment, the personal cheque, will likely vanish in my lifetime.

3. Within electronic payments, direct debits are losing market share. It's possible that this may change once the SEPA transition kicks in. As the potential for pan-European payments is realised then perhaps the market may begin to use them. The pieces are coming into place here. For example, several big processors (Equens, Iberpay, Seceti Stet and VocaLink -- who together handled 18 billion direct credit and debit transfers last

year) have agreed to establish bilateral interoperability using the European Automated Clearing House Association (EACHA) Technical Interoperability Framework over SwiftNet FileAct for the exchange of SEPA payments. I'm not so sure though: will Finnish consumers give direct debit mandates to Greek utilities? If I had to guess I would think that pushed e-billing triggering a credit transfer will become the consumer's preferred mechanism.

4. Self-service is replacing branch banking. Oddly, the number of bank employees has been surprisingly stable (and surprisingly invariant when normalised). I don't know what this implies, but presumably call centres, IT, marketing and so on have all grown even as the number of "front line" staff has declined.

5. Debit cards usage is growing faster than credit card usage, both in terms of payment volumes and values. In several countries, credit card payments are less than a fifth of all card payments.

6. ATM withdrawals are getting steadily more expensive. The average number of withdrawals per ATM per month has fallen by a third in recent years.

In all of these statistics, new "alternative" online payment mechanisms and mobile payments are essentially still invisible. I doubt this will be true a decade from now.

Banking is free like the NHS is free [17/12/2007]

Research based on the typical charging structures for banking in other countries indicates that should the UK banks be forced to scrap "free" banking then customers would be paying:

- 32.9p per direct debit;
- 34.2p for each standing order;
- 23.9p for getting cash out of the bank;
- 53.8p for card transactions; and
- 44.7p to process a cheque.

They also add on a monthly charge for running the account of £4.13p. That sounds like a lot, but wouldn't it be better than having the costs hidden? By making the charging open and up-front, banks would be helping the market to function more efficiently. The pricing of payment services would provide information for consumers to make informed choices -- where there's no proper pricing, there's no proper market. But how does a card transaction cost 54p when a cheque costs 45p? Surely, insofar as banks know what anything costs, they cannot possibly handle a cheque for less than a card transaction. How does this come about?

This is another example of how the lack of proper pricing shapes the model for retail payments. In the UK, current accounts are, theoretically, free. You can open an account and there won't be any service charges accrued as long as you keep the account in good order. You'll get charges for other things though, but those will be for other services you consume on the back of your free current account. You get subsidised to use inefficient mechanisms such as cheques and thus they perpetuate, but if banks allocated full costs to cash and cheques then consumers would go berserk and complain to their MPs and Watchdog. As it happens, cheques may not have much longer to go. The Payments Council, an independent body established to replace the Office of Fair Trading's Payments Systems Task Force earlier this year, is mulling plans to phase out paper-based cheques in favour of a UK-wide shift to automated and card-based payments. Cheque volumes now comprise 13% of UK non-cash payments compared with 64% at their peak in 1990. Based on current trends cheque volumes will fall at an average of over seven per cent per year over the next ten years so that cheques will account for only one payment in 50 in the UK market. Cheques are still widely used for person-to-person payments and payments to and from smaller businesses.

I thought it worth remarking on the cheque situation because of the council's suggestion that they will consult on, and I quote, whether the industry allows changes in customer behaviour and market forces to determine the rate at which cheques decline or whether there is a "proactive effort" to phase out cheques within a stated timescale. And, in particular, the Council's statement that is "minded to pursue the second, more proactive option" due to the availability of automated payment options and increasing use of new technologies such as mobile and contactless payments. Cool.

In the US, the Treasury Department is taking action to drive cheques out of benefit payments and is going to award a contact for a bank to administer a prepaid card programme to reduce the remaining 20% of benefit payments that are not direct deposit. The programme will begin shortly and go nationwide within six months. The reason for the programme is obvious. Many cheque recipients are unbanked. Since a typical electronic direct deposit into a bank account costs the Treasury about 9 cents, while a check disbursement costs about 89 cents (i.e., an order of magnitude more expensive), these people are wasting tax dollars (to the tune of $100m+ per annum). They're not going down the proactive route yet, so benefit recipients will be able to choose whether or not to continue wasting tax dollars as the Fed is not prepared to make the transition mandatory "right away". Still, as in the UK, it's only a matter of time.

Making prepaid work [23/01/2008]

[Richard Allen] Why would anyone use a prepaid card? I've been doing a survey of some UK products in that space. (You can do your own research at Which prepaid card.) Typically, it costs £10 to get a card, a pound or so just to load some value, 50p minimum to buy something with it, a couple of quid to draw money out of an ATM, 3% currency charges for overseas use, and so on. Many of them charge a monthly fee of around £5 in return for lower charges, but they're still expensive one way or another. Yet the market is still growing. Some of that growth is explained by the growth in online gaming, but I wonder if remittances might also be a strong growth driver. One of the cards you can get is actually two cards that are specifically designed for remittance purposes. You send one card to your Uncle Eric in Back-of-Beyond and top-up your card with value. You then "text" Uncle Eric some value (that bit is really bonkers and incurs a 2% fee) and he can take it out of any bank or ATM (with a MasterCard logo).

How much does it cost? If you ignore the cost of the card, sending £100 to USA will actually cost you about £107 and will yield approx $190 at the other end (based on $1.96=£1 exchange rate). Expensive? Well, compare it with Western Union, the market leader. It charges £114 to send a £100 that appears to yield $185. I made similar comparisons for India, Poland and Argentina. Shopping around, there are some good alternatives. I could just get a normal prepaid card, send it to Uncle Eric (with the PIN, of course!), then add value at a UK Post Office thereby skipping the nutty "text" bit and save another £2. Some cards, such as the sensational, soar-away Sun prepaid card, do not charge for foreign currency transactions, thus saving another 3% or so, and some come with a paying-in book and second card (for

Auntie Ethel). I reckon that we can now get $195 to Uncle Eric at a cost of less than £103. That's better than using your average credit card! We can do all that without a single bank account or credit record between us: the infrastructure is already there - it's called MasterCard (most of the prepaid cards I looked at were MasterCard/Maestro-branded). We just need to find ways of using it more effectively.

[Dave Birch] It's interesting to see organisations like The Sun expanding the market rather than bank brands. In the US, the arrival of the Wal-Mart MoneyCard, a prepaid Visa debit card, was expected to drive the market on, largely because the unbanked go to Wal-Mart far more than they go to banks. But a recent survey by Synergistics Research found that about 20% of consumers were aware of the card, but only about 10% likely would use it. Moreover, only 1% of those surveyed had purchased the card. Wal-Mart introduced the card as part of its plan to roll out 1,000 MoneyCenters inside Wal-Mart stores. The card can be reloaded at any of these and also at 40,000 Green Dot Financial Network outlets. So how do the charges compare to the UK examples? Well, Wal-Mart charges $8.94 to obtain a card and waives the $4.95 monthly maintenance fee when a cardholder loads at least $1,000 that month onto the card. Wal-Mart also waives the $4.64 loading fee for customers who cash checks at Wal-Mart. ATM transactions cost $1.95 and operated-assisted telephone calls are $2 each. According to Steve Verdier, the senior VP of congressional affairs at Independent Community Bankers of America, this makes it more expensive that most banks' offerings:

"If unbanked consumers want to keep their financial lives simple, the fees and complexities of Wal-Mart's MoneyCard do not meet that objective... The survey results show only a fraction of consumers have purchased a Wal-Mart MoneyCard, but banks should not discount its threat yet. The MoneyCard still has the potential to divert a lot of transactions away from traditional banks."[9]

It's a market worth fighting for. The total for load volume including all "open" (i.e., Visa/MasterCard/Amex etc) and "closed" schemes will reach $421.5 billion by 2010. The closed market will represent $240 billion of that with open solutions around $182 billion. The growth in open solutions is significant: a couple of years ago they were a seventh of the market but they are growing at more than 50% per annum (closed solutions are growing at less than 10% per annum).

---

[9] Few consumers report buying a Wal-Mart MoneyCard, *CardForum.com*

With this vigorous growth and competition, one might reasonably hope for more innovation as well.

Yet as Richard's introduction indicates, and as has been discussed here once or twice, the potential for the prepaid "cards" market looks terrific but the implementation of prepaid cards has been a little patchy. This is because the open products are built on top of the systems developed for credit and debit cards. This leads to problems from time to time. Step by step, the terminals, networks and hosts need to be improved to deliver better service for prepaid products and therefore help the sector to grow. That's not to stay that the schemes aren't already taking steps in this direction. One of these steps in the US is sorting out authorisation problems, so the news that Shell Oil and its 6,000 stations committed to Visa's "partial authorisation service" is welcome. The service is designed for customers making a purchase that is larger than the balance remaining in the prepaid account. Instead of declining the transaction (which is unpopular with retailers as it may mean a lost sale and confuses consumers) pumps will be programmed to dispense petrol or diesel to the value remaining. So instead of doing a standard (let's say) $50 authorisation -- which is what they do with credit cards -- the terminal recognises that prepaid products need to be treated differently.

I still think, however, that the most important step forward for prepaid products is integration with mobiles. Javelin highlight the example of SMS alerts, but I'm sure there are other possibilities (such as targeting better services for remittances). The reason I'm so sure about this is that knowing the balance on a prepaid product is absolutely critical to its use and the mobile screen provides no better place to show the customer that balance, either because the card is integrated into the phone (e.g., through NFC) or because the account is (e.g., through SMS).

Freebanking and free banking [14/02/2008]

Foreign readers may be unaware that banks in Scotland and Northern Ireland issue their own banknotes. In the England and Wales (and everywhere else in the entire world), banknotes are issued by the central bank. As *The Economist* points out, feelings run deep. Sir Walter Scott is commemorated on banknotes in Scotland precisely because he fought off the Bank of England's 1826 attempt to stop Scottish banks from issuing their own notes.

There are nearly £3 billion-worth of Scottish banknotes in circulation (and half as much in Northern Irish banknotes). For odd historical reasons, the issuing banks have to back their note issue with a deposit of 95% the value of notes outstanding, but only at the weekends! Seriously. So during the week they can lend the money out and earn seigniorage. The Scottish banks currently earn good money this way so the change

> *"would lose Scottish banks some of the £65m they now earn in interest and "seigniorage" (income from selling their notes to other banks)."*[10]

The Treasury, presumably still wondering what to do about Northern Rock, wants to spoil the party and force Scottish and Northern Irish note-issuing banks to keep the deposit backing the note issue at the Bank of England all the time, just in case (e.g., RBS goes bankrupt but not on Saturday or Sunday). In England and Wales there is a different system: the Bank of England, the most profitable nationalised industry in British history, backs its notes not with deposits of euros or gold bars but with fixed-interest instruments bought from the British government and remits the interest earned to the Treasury.

I don't imagine that I might agree with Alex Salmond, leader of the Scottish National Party, on much beyond the issue of independence for Scotland, but I do agree with him on his defence of the Scottish note issue: he said that there's no need for the Treasury to take this action because Scottish banks are among the most stable in the world. The SNP's defence is robust...

> *"The changes suggested will cost Scotland's financial sector £80 million a year. This is daylight robbery by the UK Treasury and will provide Scotland's financial sector no advantage whatsoever."*[11]

As it happens, I have a particular interest in the history of Scottish banks because of the lessons of that period of "free banking". This does not, as you might think, mean that Scottish banks were once operated as charities but that they were free to compete in note issue. And the result, as most historians would confirm, was a period of incredible innovation when the more tightly regulated London and

---

[10] Scottish banknotes Under threat, *Economist.com*

[11] MP Warns Treasury - 'Hands Off Scottish Bank Notes', SNP - Scottish National Party

country banks failed more often than the less tightly regulated Scottish banks did (I know this is an appalling précis of a complicated and interesting period, but I'm trying to make a bigger point).

Scotland had an enviable track record of innovation in the finance and banking sector right up until the time when the Bank of England's outrageous monopoly was extended north of the border, this prompting Sir Walter Scott's famous last-ditch defence of Scottish notes. Lawrence White's fascinating "Free Banking in Britain: Theory, Experience and Debate, 1800-1845" is a great place to begin if you're interested in delving further into this period in the history of money. Anyway, here's your handy cut-out-n-keep guide to innovation in Scottish banking:

- 1695 - Britain's first joint stock clearing bank, the Bank of Scotland, created by the Scots parliament.
- 1728 - The first overdraft is granted by the Royal Bank of Scotland
- 1750 - The British Linen Bank (Scottish, despite the name) starts to build the world's first branch network.
- 1777 - World's first multi–coloured bank notes printed by the Royal Bank.
- 1810 - First savings bank established in Ruthwell.
- 1826 - Royal Bank of Scotland launches banknotes printed on both sides.
- 1845 - Westminster, despite Scottish protests, legislates against private note issue. Since this date no major commercial banks have been formed in Scotland.

The connection between freebanking and innovation seems clear. When a previous wave of innovation (paper money) swept through the British economy, freebanking Scotland was far more successful than England in exploiting that technological change to make the economy more efficient (and more stable). By 1850, when 90% of all commercial transactions in France were still being settled in gold or silver (as were a third of those in England), 90% of all commercial transactions in Scotland were being settled with paper (see Niall Ferguson, "The Cash Nexus". I wonder if regulation might prevent innovation in the next wave of technological change around NFC and mobiles, prepaid and e-gold?

Setting the right example [29/02/2008]

As you may recall, the US Treasury Department is introducing a prepaid debit card that will be used to deliver benefit payments to social security recipients. According to the Wall Street Journal, the Treasury selected Comerica Bank as the card issuer for the programme, which will see social security recipients who don't have a bank account given a "Direct Express" prepaid card that will be loaded directly with welfare payments. The move is, in a way, obvious because the prepaid card market is as a key place to bring financial services to the unbanked. Note that as many as 40 million US households either have no bank account or make little use of banking services, according to research conducted by Chicago's Center for Financial Services Innovation. The card is being introduced to provide benefit recipients with faster access to money and eliminate some security problems, like stolen cheques, but it will also save money because it must cost considerably less to make an electronic payment than to print and mail a cheque anyway.

This really should be government policy in the UK as well. The government mails out hundreds of thousands of cheques every month and I'm sure plenty -- if not the majority -- of these go to people who have a bank account anyway, who don't have a bank account but should get one and stop wasting taxpayers' money, or who don't have a bank account and don't need one but should get a prepaid card instead (if they weren't so expensive here) and stop wasting taxpayers' money. Given the significant savings, perhaps the government should even go down the BT route and give people more benefit if they are paid by direct debit, sharing the cost savings with the customers, so to speak?

Chapter 5: Retail and Wholesale

Creating a new payment mechanism is easy. Distributing it to consumers is easy. Making it economically secure is easy. Getting the public interested is easy. Getting retailers to accept it: that's another story.

Pincer movement [27/02/2007]

Our friends at Payments News alert me to the news that DoCoMo and McDonalds have got together in Japan and created a joint venture of offer electronic payment services, initially to McDonald's own stores. I'm highlighting this one -- amongst all the other mobile payment stories floating around at the moment -- because is brings together two of the categories of organisation that can feasibly attack the banks' retail payments business.

Isn't this a nightmare come true for the payments guys in banks? The retailers and the mobile phone operators getting together to provide a new solution to a problem that is not central to either of them but as a by-product of achieving some other goals -- perhaps customer intimacy or reduced churn -- chips away at legacy payment systems provided by banks and while the payments guys are concerned about it, the bank isn't, because it's a bank line of credit that the customers are using to fund their mobile phone / retailer payment schemes. So are the Japanese banks thinking that they should pull out all the stops to fight tooth and nail to keep the retail payments franchise or are they just, like, whatever. Was Dan Schatt of Celent right to say that banks could lose customers because of the combination of mobile and contactless technologies? That's not so clear to me: if I stop using my bank's debit card and use my mobile phone instead, then doesn't that save the bank money (in the UK)?

The battle isn't just about cool technologies, although cool they certainly are. Even a management consultant must realise that one of the keys to the deployment of the DoCoMo payment schemes in Japan is the fact that the consumers are beginning to see paper money and plastic cards as just so 20th century. It's about cool technologies and alternative business models. So whatever the spreadsheets might say about the transaction income that the telco might earn (too small for a bank to make that kind of investment in a new payment solution) and the merchant service charge saving to the retailer (too small to make merchants invest in new terminals), this pincer movement will succeed because it provides a payment solution that's just better.

Cheap as chips [13/03/2007]

I am frequently, and with good reason, accused of being over-optimistic about the ability of digital money to replace to cash. But now Peter Ayliffe, the head of Visa Europe, has said that within five years credit and debit cards should be cheaper and more convenient than cash and that, as I have long anticipated, retailers could start surcharging customers if they choose to buy products with cash, because of the greater cost of processing these payments. The British Retail Consortium (BRC) dismissed his view and said that Merchant Service Charges are still too high because of the interchange component. One member of the consortium said that the estimated interchange was 4p per transaction. The retailers object to the interchange because they say that it is used to fund stuff like cashback and frequent flyer miles rather than payment processing. "There is a duopoly between MasterCard and Visa in the UK. Their setting of fees is anti-competitive" said Nick Mourant, treasurer at Tesco, which currently handles about one-eighth of all retail payments by volume in the UK and has 31% of all UK supermarket spending. The payments industry might reasonably point out, however, 97% of all cash withdrawals at ATMs in the UK are free: so someone is paying for the machines, networks, security guards, armoured trucks and everything else that goes with ATMs and it's not the people using cards. If it's not going to be customers, then why shouldn't it be retailers?

The organisation that makes serious money out of cash is the Britain's most profitable nationalised industry, the note issuing business of the Bank of England. According to the BBC today, the new Bank of England £20 note -- which features that well-known Englishman, Adam Smith -- costs 4p. That's quite a margin!

Note to foreign reader: the apparent outburst of atypical xenophobia in the reporting of the new £20 note design is because, for bizarre historical reasons, Scotland has its own banknotes that are different to English banknotes. And Adam Smith, as every fule know, was Scottish.

Who will pay? And how? [01/08/2007]

It's all very well for informed observers such as myself to call for a more efficient payment system, but the economics have to work out as well. Given that merchants already feel that they pay too much (whether it's true or not, that's what they feel) then finding ways to deliver more value to them has to be a priority in the design of new systems and services. In America, the Merchant Payments Coalition (MPC) have been complaining that the collective setting of interchange fees by Visa and MasterCard is a violation of federal antitrust laws and saying that they favour a payment system that is transparent and open to competition. Well, you might think, what's stopping them? You can't help but observe that a decade of growing complaints from merchants, and the ready availability of the core technologies required to create viable alternatives (i.e., chip cards, mobile phones and the Internet) no large-scale rivals have emerged. Perhaps the truth is that merchants are happy with the bank-centric payments model and the complaints about interchange ARE just posturing for lower prices after all. Having been at a recent meeting between a bank and some large UK merchants, however, I think there's more to it. It's not just the size of the interchange fee that annoys merchants; it's what it's for. US merchants paid $56 billion in interchange fees last year and small retailers have seen interchange costs jump by 16 per cent a year on average since 2000 but a good chunk of those fees don't go to cover the cost of the payment plus a profit, they go to pay for frequent flyer miles, cashback and other issuer incentives. In fact, in the US, almost half of the interchange goes to pay for issuer rewards.

So are merchants stuck, at the mercy of a conspiratorial oligarchy, unable to cause or benefit from change? Well, not really. Things are changing in the retail e-payments space, of course. In a survey of the top 100 largest e-commerce sites to see what payments they accepted, acceptance of "alternative" payment mechanisms such as Google Checkout, PayPal and *Bill Me Later* had gone up 267% in six months, so consumers and merchants are getting more choices. Wal-Mart's decision to support e-cheques (which they think will save them a BILLION dollars per annum) will presumably cause other merchants to look at the possibility. Apparently a couple of retailers are going to trial Bill Me Later in physical stores as well.

The entry of significant new players such as Google must have an impact. Google Checkout is, in fact, quite a useful example because their business model is somewhat different from other payment companies. Google is prepared to run Checkout at break-even, or even at a loss, because it sees the service as a useful way to bring more advertisers to its all-important *AdWords* business, which charges retailers for search-related "keyword" ads. Checkout has already signed up a quarter of the top 500 online retailers, largely thanks to its offer of free payments processing until 2008. Once the promotion ends, every dollar a merchant spends advertising with Google will entitle it to $10-worth of free processing. This could be more of a window into the future. Just as in the case of DoCoMo, payments is not a business only about transaction fees and revenues but is an integrated part of a much bigger play.

The current situation is not mandated by the laws of nature, but has been formed by a particular set of circumstances. There are people working to change it and the payments cards industry cannot just assume that it will continue to dominate. This isn't to say that people won't be playing with cards in the future: they just won't be cards from their bank. In the US and the UK, for example, it may well be that some kind of identity card (or, more likely, some kind of identity card stored in a mobile phone) becomes a platform for a much wider variety of payment options.

He overshoots, he scores [17/10/2007]

Deloitte, a management consultancy, have published a report called "is the retail payments industry heading for disruption?". It looks to me as if it is based on the disruptive innovation concepts of Clayton Christensen (our favourite guru). I think this is a very useful way to look at the evolution of the retail payments sector -- I have used the same analysis myself for a couple of years in a course I teach at the

The Digital Money Reader 2008

Visa Business School -- and it can help with product and service development in very practical ways. Deloitte says that

"Credit card companies are showing classic signs of "overshoot," which makes them vulnerable to disruption, especially disruptive innovation. "

I agree, but I think this is only part of the story, and the example of EMV helps to illustrate why.

The transition from magnetic stripe cards to EMV chip cards has, I think, left many card portfolios caught between two stools. They have overshot a mass of consumers who don't need (and are not prepared to pay for) any chip-based services as well as a mass of merchants who (in some cases incorrectly) don't see the need to pay more in order to cut down other people's fraud. Meanwhile, they have undershot a smaller number of more sophisticated customers who would like to use their chip cards to do new stuff and might even pay for it -- I would happily pay $20 for a card reader I could plug into my computer so that I could log into my bank using my debit card if it meant that I never had to remember a password again and that Ukrainian fraudsters could not loot my account -- if offered. Similarly, as the discussions with Aneace often come back to, they are also undershooting the merchants by not delivering additional payment-related value to them either.

I think what this all means is that the very idea of a single payment product (card product, in this case) for all customers and all merchants might be rather old-fashioned. Right now, it might seem quite annoying to have to choose between different products depending on who and where you are. But look into the mobile phone-based future: I wander into a coffee shop in Australia to buy a latte. I wave my mobile phone at the point-of-sale terminal: now the phone knows where it is, the issuer knows the phone, the acquirer knows what merchant it is, and so on. The phone also knows what payment instruments it has available, my ranking of those instruments (based on which one gives me the most frequent flier miles) and other factors (e.g., the balance in a prepaid account) that might be relevant. They are perfectly capable of deciding between themselves which specific instrument to use in these circumstances: instead of choosing a payment instrument, I will choose a payment strategy and let my stuff get on with implementing it. I'm not sure if the marketing guys in card issuers have taken on board that they will be marketing to my stuff, rather than me, in this future...

Cards and costs [22/10/2007]

Retailers just won't let it lay about the cost of cards and there are new articles about this every day. In the US, gas stations are a particular focus of discontent (as they have been for some time, in fact). What bothers the owners is that on a petrol sale, the card companies make more money than they do. For example, on a $30 sale with petrol at $2.89 per gallon (that's approximately zero per Imperial gallon, for British readers), the retailer will get 39 cents but (as the retailer sees it) the bank gets 69 cents. I saw a quote from another retailer recently that if a customer wants to buy a pack of gum with a card, he'd prefer them to just steal it because he loses less money that way. Not exactly a devoted customer base. It's not just in the US though. In Dubai, all petrol stations have banned cards and all Emarat, Enoc and Eppco stations accept only cash or own-brand cards. Denzil Lawson, the General Manager of MasterCard Middle East & Levant, said

"We continue to consult with all parties concerned towards finding an effective solution... MasterCard is disappointed with the announcement by the fuel companies in Dubai that they will stop accepting payment cards, denying their customers the convenience and safety of using payment cards."

If contactless transactions are to eat into cash, then the industry is going to have to do better. Not necessarily offering a product that is cheaper than cash (although it is, when cash is priced properly) but offering a product that delivers better value than cash. One rather obvious way of doing this is to point out that people spend more money with cards than with cash, but it's a sensitive issue, and with good reason: there's a fine line between trying to say that if you're going to spend money, you might as well do it with [our] card, rather than with cash, and trying to persuade people to spend more money which, in some circumstance, may not be the best thing for them do. Certain parties (e.g., politicians) would happily jump all over card companies for trying to persuade consumers to spend more (especially if it involves high interest rates).

But there is another side to the argument. Is it really true that cash, rather than "cards" promotes responsible spending? As one of the commentators notes

"Debit cards, used in conjunction with digital balances from my bank (downloaded off the website and uploaded into a spreadsheet) made me far more financially responsible than I am now that I'm "cash only"... a decade ago when I worked in

The Digital Money Reader 2008

a society that accepts debit cards just about everywhere (Australia) I could tell you exactly how much I was spending on lunches at work. And movie tickets. And impulse purchases. And everything else.

And I was able to modify my behaviour to meet changing budgetary needs."

This is a very thought-provoking input to the debate on the cost of cash: should the social cost of cash be extended to include lack of accountability and audit not for governments but for individuals? The commentator goes on to note

"Nowadays I live and work in China, probably the closest thing to a cash-only society married to hyper consumption that exists on earth. And my wages (cash -- nice red 100 yuan notes in a big stack) sometimes last the month. And sometimes they don't. And I've really no clue why or how or what or when. Give me debit cards any day of the week..."

That same article makes another point. Here's a fun calculation to make: suppose you were, for some reason, convinced that using only cash would be beneficial. On average, how much would you have to draw out each time you went to the ATM? Well, in America that answer appears to be $1,200 so that you would on average have $600 in your wallet at any one time. That's a big interest-free loan to Uncle Sam if you ask me.

So where can this argument go? Merchants prefer cash, because consumers bear the cost. Since banks can't charge the proper cost of cash, they have to provide services to merchants that make cash more attractive. An example is the new Bank of America in-store cash management system that gives merchants secure hardware for depositing notes and credits them immediately (so they have use of the funds) rather than when the secure hardware eventually gets back to the bank. It looks as if the cards business is going to have to continue trying to come up with some genuine innovation to deliver value to the retailer because there is no possibility of competing with (subsidised) cash on a purely cost basis.

Changes to the card payments landscape in Europe
[07/11/2007]

I've been chairing the International E-Payments Intensive in the City, which is how come I saw a typically excellent presentation by John Chaplin of First Data. I've known John since his Visa days and I've always found his experienced and measured perspective on the payments landscape of immense value. Once again, he really made me think. John was talking about the impact of the Payment Services Directive (PSD) on the European payments card landscape. One key point that he made, which I've been reflecting on, is that that landscape just hasn't changed that much in the last couple of decades. The market is not that open, particularly because the rules of the club favour the existing members. But all this is going to change because of the PSD. Isn't it? Well, there are plenty of major pressures for change that are nothing to do with the PSD. Banking consolidation in the Scandinavian and Benelux regions is showing how thinking might change from national to regional and sub regional organisation and then to pan-European organisation at the time when the IT infrastructure (built in the 1980s) is up for renewal and SEPA is pressuring them to change. There are commercial pressures that are nothing to do with regulation. There are technology developments. All of these combine with PSD to create the potential for change. But might there be disruptive change?

I found the last part of John's presentation to be especially interesting. John was talking about the potential for disruptive innovation in the European retail payments space and one of the scenarios he discussed was the melding of debit and ACH products to extend near-real time account-to-account transfers to POS. I can see at least two technology-driven ways that this could happen:

- The mobile handset. The mobile handset is the obvious means to implement secure, authenticated payments. I go to a shop, buy something, wave my phone over the POS, the bill shows up on my phone, I enter my PIN to pay it and the bank instructs an FPS transfer and confirms to the shop. This means that shops and banks have to agree on some sort of (presumably) XML-based standard for such data. (As it happens, there already is one: the Internet Open Trading Protocol (IOTP) that consumed a substantial fraction of my life a decade ago and may be better known to you as RFC 2801.) There are plenty of other models: the phone might implement a prepaid account automagically topped up from the customer's bank account or line of credit: you buy a pair of shoes for fifty quid, wave your phone at the POS, the phone grabs fifty quid from your bank account and then immediately sends it to the shop. This seems no big deal, but note that in this scenario, the money is switched between your bank account and the shop's bank account outside of the bank network (i.e., by your phone). It's more radical than it seems at first glance. In any case, it's only one of a number of potential implementations, all of which serve to support the main point that the mobile phone will inevitably become a means of instructing payments.

- The identity card. Suppose I'm a big retailer in the UK and suppose (this is a fantasy, remember) that the government has implemented a smart identity card with biometric PIN augmentation and it actually works. I register with the retailer by giving them my bank details (I might be incentivised to do this by a lavish helping of loyalty points) and authenticating myself with the card. Next time I go to buy my groceries, the retailer merely gets me to authenticate myself with the card. If I have a track record, they may not even bother to authorise the transaction: I'll just save them up and drop the whole lot via ACH in the middle of the night. If you don't have funds to cover the transaction -- well, I have your ID card details so I can blacklist you, or have you blacklisted by all retailers or whatever. There's no getting away! This kind of the service has begun to spring up in the USA, using the REAL ID drivers' licence.

Therefore, one possible future is that banks disintermediate payment networks themselves. Whether you think this likely or not, you can see the rationale behind the thinking. In the 1950s, no bank could have built a network to every retailer, so it made sense to begin developing networks to connect banks and retailers. Now, however, every bank is connected (in principle) to every retailer because of the miracle of the Internet (and mobile, wireless, cryptography, smart cards and so on). They are also connected to customers and everyone else besides. Hence the alternative vision: when the customer pays the retailer, the retailer never sees any payment instrument or information because the retailer transmits the invoice to the customer, the customer instructs the bank to pay it, and the bank sends the money to the retailer's bank.

It isn't only John who has spotted the potential for change here. Other observers also note that banks are beginning to think about using networks to connect more directly with customers in the payment space. Bruce Cundiff, of Javelin Strategy & Research, says that a shift in mind-set already is beginning in some banks:

"You're seeing a lot more focus on the demand deposit account (DDA) as the cornerstone of banks' retail payments strategies, as opposed to their going out and starting a new credit card business... There's a move away from a card-based strategy. Banks are seeing the DDA as the genesis of their payments strategies"

And Bruce said this before Capital One's announcement of the disconnected debit card, which provides another way to access the customer's current account funds at POS. Building on debit is a no-brainer: Figures released by APACS show that there were 1.7 billion plastic card purchases made in the UK during the last three-month period, totalling £86.6 billion, and these accounted for 72 per cent of all plastic card purchases (up from 70 per cent in the previous comparable period). Customers continue to switch from credit cards to debit cards.

Talking about new debit cards, the Euro-Alliance of Payment Schemes (EAPS) has been set up to explore ways of linking existing national debit card schemes into a pan-European network following the introduction of the single euro payment area (SEPA) in 2008. Founding members of the scheme include Germany's electronic cash, Spain's EURO 6000, Portugal's Multibanco, The UK's Link Interchange Network, Italian card schemes PagoBancomat and European card payment processor Eufiserv. The consortium -- a not-for-profit Brussels-based company that will promote "the interests of its members" -- has developed a rule set and members have begun testing some bilateral cross-border transactions. A group of Europe's largest banks (apparently, according to Lafferty, including Société Générale, Deutsche Bank, Dresdner Bank, Commerzbank, Unicredito, ABN AMRO, ING and Rabobank) is looking at the feasibility of using EAPS as the basis of a pan-European debit scheme, a non-Visa and non-MasterCard euro "third way".

If so, they're not the only ones. Indian banks are looking at a similar move, setting up a domestic card payment settlement company, called India Pay, to compete with Visa and MasterCard. The plan, taken up under the aegis of the Indian Banks' Association (IBA), comes amid estimates that payments through cards would increase three-fold over the next five years. A domestic card payment settlement company would save the "outgo on commission paid to Visa and MasterCard", a senior banker said. Last year, this was around $50 million in India, so it's serious business.

So will this kind of additional competition benefit consumers and merchants in the SEPA zone? It's not a given, as Aneace has repeatedly argued. He's at it again, drawing attention to the situation in Singapore where the domestic purse Network for Electronic Transfers Singapore (NETS) charges merchants between 35 and 55 basis points (bp). Starting next month, this will be increased to 150 to 180 bp, to bring it in line with Visa and MasterCard debit card fees because, as NETS CEO Poh Mui Hoon says, NETS will be squeezed out of the market if it does not raise its rates, because banks may no longer issue NETS cards, opting instead for the more lucrative debit cards. Will SEPA be different? It may be. When a similar price rise was mooted in Belgium -- dumping *Mister Cash* for Maestro -- the retailers went bananas and blocked it.

What are "low-value" payments? [06/12/2007]

There are different groups vying for the "low-value" payment market at retail POS. Hence there's the potential for some real innovation. But what is the "low-value" market? I was in a meeting recently where the discussion took an interesting turn. One group of retailers were unhappy with the £10 limit (fifteen euros on the continent) for contactless payments in London and the suggestion popped up -- which I thought was reasonable -- that the low-value cut-off might well vary between retailers or categories. But it might also depend on the channel. In the mobile world, the Payforit scheme has a £5 maximum purchase value but some operators are already saying that this should be raised to £10 (as I'm sure it will be soon) because the fiver limit doesn't cover a broad enough range of content. We don't want to end up with a confusing landscape for consumers though: it would, surely, be more sensible to have a universal definition of low-value payment across all channels and categories so that both customers and shopkeepers knew exactly where they stood: if the payment is under X then there's one set of rules and rights, above X then there's another set of rules and rights (e.g., Consumer Credit Act-style rights). This would also simplify implementation and customer education at the same time.

Incidentally, talking about low-value payments, I saw that pioneer e-purse *Chipknip* is steadily vanishing from the Dutch retail landscape. It's now been removed from attended POS and is being replaced by debit cards. Retailers didn't warm to it after a decade and customers didn't like having to find places to load it and they never knew what their balance was anyway (life will be so different when we all use phones instead of cards). But it did find a predictable niche in unattended environments: parking, vending and catering. That sort of thing and the product has a stay of execution because of that. I expect it will gracefully hand over to mobile proximity payments in a couple of years' time and then retire completely.

Anyway, the reason I remembered that *Linkdump on Payments* piece was because of this comment:

"We should also not forget the headlines of 10 years ago. Merchant lobby groups at that point of time explicitly stated that they were going to boycot the use of the Chipknip in the stores. Well, they lived up to their promise. It would be interesting to know if Neelie Kroes or any of her staff at DG Competition would also consider such collectively enacted boycots an abuse of dominant market position?"

What an interesting line of enquiry! Perhaps the Commission, instead of constantly blaming banks for the lack of competition in retail payments, slow progress toward SEPA and high merchant service charges, should cast the net more widely: why should merchants be excused from investing in the future of payments if the Commission believes that new payment schemes are important for European consumers?

Chapter 6: Real and Virtual

The difference between "real" and "virtual" money is getting ever smaller. Perhaps the rapid evolution of virtual money can tell us more about the future of e-payments than is first apparent.

Economic report [02/03/2007]

I'm looking again at the economics of virtual worlds and the Korean situation is once again much in my mind. An analysis of their virtual economy may contain some useful pointers. But what are they? Let's focus on the cross-border money transfers (cross-border in the sense of "real" world to "virtual" world). In 2006, these totalled US$830 Million. Around 80 percent of these transactions were mediated and 20 percent direct (player to- player). Looking at the kinds of games involved and the kinds of transactions...

Game Type	Game Items	Game Currency	Game Accounts
MMORG	18.5%	78.9%	2.6%
Action games	57.3%	41.5%	1.2%
Puzzle/Poker	33.6%	61.4%	0%

Unsurprisingly, money dominates. And, as a deeper look at some related figures shows; the foreign exchange is to support trade, not speculation.

Another source of up-to-date numbers is Sony, which has released 2006 figures for real-money trades (RMTs) on the Sony Online Exchange (SOE), which is where people trade *EverQuest II* virtual assets. The key numbers, according to *PlayNoEvil*, are that time spent on customer service calls related to virtual asset trading went from 40 percent to 10 percent, which represents substantial savings in one of the areas where a games company has controllable costs and, in itself, is the business case justification for allowing and managing RMTs. SOE also made around $275,000 in listing fees and commissions). I found the comment by Edward Castronova (I've just finished his book on virtual worlds) interesting. He said "This is a little disappointing". This is because he has traditionally opposed virtual asset trading because it goes against the rules of most games. "I was hoping that the other servers would have less (of the trading). But that didn't happen at all."

I think there are fascinating lessons buried in the Sony figures. Their virtual asset auction site (which, as I've mentioned before, makes eBay look, like, so last century) generated transactions of $1.87 million during its first year. Players have paid as much as $2,000 for the right to use a single EverQuest II character and one seller earned $37,435 from 351 auctions.

I won't rehash all of the results as you can read them for yourself, but I'd like to highlight one or two:

- The top 15 sellers each took in over $10,000.

- Characters were by far the most valuable trade category. The top 20 character auctions were each for over $1,000.

- The demographics are conclusive. 34-year-olds were the biggest buyers of virtual goods; 22-year-olds were the biggest sellers so it is entirely clear that cash-rich time-poor thirtysomethings are buying goods from time-rich cash-poor twentysomethings (let's call them "students", for short).

- Auctions for coin led to a stable, real-money average exchange rate for the year of $7.35 for one piece of platinum.

Just a reminder that we don't really understand what's going on here. The author of the Sony report says that "The sellers who provide armour and weaponry feel they are providing a service to players while elevating themselves to elite status among fellow gamers" and concludes that the vast majority of players who earned money did so through the sale of items they quested or crafted within the games, rather than by buying items at auction and selling them at a higher price. In other words, there is very little speculative trading. I'm sure that will change once I show the report to my friend at Goldman Sachs!

If there is a conclusion to the current economic review, it is, as John Smedley (the President of Sony Online Entertainment) said, "there is a significant demand for a secure, sanctioned online marketplace where players can enhance their gaming experience by spending real dollars".

Chinese walls [21/03/2007]

I wonder if the focus on virtual currencies isn't getting just a tad hysterical? The news that the Chinese government has decided to restrict the convertibility of virtual currencies into Yuan because it is worried that virtual currencies from online games could undermine the country's financial system makes you think. The government there says that the redemption of virtual currencies in value exceeding their original purchasing prices will be banned (which I think is the same as the European Directive on Electronic Money Issuing, isn't it?) to prevent attempts to make a profit. What's even more interesting is that the government also says that virtual currencies cannot be used to buy real goods but only virtual products and services provided by the operators who issue the currencies. As I've said before, this whole real/virtual thing is very fuzzy.

The Chinese virtual currency market is believed to be growing at a yearly rate of between 15% and 20%, and is estimated to be worth several billions of dollars! It isn't the size of the market that makes this story interesting but the fact that the Asian perspective on virtual currencies seems to be so different from ours and I'm very curious to find out why. We've discussed before the different regulatory approaches -- laissez-faire in the UK and US compared with legislation in South Korea and China -- and I'm sure we'll come back to it again, but I wonder if anyone out there has any opinions as to whether it is simply the size of the Asia-Pacific virtual currency markets that is attracting regulators or whether it is something cultural?

A story that has everything [15/05/2007]

Virtual worlds, digital money and mobile, all in one story! ! It's all about the Japanese virtual world *S! Town*, run by Softbank Mobile, which attracted 100,000 subscribers in its first couple of months of operation. In S! Town, subscribers design and dress their avatar and room, using the virtual world's currency for purchases. Friends share pictures, download music and meet friends in the public plaza. There are community events like treasure hunts, which often have monetary prize incentives that serve to give subscribers more currency to personalize their avatar and digs. That's what's great about virtual worlds, everyone's happy. Well, I say everyone. I mean everyone except the regulators, spoilsports that they are.

China and South Korea have already initiated stricter regulation of virtual world economies, so perhaps Japan won't be too far behind. I wonder which regulatory model they'll choose though? South Korea certainly provides a useful case study for them. Apparently, the South Korean market reached a trillion won, or about a billion dollars, last year. Itembay, the leading virtual asset exchange in South Korea, saw assets worth 300 billion won traded via its website in 2005, with roughly 5 percent charged as commission. A large part of this economy rests on sweatshops: clandestine, untaxed garage businesses that hire dozens or hundreds of people to collect up in-game virtual assets for resale. One has to wonder whether the major virtual worlds operators -- such as NCsoft, NHN and CJ Internet -- are that concerned about a government crackdown on asset trading. In fact, an NCsoft official is quoted in that article saying that "We don't think the ban will severely damage us, because gamers will find another way to trade". Quite.

Japanese money supply [22/05/2007]

Why are we all so interested in Japanese e-money statistics? Setting aside that when I say "we", I of course mean "me", it's because of the clues it may contain to the evolution of electronic money in a rich mobile-centric environment. According to the Nomura Research Institute, the Japanese e-money market grew from 180 billion yen in 2006 to 690 billion yen in 2007, including Edy's 100 billion yen share and Suica's 50 billion yen share. The market is expected to be worth

2.8 trillion yen in 2011. With the spread of e-money, concerns have been raised that the money supply -- one of the elements that the Bank of Japan uses to map out its monetary policy -- may not reflect the actual state of the economy, as the money supply data does not include e-money (and nor, I suspect, does anyone else's, although I'd love to hear from anyone who can prove me wrong).

In the Japanese statistics the money supply in March was 80 trillion yen. Of this, only 4.5 trillion yen is currency from small-scale settlements, which is likely to be substituted by e-money. So e-money currently accounts for 180 billion of a 4.5 trillion market (i.e., 4 percent). Hence one can only agree with Hideo Kumano, chief economist of the Dai-ichi Life Research Institute Inc, who said that

"E-money is not likely to have an immediate influence on the central bank's monetary policy in the near future."

How different to China, where non-existent e-money in virtual worlds is already, according to the government there, threatening monetary policy.

Quasi-bank account? [07/06/2007]

Yet more new payment mechanisms. In the UK, the Post Office has already launched an electronic money transfer service which enables recipients to receive funds via a barcode sent to a mobile phone or e-mail address. The *Payout Service* allows companies to distribute cash payments at a fraction of the cost of issuing cheques, the Post Office says. Basically, companies send a barcode by text, e-mail or post to the recipient. This barcode can be scanned at any Post Office branch counter, and the recipient receives an instant cash payment. It might be worth printing out a few random barcodes and going down to the Post Office to see if any of them are worth anything -- sort of like a lottery, but more fun and available at 14,000 Post Office branches in the UK. There must be more to it, because British Gas and Unilever liked the pilot and plan to extend their use of it. Unilever used it for fulfilment of a promotion for one of its products to 22,000 customers. Joanna Weston, a Unilever direct communication executive, says:

"We didn't have a clear fulfilment process in place to make a large quantity of small payments to our customers... This could have been problematic for us, as raising a cheque is 600 percent more expensive than using the Post Office Payout service."

For people like me who can't even be bothered to go down to the Post Office branch, there's Obopay's AOL instant messenger (AIM) plugin, enabling you to make payments directly from your AIM Buddy List. The Obopay AIM plugin is accessible via your desktop or your mobile phone, so no matter where you are, you can access your Obopay account using AIM. Since Obopay comes with a prepaid MasterCard, this means that one of your buddies can send you cash via AIM and then you can go and spend it using the card. I'll see if I can find out what the charges are so we can compare it with Post Office barcodes.

I have a suspicion, though, that neither of these schemes will generate the volume that Wal-Mart's new Wal-Money MoneyCard will. According to today's *Financial Times*, Wal-Mart are going to launch a prepaid card (it will actually be a prepaid Visa product from GE Money) targeting the 60 or so million unbanked in America: they want these people to use the card as a "quasi-bank account" and (assuming that you can get one just by wandering in to Wal-Mart and picking it up -- no REAL ID or any such silliness) then not only will they do so, they'll do so enthusiastically because they go to Wal-Mart all the time already. Given the we were discussing only recently the possibility of a prepaid cards as a solution to the problem of the high cost of payments for the unbanked (i.e., the apparent law of payments that says the poorest people must pay the highest transaction costs) I think Wal-Mart are on to a winning proposition and it can only be a matter of time before (e.g.) Tesco do the same in the UK.

Real profits, but for how long? [19/06/2007]

Something you may not have noticed, but there was another milestone passed on the road to the future of banking a few weeks ago, when *Project Entropia* auctioned banking licences for its virtual world. In fact there were five licences sold, with the highest bid at $99,900 going to "Yuri", an undoubtedly fit and proper avatar. Financial services follow the money, even when it is virtual. Last year, a player set up a bank in another science fiction game, *EVE Online*, but that one was unsupported and unregulated by the game's operator, CCP hf of Iceland. The player tried to abscond with the deposits, but CCP froze his account before he could sell them for "real" money. EVE Online has been attracting more interest, this time from the Financial Times, which picturesquely calls it a galaxy far far away where rampant capitalism held sway, free from the restraints of Sarbanes-Oxley legislation, SEC inquiries and European Commission investigations.

Where there are "large-scale scams, widespread corporate espionage, military-industrial alliances and interplanetary wars".

"Eve seemed like a playground for totally unfettered hardcore capitalism, with none of our justice systems or controlling bodies."

according to Trey Ratcliff, a former player and CEO of John Galt Games Note, by the way, that EVE Online has 200,000 players paying a $15-a-month subscription. Jason Schripsema, CEO of SolarBOS, a maker of solar electric products, says he became fascinated with manufacturing and marketing products for other players. He learnt valuable lessons about how to maximise profits and prioritise projects, and says

"Eve is a good training ground for anyone interested in business – the markets really work."

Dan Speed, acting economist for CCP, says the game is "hypercapitalistic"; rife with corporate espionage and wrongdoing. One group infiltrated a corporation, assassinated its chief executive and carried out a heist. Another staged a successful IPO to raise money to build space stations. Investors lost everything when the outposts were attacked and taken over by a rival. I thought it was amusing that Mr. Speed goes on to say

"Yet honest players survive and they are earning virtual qualifications for real-world jobs."

What "real-world jobs", I'm dying to know. Has the East India Company been advertising on Monster.com? Is Sir Walter Raleigh about to launch an expedition to El Dorado? Is "The Apprentice" now featuring John D. Rockefeller?

Meanwhile, back in the real world (well, America), the numbers are in on the bank card business for last year:

- Purchase volume on consumer and commercial cards last year reached 1.29 trillion, up 9.3% from $1.18 trillion in 2005. Total charge volume, including cash advances, reached $1.53 trillion, up 8.5% from $1.41 trillion.

- Total revenue among issuers of Visa and MasterCard consumer and commercial credit cards last year reached $114.99 billion, up 5% from $109.98 billion in 2005.

- Penalty-fee revenue dropped 27%, to $6.44 billion from $8.87 billion in 2005, as fewer consumers were delinquent on their card payments.

- Expenses dropped 4% last year, to $86.72 billion from $90.48 billion in 2004. This was driven by a 31% reduction in charge-off expenses, which fell to $24.12 billion from $35.13 billion in 2005.

- Issuers' collective after-tax return on assets was $18.37 billion, or 2.97% of average outstandings, up 45% from $12.67 billion and 2.09% in 2005.

Next year is going to be harder, with a squeeze on interest income. While outstanding US credit card debt was more than $750 billion in November 2006, according to estimates based on Federal Reserve figures, and there are more than 640 million credit cards in circulation, perhaps as things get tighter in the real world, the virtual one will look more attractive!

Climate Change, Whatever [13/12/2007]

It's odd how memory works. I read in the newspaper that several thousand people have burned millions of gallons of aviation kerosene flying to Bali (these things are never in Barnsley, are they) to discuss climate change, and it reminded me that several months ago, amongst all of the vital global stuff being discussed by the great and good at the World Economic Forum in Davos, Bill Gates told a breakfast meeting that Microsoft is developing an online payment system that will be cheaper than credit card transactions, making it possible for companies to charge small fees for web-based content and services they now offer for free. Apparently he described a system that would undercut credit card fees, making it profitable for an online newspaper to charge small fees for individual articles, for example. He said: "If you want to charge somebody $0.10 or $1 a month, that will just be a click...you won't have to manage some funny thing or pay some big credit charge, where half of it goes to the clearing."This sounds like a great idea, and I'm really looking forward to trying it out.

Microsoft is only one of the non-banks trying to boost e-commerce by developing "better" payment systems. Now, I'm wholly in favour of competition as a way to improve things rather than regulation or legislation, and because of the nature of innovation in large organisations -- much remarked upon here recently -- tend to think that it will be a non-bank that comes up with a practical way to crack the micropayments problem. Personally, I always liked the old DEC Millicent idea: when you put the cursor over a paid link, the cursor changes to a little currency sign to warn you that 10 cents (or whatever) is going to be deducted from your prepaid purse when you click on the link. But the user interface isn't the whole of a new Internet micropayments payments system -- if it was, we'd have more of them by now. I've often remarked on this absence of a decent micropayment mechanism in the online world, but it's undeniable that all efforts to date were somewhat unsuccessful (to put in mildly) and the concept has been hibernating since the dot-com bust. There has always been one reasonable criticism, and that is (essentially) that customers don't like micropayments, partly because they don't like uncertainty. Yet micropayments have arrived -- just not in the way they were originally envisioned. I buy songs on iTunes for 79p, which is undeniably a micropayment, and the system seems to work OK. Similarly, website operators can earn small amounts whenever someone clicks on the ads on their pages. The expectation was that a handful of companies would provide platforms -- or perhaps a single ubiquitous platform, such as the Microsoft one discussed above or my old favourite, the red button -- that would let users pay a penny, a dime or a dollar for a bit of content. In the "old days", content owners such as newspaper companies were looking forward to using such a system, but the problems were insurmountable. At the same time, advertising provided a much better income than was envisaged. While the sub-one cent transaction didn't arrive via payments, something like micropayments grew up at the advertising payment end -- where payments can be effectively aggregated -- rather than the consumer payment end. The result was that many micropayments companies shut down or gave up and changed business models. The names are familiar to Digital Money denizens: *DigiCash*, *CyberCash*, *First Virtual Holdings* and *Peppercoin*. They used various systems, but in general users loaded prepaid accounts with credit cards and then drew from those accounts. As the Times article notes, in the mid- to late '90s, electronic cash had become such a popular concept that some politicians worried that it might threaten the stability of the nation's currency. And I don't doubt that, one day, it will (if politicians haven't destabilised the currency themselves already). Consumers were reluctant to pay even a tenth of a cent for something they believed should be free, leading to the paradox of "free" music but expensive ringtones. Clay Shirky, at the time, put forward another theory: There is a certain amount of anxiety involved in any decision to buy, no matter how small. So micropayments wouldn't work because it requires too much mental transaction cost on behalf of the buyer.

There's undoubtedly something in this, but again it cannot be the whole story. I, for example, expended absolutely no mental effort whatsoever when I bought The Moody Blues "I'm just a singer in a rock and roll band" from iTunes a couple of days ago. I heard it on the radio driving home, remembered how much I liked it, spent seven seconds searching for it on iTunes and clicked the button to buy it. Since I know that songs on iTunes cost (essentially) nothing, I buy them. But why have "closed" systems like iTunes worked? Why can't I use my iTunes account to buy stories from the Financial Times archive, for example? Perhaps there just isn't enough margin in the transactions to make the inclusion of any third-party viable. Or perhaps it's just early days. It's not all about the online world. Introducing micropayments in the physical world provides for another way of thinking about problems. I say this because I heard a fascinating example from Singapore the other day. The story concerns university campuses and printing. Colour laser printing is expensive, so the colour toner cartridges were kept locked and when students wanted to print something they had to go and get permission and load the cartridges. An enterprising company built an EZ-Link unit for HP colour laser printers, so that students could use their EZ-Link (contactless transit) card to pay for printing. Result: everyone's happy (all the students have EZ-Link cards anyway), no-one wastes times loading and unloading cartridges, students don't waste paper and toner printing things they don't need to and the company running the microtransaction services is doing rather well. This subject deserves more thinking, deserves revisiting in the light of changing technology and more sophisticated media because price is information. A market without prices isn't a proper market, whether its students printing from laser printers or online content. But a market with prices is still hopeless if there's no efficient, workable payment mechanism. I don't, as a consumer, especially care whether my one euro charge for accessing some great web content is billed to my mobile phone bill, broadband bill, prepaid account or anything else, so long as it's easy.

Getting cash on the web [15/01/2008]

There are plenty of people out there who want to use cash on the web. Not digital cash, or electronic cash or virtual cash but actual cash. (This shows how the variety of e-cash solutions introduced over the years have failed because of execution and implementation, not because of a lack of consumer demand) There are companies who are trying to find ways to help them to do this, such as Click and Buy in the UK, for example. Similarly in America. Chase Paymentech and

Green Dot Corporation have announced an agreement to offer Chase Paymentech-processed merchants an alternative cash payment solution that gives them the ability to accept cash transactions through their existing online and phone interfaces by accepting Green Dot's *MoneyPak* as a form of payment. They say that research from McKinsey shows that cash accounts for more than 60 percent of all consumer transactions. So there's plenty to play for. Green Dot run one of the largest retail-based cash acceptance networks in the United States, and MoneyPak would be the first cash-based payment solution available for use by Chase Paymentech's merchants. Available at more than 40,000 retail outlets nationwide, including Wal-Mart, Walgreens, CVS/Pharmacy, Rite Aid, Radio Shack, Kroger, Ralphs, Food4Less and Fred Meyer, consumers can purchase a MoneyPak for $4.95 (suggested retail price) at any Green Dot retailer location and move that money wherever MoneyPak is accepted as a form of payment or funding. I've never used it, but I assume that they can reload their MoneyPak at the same outlets. Choice is a good thing, and I'm sure that consumers having the ability to choose between prepaid "open" (i.e., Visa/MasterCard) payment cards and non-bank alternatives is a thoroughly good thing.

Talking about alternatives, it's worth noting that new cash-replacement prepaid services (such as the MoneyPak), e-billing services and other new entrants continue to add to the possibilities in the world of "alternative" online payment options. These ranks are led by PayPal. In less than a decade it has taken nearly a quarter of the US online payments market (it handled more than $12 billion in payments in the last quarter). While the majority of its processing volume still comes from eBay, non-eBay payments are already 45% of the total and still growing.

Taken together, these alternatives are nearly a third of the online market and the powerful combination of consumer fears about security and consumer laziness are driving them. As everyone's favourite case study, PayPal, demonstrates perfectly. Consumers know that if I they see the PayPal option on a payment page it means that they have only to enter a password and hit OK and then they're done. No name and address, no going in to the other room to get a card from their wallet, no expiry date or CVV or the rest of it. This is why I use PayPal whenever I see it offered: because I am lazy, and therefore entirely representative of the mainstream consumer base.

I'm not altogether sure whether "alternative" has any real meaning in this context any more. In a couple of years, credit cards will be lucky to get half of a market that they started off with 98% of a decade ago. Broadly speaking, since those heady days when they saw off DigiCash and VisaCash and *Cybercoins* and goodness knows what else, there has been essentially no innovation whatsoever from the credit card world. Those of us old enough to remember the dead-end of Secure Electronic Transactions (SET) might have thought at the time that some other new initiative would come along and pick up the baton (adding smart card readers to PCs, that sort of thing) but that never materialised. The "band aid" of 3D secure hasn't transformed the space as the schemes perhaps would have hoped. As is generally the case, I think, organisations have a tendency to label fiddling around at the margins of core business as "innovation" and get on with it. This serves tolerably well as a strategy, up until the moment the core business goes away. When the alternatives have more than half of the market, I suppose we'll have to start labelling credit cards as "alternative" instead.

What is different about virtual banking? [22/02/2008]

I happened to be speaking to someone from a developing economy recently, and they said that (and I quote) "it would be a dream to be regulated by the FSA". What they meant was that however much people might complain about regulation, having some regulation is better than having none, because with no regulation it's actually more difficult to get a new payment system off of the ground. Customers and businesses want to see that their payment system is regulated properly (the person from the developing economy said) and that they are dealing with reputable people and not fraudsters. This applies to developing markets in cyberspace as well, which is why the regulation of the virtual payments and banking space is not only inevitable but also not in itself bad (provided, I would argue, that a thousand flowers are blooming, since it's too early to know what the "best" regime is). This shift to regulation is already happening in *Second Life*:

"In a blog Linden Labs says it will be prohibited to offer interest or any direct return on an investment from any object, such as an ATM, located in Second Life, "without proof of an applicable government registration statement or financial institution charter"."[12]

---

[12] Second Life cracks down on unregulated banks, Finextra

Now, having regulation does not, in itself, stop bad things from happening, as we in the UK know only too well: people can still make bad decisions that jeopardise other people's money...

"Gordon Brown defended the temporary nationalisation of Northern Rock on Monday morning amid widespread questions over the government's handling of the collapse of the mortgage lender."[13]

Chris Skinner pointed out the chain of events that led to the banking problems and also notes that their particular virtual environment has stagnated

"The former point relates to Second Life losing credibility when they outlawed gambling with the knock-on effect that their banking system crumbled. The latter is indicated by the fact that Second Life grew from virtually no users in 2006 to 12 million in 2008 ... but only 1.2 million people use the service regularly (in the past 60 days) and this number is declining."[14]

The number of people in virtual worlds overall continues to rise, though, and those of us in the payment business who have time to look at them continue to find new trends, new learning and new ideas. Look, for example, at what MindArk is doing with *Entropia Universe*, where they hope to get 150 million users from around the world. Marco Behrmann, their CEO, says that

"Entropia Universe utilizes a "real cash economy", which means that the internal Entropia Universe economy is linked to the real world economy. This is achieved using a virtual currency called the Project Entropia Dollar (PED), which has a fixed exchange rate, guaranteed by MindArk, to the US Dollar, where 10 PED equals 1 USD. By enabling this kind of currency exchange, both to and from Entropia Universe, a participant has the opportunity to earn real money while in essence partaking in an online computer game.

"Real currency is entered into Entropia Universe using mainly credit cards and prepaid cards. The virtual PED currency may then be exchanged back into real world currency using either a direct bank transfer, or the Entropia Universe Cash Card, which essentially is an ATM card that can be loaded with PED from inside the Entropia Universe and used to instantaneously withdraw real funds

---

[13] In depth - Brown defends Northern Rock nationalization, FT.*com*

[14] ING closes down Our Virtual Holland in Second Life, The *FinanSer*

according to the exchange rate mentioned above, from over 1 million ATM machines worldwide."

As for the numbers, he's a little less forthcoming. Entropia has some 595,000 registered accounts. He says that "almost everyone" takes part in the economy as many activities have some cost associated. The number of people depositing compared to the non-depositors is a "business secret". However, some 110,000,000 PEDs (i.e., more than a million of that other virtual currency, the US dollar) were deposited last year into Entropia Universe.

One particular area interests me greatly and that is that there are issues around identity and authentication in virtual worlds that have direct relevance to our customers' future businesses. At a seminar I gave recently I talked about the difference between phishing for bank details and phishing for WoW accounts, pointing out the perverse nature of the situation whereby as a customer I'm not that bothered about phishing because if my bank account is hacked by Eastern European fraudsters then Barclays will give me the money back whereas if my WoW account is hacked by Eastern European fraudsters then Blizzard won't give me my magic sword back. So therefore I might be prepared to pay for 2FA in WoW but not in WoB (World of Barclays). It's actually in everyone's interest to come up with a better solution that, I would argue, works for both. It's an immediate win-win because of the size of the problem. John Smedley, the Sony Station Exchange CEO, talked about the overlap with payments. He said

"They use a credit card —sometimes stolen, sometimes not — to buy an account key. They use the account for a month, and then they call the credit card company and charge it back. We have suffered nearly a million dollars just in fines over the past six months; it's getting extremely expensive for us. What's happening is that when they do this all the time, the credit card companies come back to us and say 'You have a higher than normal chargeback rate, therefore we'll charge you fines on top of that.'"

This is true for World of Warcraft payments too. What this seems to indicate to me is that entrepreneurs might be better advised to find a workable 2FA solution for WoW and then take that same solution into banking where it can then be tied to payments. As an aside, if you have nothing better to do you might find it diverting to listen to Episode Five of The Banking 2.0 Podcast, brought to you by the nice people from Voices in Business, which features yours truly talking about virtual worlds and virtual banking.

Chapter 7: Developing Markets

It can sometimes be surprising that the more recent technology innovations which would in previous times have only been available to those who can afford them are now being used to solve problems in some of the developing markets.

Alternative to what? [25/01/2007]

I heard the phrase "alternative payment technologies" at a meeting today. I wonder what it means? Payments News noted a report out from Pelorus about alternative payment technologies in the US, predicting 15-fold growth over the next five years. The alternatives they look at include contactless (which I would argue shouldn't be seen as alternative any longer), smart cards (which are what contactless payment cards are, even in the US), SMS (which is about as mass market as you can get, although I just can't see taking hold for payments in the developed world), biometrics and NFC. But I'm wondering what they are an alternative to.

The answer seems to be that they are alternatives to the bank-issued, magnetic-stripe powered plastic card. But a more interesting question would be to ask which technologies will provide an alternative to existing business models, not an alternative to existing technologies. In other words, are any of these technologies disruptive? I'd be curious to see what other people think, but my feeling is that both biometrics and NFC have the potential to disrupt the business model whereas contactless smart cards (and SMS payments) do not.

My five year predictions, for what they are worth, is that mobile payments will integrate with contactless because of NFC, that biometrics will stay a niche and that the US will start issuing chip cards to deal with card-not-present (CNP) fraud even though they won't use chip and PIN at POS.

Payments and loyalty [15/02/2007]

I was in a meeting that touched on loyalty and payments today. It reminded me that the *Wise Marketer* had a story about payments and loyalty that readers might find interesting. The report, called Making Loyalty Pay: The Relationship Between Rewards and Payments, talks about new models for loyalty with their roots in the web, mobile, biometrics and other technologies. It's very positive about them, saying that they have the potential to boost revenues for merchants, technology providers and payment providers alike, while also minimising the issuer payment revenue cannibalisation. Judging from the priorities of some of our clients, I would say that this bullish perspective is probably correct. As Aneace often points out, while banks (in particular) have yet to really take advantage of the migration to chip, the retailers are looking to banks to deliver more value and better loyalty and rewards platforms seems to be a reasonable way to create that value. Contactless, for example, should mean that customers are using cards in places where they used to use cash and so loyalty schemes had to be often-forgotten bits of cardboard and the like. With the chip, they can be automated.

Some of the report's main findings should influence the design of new payment products:

- Credit card rewards programmes have lowered overall credit card churn from 33% in 2000 to 24% in 2006. Moving forward, churn rates are likely to remain flat with the introduction of new loyalty and payment technologies and increased competition.

- More than 60% of banks will offer rewards by 2010, up from 31% in 2005, as banks take advantage of shifting consumer payment preferences and the growing commoditisation of credit card rewards programmes.

- Loyalty programme economics, traditionally centred on low redemption rates (averaging 21%) will begin to increase. Automatic redemption will increasingly be offered by loyalty programmes that leverage low cost Internet, mobile, and local advertising channels.

- Blended and cashback programmes will account for 86% of all credit card rewards programmes by 2010. Experiential rewards programmes will also grow for the high net-worth segments of the population.

- Merchant discount fees associated with card issuer interchange currently account for up to 74% of payment processing costs for a small grocer or convenience store, up from 47% in 2000. The tension over interchange is leading to new business models that address merchant payment processing costs and loyalty programme shortcomings in new and effective ways.

Banks will undoubtedly have to work harder for their money at the retail POS, but it seems to me that new technology is coming to their aid because chip and PIN, mobile, contactless and other new payment methods all have the potential to provide more and better services to both the customers and the merchants. As always, technological change means both threats and opportunities.

Digital money and innovation, again [22/02/2007]

There was a lot about corporate social responsibility in the *Harvard Business Review* that I finally got around to reading. For us technical persons, Clayton Christensen et al on innovation is a set text so it was his (and his colleagues') piece that caught my eye. He was writing about "catalytic innovations", which he says create systemic social change through scaling and replication, meet a need that is either over-served or not served at all, offer products and services that are simple and less costly, generate resources that are unattractive to incumbents and are ignored by existing players. Should digital money be in this category? There is a market out there made up from people who just need a simple payment account -- not a bank account with credit, statements and branches -- linked to a card (because cards are how retail e-payments are effected). These people are either over-served, because they have to get a complicated and expensive bank account in the developed world, or not served at all in the less developed world because there are no bank branches or POS terminals.

Some organisations seem to have spotted them. The GSM Association (currently active standardising NFC in SIM and so on) cheerfully point out that there are 6.5 billion people on the planet, that close to 3 billion of them have a mobile phone and less than one billion have a bank account. Mobile communications operators and banks joined forces on Monday to make it easier and cheaper for hundreds of millions of immigrants and migrant workers to send money home by using their mobile phones. Now, the GSMA and a group of operators are going to work with banks to provide services to migrant workers and take a chunk of the $230 billion international remittances market. The aim is to reduce the transaction costs of sending small amounts of cash to just a few percent, from a current 20%+ for amounts as small as $50. They hope to double the number of recipients of international remittances to more than 1.5 billion, while helping to quadruple the size of the remittances market to more than $1 trillion by 2012. Mobile operators plan to partner with banks; MasterCard will pilot a global hub that will link together national markets and the local payment systems run by mobile operators in partnership with those local banks. The idea is that people can load cash on their mobile, and order it to be sent to a mobile phone number in another country, where the recipient receives a message that money has arrived, making it as easy as sending a text message, much as they can with the Vodafone M-PESA scheme in Kenya, now extended in partnership with Citi so that people in the UK will be able to use their mobiles to send money to people in Kenya (with extension to Eastern European and Asian markets, such as Poland and India, in the near future).

Sunil Bharti Mittal, chairman and managing director of Indian mobile operator Bharti Airtel says that these developments will "revolutionise the money transfer industry with its advantages, such as reach, ease of use, and lower transaction costs and provide immense benefits to people in developing nations such as India", and I'm sure he's right. But will it be a disruptive innovation. In other words, will people make money in new ways, or will need people make money in the old ways (i.e., transaction fees)? India may well be a good place to find out, as it is both the world's fastest growing mobile services market and the biggest recipient of overseas remittances in the world, accounting for around 10 percent of the world market. The State Bank of India, the country's largest, is also participating in the project, so what happens in India ought to be a useful indicator of how the scheme might develop. Which reminds me. If only Mr. Leedladhar, the deputy governor of the Reserve Bank of India, had come along to the Digital Money Forum last year. Then he would have know that his forward-looking suggestion that Indians in rural areas might be able to bank and make payments using a SIM card is actually rather old hat, since M-PESA (amongst others) has been up and running for some time. He even goes so far as to suggest "This (SIM card) could function as a multi-application smart card, with some cash stored in it, in the form of e-cash."

Islamic e-payments [22/03/2007]

Islamic finance seems to be growth area generally, so I wouldn't be at all surprised to see Islamic payments growing similarly, even if I'm not entirely sure what that would mean. But with the first Islamic chip and PIN card now in the market, issued by the Kuwait Finance House in Bahrain, it might be a good time for digital money thinkers to look at the area in more detail.

I've consistently thought that there might be an opportunity here. As I wrote some time ago, once an e-payments infrastructure is in place so that the currency of the transaction becomes immaterial, then consumers might want to transact in Manchester United pounds (they already use credit cards and savings accounts) or Microsoft dollars or Islamic gold e-dinars or Cornish e-tin for reasons that have nothing to do with the drivers for the use of traditional means of exchange (e.g., liquidity, stability and so on). Once brand arrives in the world of currency, who knows where it might go.

The Islamic e-gold is a special case, though. Given the desire to transact with the convenience of a card but in a non-interest bearing currency, it would seem to be a straightforward proposition to offer a gold card that is actually denominated in gold. An Islamic person tenders their chip and PIN gold card in Oxford Street to buy a pair of shoes: to the system it's just another foreign currency transaction that is translated into grams of gold on the statement. If, at the end of the month, the person has used more gold than they have in their account then they can use some of the bank's gold for a time at a fee. Hey presto, no interest. And if said Islamic person wants their gold then they can, in principle, go to the relevant depository and draw it out (minus a handling fee, naturally). Would interested credit card issuers form an orderly queue, please?

Incidentally, old Digital Money hands will remember Douglas Jackson of e-gold, who presented his Internet-based gold payment system to us some years ago, so using precious metal as a medium of exchange but in an electronic context is hardly new, but it may be that the Islamic market provides the space for it to really grow.

The Digital Money Reader 2008

Underdeveloped markets [10/05/2007]

Payments News points me to a new research report from the CFSI (not to be confused with our own CSFI: the US one is the Center for Financial Services Innovation, our UK friends are the Centre for the Study of Financial Innovation) called "Mobile Financial Services and the Underbanked: Opportunities and Challenges for m-banking and m-payments". We often discuss the use of the mobile phone to provide financial and payment services to developing markets (a technology-driven strategy so obvious that even management consultants recommend it) -- and the overlap with other developing market financial trends such as microfinance -- but sometimes forget that there are a great many people in developed markets who are not served by current finance and payment institutions. I thought it might be useful to look at the specific financial services highlighted in the report.

I've taken the services described in the executive summary of the report and list them below with additional comments. The services are...

- Merchant Pay: In March 2006, Scarborough Research found that 50% of Americans without bank accounts had shopped at Wal-Mart stores in the previous 30 days. Indeed, large and chain retailers, such as discount and convenience stores, grocery stores, and gas stations, seem best positioned to make the kind of investments necessary to receive mobile payments -- because of both their financial resources and the particular value they receive from speeding and simplifying transactions. If these types of merchants prove to be the earliest adopters of m-payments technology, the underbanked will stand to benefit perhaps even more than other customer groups.

- Bill Pay: Consumers without checking accounts generally depend on walk-in services to pay their bills, incurring fees as high as $3 for regular payments and $7 for rush payments. You'll remember the recent discussion here about this in the context of BT. According to Mercator Advisory Group, walk-in bill payments are expected to reach more than $80 billion in volume by 2009. Prepaid card companies have already begun to allow customers to pay bills that can be funded using direct debit, usually for a fee of between $0.50 and $3.00. A significant market opportunity may exist through partnerships with major utility companies. Mobile financial service (MFS) providers could offer competitively priced remote bill payment services structured similarly to P2P transfers, as we have advised a number of clients in developing countries in the past. Apart from anything else, the unbanked often pay for utilities weekly or even daily, so there are far more of these utility payments to process than for banked customers.

- Remittances: We've long recognised the potential for mobile phone-based service in the global remittance market. In 2004, workers in the US sent $34 billion to Latin America and the Caribbean, and approximately $6 billion each to India and the Philippines. A 2002 study by the Pew Hispanic Center and the Multilateral Investment Fund found that as many as 43% of Latino remitters in the US lack any kind of bank account; a greater number may have formal banking relationships but choose to employ non-bank money transfer services. While the fees charged for international money transfers have decreased substantially in the past few years, remittances remain a relatively high margin business and a key point of entry to immigrant markets -- and therefore a potential mobile financial service well worth considering.

- Person-to-Person (P2P): Surprisingly (to me, at least) in the US more than a third of the "remittance" market is actually domestic. According to one bank, 37% of the remittances channelled through its US branches were domestic. Clearly, there is some need for secure methods to send funds domestically among people who cannot write personal cheques, deposit to shared accounts or use PayPal. Mobile transfers of funds may provide a solution.

- Prepaid Top-up and Tie-ins: Atlantic-ACM recently estimated that the total numbers of prepaid users will more than double from 24.2 million in 2005 to 55.5 million in 2010. Because prepaid mobile services are particularly popular among immigrants, lower-income consumers and those with poor or no credit (which is one way in which the US market is different to the European market), financial services linked to prepaid wireless represent a natural point of departure for MFS targeted at the underbanked, which I think is a critical part of the analysis.

- Short-term Credit: The magnitude of the $6 billion US payday lending industry is just one indication of the strong demand for short-term credit among consumers without easy access to more reasonably priced loan instruments, such as credit cards or bank lines of credit. MFS platforms could add value for credit-underserved customers by offering short-term credit instruments that could be applied for and disbursed via mobile phone. MFS providers would have access to considerable data on their current users' financial behaviour, information that would help them better price loans. They need not provide the credit, of course, since (rather as eBay does with GE) the MFS provider could simply deliver white label credit from a third-party provider to a "seller".

- Saving: service providers could help spur savings among their customers providing a convenient means to move funds between active spending accounts and mobile savings accounts. I'm not sure about this one, because it seems like the kind of thing I'd prefer a bank to manage for me at the back-end rather than be bothered about it during the day when I'm out and about.

All of these taken together explain why there's been a rash of activity in the US mobile banking and payments space.

Another template from Japan? [06/06/2007]

I gave a talk to executives at a financial services company, focusing on the relationship between banks and mobile operators. In the payments world, technology is pushing this relationship back up the agenda. In Japan, remember, they're getting over the co-operation issue by getting in to bed together. KDDI Corporation and Mitsubishi-Tokyo-UFJ Bank have created a joint venture -- the "Mobile Net Bank Development Corporation", MNBDC -- in preparation for the two companies to launch a mobile-centric bank, Shinginko (which just means "new bank" in Japanese). MNBDC has already started building the systems for the New Bank and, subject to regulatory approval, products and services will be offered to the public soon. The idea of Shinginko is to offer a full line-up of financial services to individual consumers, capitalising on the strengths of the mobile phone as a channel using operator expertise. We once did some work for a UK joint venture like this but it never went anywhere because the goals of the bank and the operator were too divergent. Perhaps in Japan, and with a few more years experience, it will be different. There is certainly an appetite for mobile banking in the region. As Ericson Chan, group head of systems development for consumer banking at Standard Chartered Bank, noted recently, although many of the bank's current customers may not be comfortable with using smartphones to make payments, the next generation of consumers are apt at doing so. Banks aren't the only option for operators looking for partners to expand payments services: in Italy, Vodafone has joined forces with Poste Italiane, home of the prepaid scheme that we look at from time to time. Poste Italiana sees scope to link up the new mobile virtual network operator (MVNO) customers with electronic payment cards, for which the post has 9 million customers, allowing customers to make payments using their mobile phones. Mobile phones can be filled up with 200 or 500 euros of credit, which can then be spent in retail outlets. I'm not sure whether customers would really want to use SIM-based services for this kind of thing so it's not transparently obvious that this side of the venture will be successful. When the NFC handsets come along though, this could be big.

Glancing across the pond, it's not entirely clear what the demand for US mobile banking is likely to be in the coming year or two. I thought *NetBanker*'s explanation for the widely differing forecasts was very good... Imagine the difference in response to these two questions:

1. How would you like to press a button on your cellphone that gave you instant, secure, free access to your bank account balance so you didn't ever bounce a check again, or

2. At some point in the future, you might be able to download and install a Java application over the air for your mobile device that provided a subset of the functionality of online banking ported to a 2 inch screen. And, as long as you never left your phone somewhere by mistake, it should be as secure. How excited would you be about that?

Quite. But don't listen to me about forecasting mobile services: as is occasionally pointed out by friends and enemies alike, I didn't think prepaid mobile would be a big deal. ("You're going to ask people to pay up front for a more expensive phone service? No way!") Nevertheless, banks and service providers are rolling mobile products that let customers check account balances, pay bills, transfer money and receive alerts about deposits and payments by mobile phone. By the end of 2007, TowerGroup (part of MasterCard) expects that eight of the ten largest banks will offer mobile banking and bill payment of some kind and predicts that, eventually, up to 25% of existing Internet banking customers will adopt mobile banking.

Celent Communications' US Mobile Banking: Beyond the Buzz report says that estimate is too low. By 2010, Celent predicts, 35% of online banking households will use mobile banking, compared to just 1% today They say that consumers will be attracted by new capabilities such as mobile payments at the physical point of sale, which may well be true but is not obvious. Mobile (i.e., NFC) payments look a no-brainer because they're quick and easy, whereas paying a bill on your phone is neither. Having said that, I was talking with someone the other day about a home shopping using mobile phone experiment and they told me it had gone quite well: people really don't care if it takes a few minutes and a few keystrokes, provided they're watching a shopping channel.

M-PESA at the RSA [21/06/2007]

I dropped in at the RSA for another seminar, this time including Nick Hughes from Vodafone talking about one of our favourite projects, M-PESA. He gave an excellent talk about the role of m-payments in improving the life of people in developing countries. A few points he made to establish context (my paraphrasing):

- The average European cow gets €2.50 per day in subsidy and 75% of Africans live on less than that: they don't have much spare money.

- In Kenya, 30% of household income goes on what we in the West would call bribes.

- A fifth of working Kenyans send money from the cities back to the countryside but there are few banks or ATMs. High transaction fees for sending money hit them hard.

- In Kenya, mobile phone penetration is already 30% (in South Africa is it 60%).

As The Economist pointed out back in March 2005, poor countries don't need a PC in every home, they need more mobile phones.

They've certainly done something right. There are already 477 agents live where you can take in cash to top-up your M-PESA account and the number of people signing up has accelerated to currently 2,500 per day (it was 1,500 per day last month) and there are now around 140,000+ customers. Safaricom are now targeting a million customers by the end of this year. They've processed around a million transactions. The average customer is already doing 3-4 transactions per month. The average P2P transfer is for £23 (say around $40). By the end of May, a billion Kenyan shillings had been through the system. Nick mentioned that the scheme is now being trialled in Afghanistan and Tanzania and will soon begin trials in Sri Lanka and also gave some examples of the scheme's use, which I won't repeat here, except to note that they demonstrate how a good, functional payment system makes life better for the average person.

As a complete aside, the other speaker who was talking around innovation and community was from Lego. Since there is no nook and/or cranny in my house that does not have a Lego brick in it, I was actually quite interested in the discussion about how Lego has transformed its fortunes, partly by becoming part of a community with its customers. I can testify as a parent that Lego deserves every scrap of praise it gets, both for providing what is undoubtedly the best play time per dollar invested toy value ever and for integrating the real and virtual worlds so thoroughly and effectively. Incidentally, if you think this has nothing to do with digital money, you are very probably wrong. On one of his slides was a mention of the Lego virtual world that is about to be launched where (if the general pattern of virtual worlds is anything to go by) real money trades (RMTs) will be inevitable and, if my household is anything to go by, on a vast scale.

Economics 1.01 [13/07/2007]

Using a reasonable model, the global RMT (real money trade) market looks to be around $2 billion, which implies a virtual Gross Domestic Product (GDP) of around $27 billion. Note that this is significantly greater than the GDP of many countries. In fact, according to the World Bank, it puts the virtual realm somewhere between Lithuania and Sri Lanka. Not, let me repeat, in terms of GDP per head but in terms of absolute GDP in 2006. About twice the size of Iceland, in economic terms.

In case you think that all of this is a bit of nonsense and that South Korean students selling magic swords to Japanese businessmen isn't an occupation for real persons, you might note that Microsoft says that virtual asset sales on XBox Live have now reached $125 million. That's about $18 per user or, as PlayNoEvil points out, a lot of horse armour.

And if you think that, well, that's not a lot of money so why would anyone really care about it, look at what's been going on with QQ in China. In the first quarter, it had QQ recorded 28.5 million peak concurrent IM users and a QUARTER OF A BILLION active accounts. No wonder that the Chinese central bank and 14 ministries had a crackdown on QQ coins being used for non-virtual purchases. Here's another extract from that Wall Street Journal piece:

"Economists say virtual currencies work like any other currencies, so long as people trust the institutions behind them. The US dollar, which lost its gold backing in 1971, survives because people trust the US government.

The trouble starts when a virtual currency that isn't backed by a trusted government, becomes linked to a real one that is through an exchange rate. Virtual currency brokers call that RMT, or real-money trade. When that happened to the QQ coin, it effectively turned into a parallel currency operating alongside the yuan, says Yiping Huang, the chief Asia economist of Citibank.

The creation of too many QQ coins, he notes, could, in theory, create a surge in China's total money supply, leading to inflation."

You can't help but be fascinated by this. Or at least you should be fascinated by it if you're interested in digital money.

Gold opportunity [18/07/2007]

I've written before about commodity currency and, while I don't particularly see why gold should be the focus of such initiatives in the modern world, there's no doubt that its allure is unwavering in some territories and cultures. A specific example that I've previously discussed in many different contexts, is the idea of creating an electronic gold currency to serve the Islamic e-finance world. This has certainly been kicking around for a while (the Gulf States have been discussing a single currency and its virtual equivalent, the e-Dinar, for some time) and it was only a matter of time before an implementation arrived. Well, a Malaysian start-up has done it and entered the fray with c-*gold*, a digital gold-backed currency that has already started to gain acceptance. It works in a similar way to e-gold but is apparently going to develop a physical world presence as well, with stores (presumably to "top-up") as well as mobile integration and so forth. The *DGC* (Digital Gold Currency) blog's comment is very positive

"What I considered so unique to c-gold is their over-the-counter bailment's and redemptions. This operation is handled at brick and mortar locations. Verified, account holders simply drop off a bar and pick up a bar when funding or redeeming

their digital account. There is NO surcharge or extra fees for this operation. Bars are also shipped worldwide and the service is fast Nice!"

Given that the minimum bailment is 1Kg, you won't be popping in and out much but I assume that once people are confident that their c-gold can be redeemed on demand for real gold, then they won't bother with the real stuff. I also noted the comments about transparency, which I think is essential to getting something like this into the mainstream. For c-gold you can see their daily holdings right down to the bar mark and number from the website.

This is not to imply, incidentally, that digital gold is just for the Islamic community or that gold is the only commodity that may be used as a store of value. It may well be that digitised commodity money is in the future for all of us. Ben Steil, director of international economics at the influential Council on Foreign Relations (who wrote that Financial Times piece) certainly puts forward some challenging views. He says, for example, that

"As radical and implausible as it may sound, digitising the earth's 2,500-year experiment with commodity money may ultimately prove far more sustainable than our recent 35-year experiment with monetary sovereignty."

Mr. Steil was also quoted in *Foreign Affairs* (May 2007) saying

"Governments must let go of the fatal notion that nationhood requires them to make and control the money used in their territory. National currencies and global markets simply do not mix... in order to globalise safely, countries should abandon monetary nationalism and abolish unwanted currencies, the source of much of today's instability."

Now that's what I call thinking out of the box. Neil McEvoy and I wrote a paper for the Financial Cryptography conference in 1997 that touches on similar ground[15].

Chequeing out [12/09/2007]

Here's another milestone that will probably pass unnoticed. The US Federal Reserve will stop processing paper cheques in 2010. From then on, they will only handle "Check 21" (i.e., captured images and details) and I'm sure that the numbers of those will continue to fall.

---

[15] http://digitaldebateblogs.typepad.com/digital_money/FC97_LNCS.pdf

For some people, that's a problem. If, for example, you make equipment to print and process cheques as does Panini North America in Dayton, Ohio. Their president, Douglas Roberts, says that

Checks will take us into 2010, 2011, but we need to be selling something in 2009 beyond checks... Checks will be a maintenance-only industry.

There's something really unusual -- in the big sense of the word -- rumbling along here. In the course of human history and the march of commerce, new forms of payment have been invented from time to time. Coins, notes, cheques, cards, EFT, PayPal and M-PESA. But over time they have sat alongside one another. We've seen them change their market shares, obviously, but they all continue to exist. In the last couple of days I've used coins as well as chip and PIN cards, PayPal as well as online bank transfers. As each new mechanism comes along, we carry on using the old ones. We've never seen one of them go away. Never. But in the case of cheques, it seems to me to be entirely plausible that they disappear within my lifetime.

Last month, I tried to book a flight on British Airways website. Every time I pressed "pay" (or whatever it says) it went wrong, so in the end I had to phone up their call centre and sit on hold (on an 0870 number) for ages before I could book the tickets for the whole family. BA punish you for doing this not only through the 0870 charges (note to foreign readers: 0870 is not free) but also by surcharging fifteen quid per ticket for phone bookings. I complained to their customer service centre and got a refund. I assumed that, since BA knew perfectly well which card had been used to pay for the tickets they would simply refund the money to the card. But to my surprise (and slight annoyance) they sent me a cheque. I was looking for it over the weekend but I can't remember where I put it.

I'm almost an anomaly. Half of all British adults didn't receive a single cheque last year. In the last decade, APACS figures show that the number of cheques written in the UK has halved, to the point where the billion cheques written account for only one in ten of all non-cash transactions and only one in thirty of all retail non-cash transactions. APACS predict that the fall will continue but slow, so that in 2016 us Brits will still be writing 840 million cheques per annum. Maybe. But on the other hand, perhaps by 2016 P2P payments will have moved entirely to NFC phones and bill payments will be pushed to the handset, and there will be nothing for cheques to do. Except for the giant ones they give to lottery winners, but that's a bit of a special case.

eBay to east Africa [27/10/2007]

The microfinance story continues with the new that eBay has launched *MicroPlace*, a website that enables US customers to invest in microfinance projects. The site acts as a broker, allowing customers to buy microfinance investments for a minimum of $100 from microfinance security issuers. How fun. Investors can choose the country and microfinance institution that their money goes to. At launch the site will allow people to direct investments to Africa, Eurasia, Latin America and Southeast Asia. As soon as the scheme is extended to the UK, we will make a Digital Money blog investment in Africa on behalf of all of our readers. I know just how worthwhile microfinance is because of Consult Hyperion's work for Vodafone in Kenya. Kenya continues to provide a fascinating case study on the evolving competition and cooperation between banks and mobile operators in the world of payments. Safaricom's m-payment scheme M-PESA has been signing up 2,500 customers per day. Just to put this in context, Barclaycard in Kenya issued 7,000 cards last year. Kenya has about 70,000 credit card users, up from 10,000 in the eighties, and nine million mobile phone subscribers. As an aside, there is an obvious corollary to this kind of development: whereas phishers in the UK target banks, in Africa they have started targeting mobile. Bad guys have conducted fraudulent transactions on ABSA accounts by swapping the customers' SIM cards. It was actually quite a complicated fraud, defeating a security measure implemented by ABSA where a one-time password is sent to a customer's mobile phone. By swapping SIM cards (an accomplice inside the phone company moves the mobile number to the new SIM), the fraudsters could intercept that password and move money. Repeat after me: one factor bad, two factor better...

The volume of mobile payments in the developing world is steadily increasing. Take a look at *G-Cash* as an example: more than a million customers and more than $100 million per day in payments. Now Western Union and the GSMA are going to develop a commercial and technical framework that mobile operators can use to deploy services that enable consumers to send and receive low-denomination, high-frequency money transfers using their mobile phones. The first commercial services that make use of the framework are anticipated to be rolled out beginning in the second quarter of 2008. The idea, essentially, is to allow mobile operators to connect to the Western Union network (which handled 17 percent of the global remittance market last year) so that the operators can offer mobile-to-cash and cash-to-mobile services. It's undoubtedly worth a look from their point of view: according to ABI Research, the mobile fund transfer market will see a near $8 billion revenue opportunity for mobile operators by 2012 (up from just over $10 million in 2006).

What kinds of competitors? [30/10/2007]

PayPal has been pottering along nicely. The steady growth of their off-eBay business means that they are sitting side-by-side with traditional online acceptance brands (Visa, MasterCard, Amex, Discover, et. al.). Competitively, payments companies and their issuers have looked at this as an online phenomenon. Rightly so, as it has been. Online transaction volume is just north of 10 per cent. One of PayPal's new products is their virtual debit card, a response to customer requests that PayPal be accepted at more online merchants. If you want to buy something at a merchant that accepts cards but not PayPal, PayPal will generate a one-off MasterCard number for you. Now in testing, the virtual card is expected to be rolled out in the US by Christmas. They are also steadily putting together other services that may pose a genuine threat to incumbents, according to Aite Group payments analyst Adil Moussa: deferred-payments options and mobile payments. But why? Surely a bank can work out how to offer a good mobile payments service can't it (or, more likely, wait until someone else has worked out how to do it and then buy it, rather as RBS did with WorldPay and Bibit). Why is it considered a threat to banks? Similarly, the deferred-payment option is already provided by banks in some countries, and if customers show that they want deferred-payment options that it doesn't seem wholly implausible that MBNA or HSBC could provide them. In this particular case it's not actually PayPal that provides the underlying instrument, it's GE Money that is delivering the credit behind the deferred payment and since (as a general rule) providing credit is the most profitable part of the payment process for banks, that is why banks might be eyeing PayPal more nervously than before.

I wonder if the next cycle of nervousness might involve other more novel underlying instruments? We've noted before the kerfuffle about virtual currencies in China, for example. These are now far from niche. The "QQ currency" is substantial: while it was created for use on the web, it is being used in other kinds of commerce (which, since

I think that stimulating trade is one of the good things that a payment system should do, is probably a good thing overall). The Chinese government had a bit of a crackdown on QQ coins with the predictable (to economists) result: the price of the money went up (in fact it went up by 70% against the Yuan) which clearly indicates that there is a significant unfulfilled consumer demand for the new currency.

Now, QQ may not mean much to consumers in the UK, but just suppose that eBay or Tesco or Google were to create their own currency for special purposes and then it were to be adopted more widely? I think this might be rather fun. And rather likely, since the marginal cost of the "n+1"th currency in the electronic world is very low. Just because this was tried before and didn't work -- Beenz, Flooz and others -- doesn't mean that what Javelin call the finite-to-universal currency phenomenon couldn't happen in the future especially given the brand and presence of the big web players. Why would they do this? Well, a few years ago, I contributed to an excellent book by Forum friend David Boyle: The Moneychangers. One of the other chapters is by noted lateral thinker Edward de Bono. It's called "The IBM Dollar" and is based on a 1994 pamphlet he wrote for the Centre for the Study of Financial Innovation (CSFI) -- in fact it was the first CFSI pamphlet I read -- and sets out some reasons as to why a company might want to issue its own money. Well worth a read: in fact, I'm going to read it again myself.

SEPA update [06/02/2008]

Unlike many of you, I am very fortunate to have access to a) a euro bank account and b) someone that I can ask to waste their time on payment-related lunacy. Put these two things together and a SEPA experiment was born: I decided to celebrate the birth of the SEPA zone and send some euros to one of our Forum friends in the Netherlands, thus becoming (I hope) the first blogger to originate a SEPA Credit Transfer (SCT).

Well, my plan fell at the first hurdle because according to our bank (who shall not be named in this piece, but it's one of the UK's big four) "SEPA transfers are not available online". Yes, that's right. Getrude's dream of a friction-free payments landscape was in tatters, and it was only day 1. Someone had to physically go to the bank in order to do a SEPA Credit Transfer.

Most normal consumers would, of course, have given up at this point and forgotten about the whole SEPA thing. But I'm not a normal consumer. I have a responsibility to Digital Money Denizens and will leave no stone unturned, no path untraveled in order to send some euros to Amsterdam. So I sent someone down to the bank (not because I was lazy, but because I was out of the country).

She came back with a paper form to fill out. This was done, and the form was returned to the bank on a Tuesday, and on Friday I received confirmation from my Dutch colleague that the money had arrived in his account.

So, in summary, sending 50 euros to Amsterdam in the exciting new world of SEPA took two trips to the bank, cost £15 (i.e., a transaction fee of 40%) and took three days. Next time, I'll use PayPal.

Part 3 – The Social Axis

Chapter 8: The War on Cash

There is no functioning marketplace without price. The fact that the cost of cash is hidden from consumers stops the world of retail payments from evolving the way that other markets evolve. These posts explore the costs of cash and what may be required to create a level playing field.

Tokyo end-game [14/02/2007]

Someone after my own heart writes from Tokyo to say that as more deals are thrashed out to allow interoperability and a single contactless payments standard starts to look a realistic possibility, the Japanese could be facing a future where anyone without electronic money or the desire to embrace technology faces becoming a second-class citizen? "Ugh – real money? No thanks, it's filthy".

The pace of digital money development in Japan seems to be accelerating, which is why I keep coming back to review it again and again. DoCoMo (i.e., the mobile phone company, not the banks) is still in the forefront of the Japanese digital money revolution. It has 52 million subscribers and 20 million of them already have handsets with "osaifu-keitai" -- portable wallet -- functionality built in. This allows their phone to function as an Edy e-purse, DCMX credit card, train ticket and so on, all through the convenient contactless interface. The DCMX credit card now has 1.5 million users. DoCoMo also has 100,000 POS terminals in place in Japan that allow customers to use the portable wallet functionality of their phones, and it expects to have 150,000 in place by the end of next month. And they're going to keep going. As the investment site *Motley Fool* says, "It's important for the company to continue building out the network effects here because the financial success for DoCoMo is not in the phone sales, but in the transactions".

I wonder how long it will be before the prevailing mental model of mobile operator additional revenues in Europe shifts from dreary "content is king" plays (or should I say, "content demonstrably isn't king" plays such as Telefonica's multi-billion write-down on Big Brother format keepers Endemol) to something based around transactional markets and the value-added services built on those markets? The equivalent European technology platform (i.e., mobile and NFC) seems to be gaining ground, with yet more trials and pilots underway already. Perhaps the paradigm shift is near.

Competition for cash [15/03/2007]

Some unrepentant e-cash fanboy was quoted saying that "society will eventually end its love affair with cash and embrace technology - as in Japan where mobile phones, not bank cards, are replacing coins and notes". It this a reasonable comment or techno-blinkered boosterism? We need, as Aneace says, to find some figures on actual transactions performed with mobile phones. Let's look at Japan.

The main alternative to cash in Japan is the euro-dollar-yen (Edy) stored-value e-purse run by bitWallet, but in the last couple of years four other competing contactless payment schemes have launched. Edy now has to compete with DoCoMo's DCMX credit product, the Suica combination train and e-purse scheme and the new PASMO combination transit and e-purse scheme. Seven-Eleven Japan is about to launch another contactless payment service, called "nanaco," in 12,000 stores. Phew.

But, you might note, Japan is a cash-oriented society. In Japan, 90% of retail payments are cash whereas in the UK it is 60% (although, obviously, a much higher proportion of small payments). But on the other hand, 90% of payments in the UK used to made in cash, so maybe we're ahead of the curve.

In February 2006, Japanese consumers performed 15 million transactions with the nearly 27 million Edy cards and Mobile Edy applications on wallet phones in circulation. For comparison, I think Visa has around 70m+ cards in circulation in Japan and just one major card issuer, Sumitomo Mitsui (which is partly owned by DoCoMo), handles about $3 billion per month. Nevertheless, the Edy volume is more than double the 11 million monthly transactions made a year earlier. 80% of Edy users carry cards, 20% use Edy on phones (all the telcos -- DoCoMo, KDDI and Softbank -- have EDY handsets). There are nearly 50,000 merchant locations that accept EDY.

While the EDY application already runs on a number of banking cards, bitWallet is about to extend the reach significantly. ATM cards issued by Japan's postal savings bank are the next stop: and this is vitally important because the postal savings bank is huge there. Japan Post has agreed to put *EDY* as well as Suica onto some of the more than 70 million magnetic stripe ATM cards it is replacing with chip cards. And bitWallet will try to expand the merchant network to gas stations, retail shops and restaurants along Japan's toll motorways.

What I find particularly interesting about the latest figures is that Japanese consumers are already buying goods and services over the Internet by tapping their *EDY* cards or mobile phones on readers connected to or built into PCs and as we have discussed before, bitWallet hopes to increase use of Edy for e-commerce, along with payment by the e-purse for downloads of games to PlayStation 3 consoles. As in Europe, where we expect NFC interfaces to be built in to a variety of consumer electronics, more devices (such as set-top boxes) will be sprouting contactless interfaces to support small payments in the future.

So what does all this mean when it comes to figures? Well, here's the key one: the Feds say that the Bank of Japan reported that the total amount of coin in circulation has started to fall for the first time on record.

Negative added value [17/04/2007]

Cash really is a waste of money. In the USA, the government has been losing money on every new copper coin, as the costs of producing a one cent coin is about 1.4 cents. Now, because of the cost of nickel, the five cent coin costs 5.73 cents. This makes minting coins an astonishingly bad business: it may well be unique in the amount of value destroyed in the production process. I wonder if there's a business school course somewhere about managing businesses with negative added value: the final product is actually worth less than its raw materials.

I do remember hearing about this phenomenon before. It was many years ago when I was teaching an MBA course in IT Management and I can remember some of the (mature) students discussing negative value in the context of the Trabant, the famous East German mass-market car which was so rubbish that building them destroyed the value of the basic raw materials, let alone anything else. I did a quick Google to see if I could find a reference to this and found that negative added value is well-known: in fact, during the 1990s, **all** of the world's leading automobile manufacturers (with the exception of DaimlerChrysler) earned a negative added value!

You really do learning something new every day.

More from the war on cash [02/05/2007]

Linkdump on Payments pointed me at McKinsey's "golden rules" for the "war on cash". These are:

- The stakeholders must agree that substituting debit cards for cash is beneficial to society (This consensus will be hard to reach, as the parties involved do not agree on the true costs of cash and the other payment instruments involved).

- The debit product must be enhanced.

- Acceptance of debit cards must be vigorously promoted, both in terms of personal acceptance of cards and in the world of remote commerce (mail and telephone order, e- and m-commerce).

- Banks must develop segmented card offerings.

- Cash needs to be priced appropriately. The fact is that, today, the pricing of cash is not in line with its costs. Consumers and merchants in most countries do not pay the real cost of cash, and so merchants and consumers have no reason to reduce their use of cash. One problem is that there is no clear ownership of cash. Another is that governments often position cash as a public good -- to be offered free by banks -- thereby inhibiting an economic debate on cash versus other instruments.

- Finally, we will need to see significant targeted marketing efforts to promote debit over cash.

If by "debit" they mean debit products, pre-authorised debit products and prepaid products, then I think I agree with all of these points, especially the ones about segmentation and costs.

Even though I agree with all of those obviously sensible points, they do presuppose that it's debit cards that are the means of exchange that will replace cash. It seems to me that there are other possibilities. Mobile phones, for example. Consider the case of the parking meters in Westminster, where cash is being replaced by mobile phone payments. Remember that the local authority there is planning to replace all its parking meters within 12 months following a six month trial last year when they introduced cashless parking in the West End and Harrow Road to reduce theft from parking meters as well as to make life easier for motorists. This leads me to think of another "golden rule": take away the cash alternative or price it appropriately. Make motorists who pay in cash cover the cost of the thefts.

When payment services are free, consumers do not just get a bargain, they do not get clear signals about the costs of producing the services. However, as a study of the Norwegian market suggests, the negative consequences are limited if only the most efficient payment services (i.e., not cash or cheques) are free. The Norwegian banks that offer free payment services primarily offer electronic services and similarly, most customer retention and loyalty schemes only offer a discount for electronic services. This means that customers are motivated to choose the most cost-effective payment services, which is all to the well and good. There may be a downstream problem looming, though. A lack of profit opportunities in the payment system, particularly under SEPA I would think, may make it less attractive for banks to invest in the development of new payment services. I've decided to call it the non-innovator's dilemma: extensive use of efficient free services such as debit may have negative consequences for the efficiency of the payment system in the long term, while nimble competitors pop up with new services that take away customers.

Transport tales [08/05/2007]

I was on a train, in the UK today, and I was in the line at the buffet car trying to buy a couple of coffees. The guy in front me bought a drink and a pastry, which came to £2.10 and all he had was a ten pound note. The guy serving didn't want to take the note because it would use up all of his change, so he asked the customer to pay by card instead. Which he did. And he signed for it, because it wasn't a chip and PIN terminal, even though it was clearly working off line. How much easier life would have been if the customer had used one of these new "contactless" credit cards that I heard about on the BBC this morning while I was getting ready. The supreme irony, of course, is that I paid my £2.90 with the exact change.

Meanwhile, two of my colleagues went to a European city and set themselves the goal of not bothering to get any euros, thereby living the cashless dream. They almost succeeded. They used chip and PIN for everything from meals, to taxi rides to 1.40 euro transit tickets. But on the last day, they were almost defeated. The toilet cubicles in the restaurant had locks on and you needed a 20 cent coin to get in. My colleague crossed his legs and went back to his table. The waitress, presumably noting his odd gait and being familiar with the toilet cubicle cash catastrophe that had befallen him, reached into her pocket and gave him 20 cents! Mission accomplished: a trip to Paris with no euros.

They were actually in that city to talk to some ticketing guys in connection with a project we are working on. I won't say which transport company was involved, but I will share their figures. For a ticket sold at a ticket office, the cost of sales is four-fifths the average ticket price. For a ticket sold at a vending machine, the cost of sales is one-eighth of the average ticket price. For a ticket sold online, the cost of sales is one twentieth of the average ticket price. So it's no surprise what the company's ticketing strategy is.

More on Moore's Law [01/06/2007]

Money used to be stuff, now its data. Some people are sad about this, nostalgic for the good old days of the Gold Standard: As John Maynard Keynes once lamented, when "it appears that value is inherent in money as such", governments are able to steal from the populace by inflation, which is sort of a bad thing. On the other hand, when money is minted from silicon, the economics of handling cash (which today involves armoured vans and security guards) are driven by Moore's law. As that commentator notes, electronic information is instantaneous, weightless and exact. No longer the fumbling through coat pockets while a line of waiting customers quietly fumes. He goes on to point out that retailers get rid of both cash floats and cash frauds *such as charging $4.99 so that the $5 bill most people hand over has to pass through the till for one cent change rather than being trousered by a shop assistant* (my italics). I have to say, given the discussion about 99p coins, this had never occurred to me until I read it in this article, which I came across while searching for something else entirely. Is it really true? I had always thought that the origin of this irritating practice was to make goods appear cheaper, because 4.99 somehow sounds a lot less than 5. But the anti-trousering theory sounds, frankly, more plausible. Does anyone out there know?

As was mentioned in a previous discussion about the cafe that won't take cash, cash fraud is an important driver for digital money and must be one of the reasons why retailers are probably on balance OK about it going away, despite its perceived low cost and the amount they have to pay in the merchant service charges (MSCs). In the big picture, this is a trend already under way, and the introduction of contactless and mobile payments simply builds on the foundations made by debit. Debit is growing very strongly. The recent figures issued by Visa show that the total volume for Visa consumer debit and prepaid programs, including cash transactions, grew by 17% in 2006, reaching US$2.68 trillion up from US$2.29 trillion in 2005. Debit and prepaid now account for 60 percent of Visa global total consumer volume and over 67 percent of the number of Visa transactions, based on total consumer volume of US$4.4 trillion and 59.9 billion total transactions.

ATM anniversary [26/06/2007]

I got invited on to BBC World to be interviewed (by Zainab Badawi) about ATMs, which was quite exciting really. I had been very busy all day and hadn't really been paying attention to the package that rolled before the interview, so it wasn't until I got home that I realised that the core of the story was not only the 40th anniversary of the ATM, but that John Shepherd-Baron, the former De La Rue executive credited with inventing that machine in 1967, "now believes that the ubiquitous ATM will be made redundant within the next three to five years by the demise of paper cash". Even an unreconstructed e-cash fanboy like me wouldn't go with a five year horizon, but I appreciate both the sentiment and his support for our strategic perspective that it will be mobile phones that are the final nail in cash's coffin, not cards. Anyway, John says that the inspiration for the ATM came to him in the bath and a deal to develop the first such machine was sealed over a pink Gin with the then chief executive of Barclays. In a BBC interview timed to coincide with the fortieth anniversary this week of the installation of the first ever cash machine at a Barclays Bank branch in Enfield, North London, Shepherd-Baron explains the origins of the four-digit PIN and how the first machines actually worked (hint: they didn't use plastic cards).

One thing that struck me about this story -- apart from the fact that the machine used radioactive cheques rather than plastic cards -- is that I recall someone else getting an OBE for inventing the PIN last year. A James Goodfellow from Paisley in Renfrewshire who devised the mechanism of keying in a number code to cash machines in 1966 (i.e., a year before the machine was invented by De La Rue in 1967). James himself says:

"As a Development engineer with Smiths Industries Ltd, I was given the Project in 1965. Chubb Lock & Safe Co. were to provide the secure physical housing and the mechanical dispenser mechanism. My task was to design the means of allowing a genuine customer, and only a genuine customer, to actuate the dispenser mechanism. I reviewed many techniques, which may have achieved this aim. Areas researched included fingerprints, voice recognition, retinal patterns, card intrinsic value equal to value of money issued, magnetic strip, on line operation, imbedded resistive network on the card etc. These approaches all foundered on technical feasibility / cost / bulk or just price / performance criteria, so it was obvious that a new solution had to be found.

Eventually I designed a system which accepted a machine readable encrypted card, to which I added a numerical keypad into which an obscurely related Personal Identification Number had to be entered manually by the customer. This PIN was known only to the person to whom the card was issued."

This was, even more surprisingly, some years before the patent on ATMs was issued to Don Wetzel, Tom Barnes and George Chastain of Docutel, a company that developed automated baggage-handling equipment. According to this version of the history, the concept of the modern ATM first began in 1968, a working prototype came about in 1969 and Docutel was issued a patent in 1973.

I realise that no-one else in the world cares, but I am now fascinated to determine the genesis of the modern ATM. Any -- and I mean any -- relevant details would be gratefully received.

Don't do as I do [12/07/2007]

After 140 years, the Dutch central bank has closed its last cash outlets. From now on, the money couriers in the Netherlands must all drive to either a bank money centre or to Amsterdam (to deposit cash). But as is pointed out by the astute Linkdump on Payments, it's odd that banks in, for example, Maastricht cannot deposit their euros in nearby Aachen or Brussels. This is apparently not allowed by the central banks. Meanwhile, electronic payments are governed by SEPA and have to work cross-border as they would domestically. So the central banks that are moaning about banks not making sufficient progress in harmonising European payments are unwilling to harmonise their own cash handling because of the potential job losses. It's a funny old Europe.

As Chris Pickles points out, there are a number of initiatives running in Europe at the minute, each of which has "an intrinsic tendency towards monopoly". SEPA: why not have just one big clearing house for the EU? Securities settlement: why not just have one big Central Securities Depository (CSD) for the EU? How will customers access these services? - why not just have one big network for the EU? And so on. If you're a hammer, as the old saying goes, the whole world looks like a nail. In other words, if you are a centralised institution, then you tend to regard the solution to any problem as being more centralisation. I don't want to make any particular sort-of-political point here -- although I did once surprise an EU official who asked me "why don't you support the idea of a single currency for Europe" by answering "because I don't support the idea of a single currency for the UK" -- but I do want to note that it seems to me that the overall trend of technology is surely in the opposite: decentralisation and distribution. This is why I don't believe that the science fiction concept of some sort of "universal credit" throughout the galaxy will ever come to pass: the computers on the Enterprise will be trading between billions of currencies as it boldly goes where no central bank has been before.

Incidentally, the Monster Raving Loony Party -- who have been in vanguard of so many changes in our country -- think that Britain should leave the euro and instead invite European countries to join the pound. At $2.03, they might extend the offer to our transatlantic cousins.

Cost dynamics, again [25/07/2007]

The Swedish central bank published some detailed figures on the cost of payments and they provide useful input to the debate on the future of payments. They show that on average the variable cost of an ATM cash withdrawal to the issuing bank is around SEK1.3, compared to

SEK0.23 for a debit card payment, but that is still less than credit card transactions. As in the case of the Norwegian study we discussed before, the central bank study highlights the fact that consumers get very little information through the price structure on the costs that banks have in the provision of payment services. In particular, they say that

"the problem is that for a large number of payment instruments the variable fee is set to zero, although our study indicates that marginal costs are above zero"

On the whole, with the exception of debit card transactions (on the acquirer side) and direct debits, variable costs and fees differ significantly. Private customers only face transaction fees when making payment transactions at the bank branch-office or when using cheques (although cheques are hardly ever used). Transaction fees are almost exclusively taken from corporate customers, particularly merchants.

Delving into the figures further shows the extent of the cross-subsidy to cash. The Bank estimates that the average large retail banks' payment service profits are around SEK155m and also that all payment services except cash generate a profit. Remember that the Scandinavian payment systems are much more efficient that in the rest of Europe (or the US) because of higher e-payment usage, so the losses will be even worse in other countries.

Credit transfers as a whole give a net revenue of about SEK160 million.

Card payments, in particular from acquiring services for charge and credit card transactions, are much more profitable.. The average bank has an annual surplus of SEK460 million.

The average bank has an almost equally large annual loss from the distribution of cash to the public, of which two-thirds come from ATM services.

So, as is generally true, card payment transactions finance distribution of cash to the public so there might be considerable cost savings to be made by the banks through a more transparent and cost-based pricing. This is because such a pricing strategy would lead to changes in the pattern of demand. Consumers would have economic incentives to shift to those instruments that are less costly to produce. According to the Bank's cost estimates, they would use debit cards more and credit cards and cash less and they would increase their use of electronic credit transfers and direct debits at the cost of paper-based credit transfers. This would mean in practice, transaction fees on paper-based and electronically-initiated credit transfers and the introduction of transaction fees for cash withdrawals. Fees for acquiring services would have to decrease.

One of our heroes, the governor of the Bank of Sweden, has previously noted that the fact that Swedish banks do not take any fees for cash withdrawals may very well be the explanation for our greater use of cash and lesser use of card payments. The Bank's conclusion is that the banking sector could lower its variable costs by the best part of a billion SEK per annum by shifting to cost-based pricing.

This analysis is not limited to Sweden. If we look at the EU as a whole, in the context of the SEPA push, the big picture is straightforward, as shown below (using figures from McKinsey, July 2007). European banks lose a lot of money on the non-SEPA payment instruments (i.e., cash and cheques), they make reasonable money on SEPA instruments and they make a lot of money on payment-related (rather than direct payment) revenues. These payment-related revenues (e.g., interest foregone on current accounts) are significantly at risk if non-bank payment alternatives gain any ground. So if downward pressure on the profits from SEPA instruments together with downward pressure on payment-related profits by non-bank competitors become significant, then they money available to support the losses on non-SEPA instruments will simply not be there. In the case of cheques, the writing is already on the wall (I saw a notice in my local Sainsbury's last week indicating that they will stop accepting cheques on 31st July). In the case of cash, where next?

Coin concerns [27/07/2007]

I couldn't care less if I never saw a coin again (outside of a museum) but in other economic circumstances, they might be missed. The Bank of Mozambique is concerned at how the alleged absence of coins is being used as an excuse for raising prices. The chairperson of the Maputo Baker's Association, Victor Miguel, has said that it was availability of loose change that determined the prices that are charged. He claimed it was impossible for an item to cost one metical and 70 centavos, because 10 and 20 centavo coins are supposedly unavailable (a metical is about a nickel). Mozambique's currency was reformed last year, with small denomination coins, but retailers say they never see them (despite the Bank saying that large numbers were minted). The Bank says that retailers are refusing to get the coins because they prefer to keep the prices up. Strike another one against cash. But what if there's another explanation? I wonder if the coins have been melted down for the metal?

This is happening in other places. Bangladesh, for example, where millions of Indian coins are being smuggled in and turned into razor blades. And that's creating an acute shortage of coins in many parts of India. Police in Calcutta say that the recent arrest of a grocer highlights the extent of the problem: he confessed to melting down tens of thousands of Indian coins into razor blades and told the police

"Our one rupee coin is in fact worth 35 rupees, because we make five to seven blades out of them."

One day, the coins will be a memory, so perhaps I should salt away a rupee coin to sell on eBay in a hundred years. They probably won't be that rare though, unlike the rarest banknote in existence which is in the G&D Banknote Museum: it's the only existing 100-mark note dated 1914 from the former colony of German New Guinea. If you do find a £50 anywhere (apparently they've gone to Poland), don't spend it, save it for posterity.

A bear market for cash [31/08/2007]

WebMoney is an electronic money and online payment system (transactions are conducted through WebMoney Transfer). WM Transfer Ltd, the owner and administrator of WebMoney Transfer Online Payment System, was founded in 1998 and is a legal corporate entity of Belize, Central America. Originally targeted mainly at Russian clients, it is now used by more than four million customers worldwide. Over on DGC there was a case study on WebMoney that was well worth reading. Their service, WebMoney Transfer, is now a global system, handling billions of Dollars, Euros and of course Rubles. They recently launched a fully-backed gold currency as well, 1 "WMG" equals 1 gram of Gold. Now, as is frequently observed, the difficult part of this kind of system is getting money into it, not moving money around it. Here they have executed a physical strategy that has resulted in 120,000 locations across Russia having electronic kiosks which allow anyone to pay cash and fund a WebMoney

Transfer account. More than 25% of the total WebMoney account funding comes from these 'cash-in' kiosks.

In Russia, the use of electronic payments in both the public and private sectors in recent months has grown so fast that the Central Bank has had practically no demand for new money. Published data shows M0 growing to 3.26 trillion rubles in June 2007 from 3.07 at the start of the year. M2 figures show that almost the entire growth in the volume of money in the economy (at the level of 50 percent annually) is due to electronic payments. Indicators of the growth of turnover in retail trade in the first half of the year (14.2 percent in real terms, that is, taking account of inflation, almost 20 percent nominally) and the growth of public spending (19 percent) do not give cause to think that there is no public demand for more money. A comparison of M2 and M0 (money in circulation outside banks) shows that the share of cash in economic turnover, which has been slowly sinking since 2002, began to fall faster in 2006. it seems that a key reason for the transition to e-payments is increasing transparency in salary payments. In other words, when salaries are transparent they no longer need to be in cash. The transition is taking place on a massive scale and it reveals a "kind of paradox", as the article puts it. The rapidly growing Russian economy, in spite of 8-9 percent annual inflation, will soon not need any more money.

Read all abaht it: retailers don't really like cash [25/09/2007]

Retailers say that cards are more expensive than cash. Therefore, they can't help noticing comments such as those by Bank of England supremo -- much in the news in the UK at the moment -- Mervyn King. Mervyn reportedly said about having cash in circulation that:

"such mutual convenience is a public good, and may not correspond to the private interest of commercial banks."

In other words, everyone else is happy with cash but bankers are conspiring against the general welfare by trying to persuade people to use cards. Now, one might reasonably imagine that part of retailers apparent devotion to cash is as a bargaining chip with banks, but their suspicion is genuine enough: they don't want to be held to ransom over payments (which, for some retail categories are already a significant overhead). But are they right (as in that article) to look at contactless payments as being a wheeze to increase retailers bank charges tenfold? The calculation that they are making here (i.e., a small shop with 450 cash transactions per week being replaced by contactless) shows the retailer's costs rising to £200+ per month compared to the current £20 per month they pay for banking cash. I think there are two issues about this calculation: first of all, retailers are right to ask for differential interchange of offline EMV transactions that are replacing low-value cash, so that means the cost wouldn't be anything like £200. Maybe £50-£80, something like that. Secondly, I can't help noticing that the retailers are only calculating the cost: they don't see any upside. They don't see any benefits to them in reduced cash handling or shorter queues, they're not being offered any value-added services. As our good friends at Payments News perceptively noted, this sort of thing is a symptom of an industry (i.e., acquiring) that is competing only on price but that should instead be looking to offer something new.

Is contactless an example of something that's genuinely new and delivers something to the merchants? Well, the evidence from the marketplace at least indicates that that might be a realistic possibility. Look at this example from Taiwan, where "Watsons Your Personal Store" has reported a 77 percent drop in average queuing time now that they accept contactless payments. Their managing director says that

"Visa payWave enables consumers to complete a whole transaction in as little as four seconds, significantly reducing queuing time and increasing consumer satisfaction [and] operational efficiency by reducing the time and cost of processing cash."

So one might expect retailers to appreciate that substituting card payments for cash payments benefits everyone (except the issuer of the notes and coins in circulation, of course, because they lose the seigniorage) and increases the net welfare.

Well, sort of. What these figures show is that contactless technology is a viable -- indeed, beneficial -- substitute for cash. What they do not show, of course, is that banks are the optimum issuers and that is why there is so much interest in other organisations such as mobile operators and retailers (to pick the obvious examples) becoming issuers of cash-substituting instruments. That said, I was still quite surprised to see that the London newspaper "The Evening Standard" is going to launch its own contactless prepaid *Eros* card to the replace cash for people buying newspapers from their (i.e., the Evening Standard's) sellers. To incentivise use, the paper will be cheaper for contactless buyers than for cash buyers. There's going to be a trial this week at the London terminus I use, Waterloo, so I shall endeavour to obtain a card and report back. The scheme's creators (marketing consultancy HH&S and technology company i-movo) believe it to be a world first although they don't say what at. It's certainly not the world's first newspaper to be purchased with stored value card, because I was there on 4th July 1995 in Swindon town centre when *Evening Advertiser* vendor Mr. Don Stanley (then 72) made the first ever live Mondex sale.

One rather obvious question that any thoughtful consumer might ask, though, is why doesn't the Evening Standard just take Oyster cards in payment -- after all, Hong Kong commuters buy their evening paper using their *Octopus* card -- since everyone on Waterloo station has an Oyster card anyway? Well, Transport for London decided a couple of years ago that they didn't see a business case in doing this: after all, the Evening Standard can't sell more than a couple of hundred thousand copies in London every day. Another rather obvious question that the same thoughtful consumer might ask is that since the banks in the UK launched contactless payments in London a couple of weeks ago, why didn't one of the acquirers sign up the Evening Standard? Surely waving your Barclays OnePulse to buy a paper in 500 milliseconds is just what it was designed for. The answer, of course, is that if you're selling the Evening Standard for Xp, you wouldn't want to pay a 10p merchant service charge on a debit transaction even if the banks could offer you a suitable fixed-fee, no screen, rugged terminal (which they can't). Now if I was one of the acquirers, frankly, I have been tempted to knock up a terminal like this (just use a mobile phone with a bit of POS software on it to start with) and sign up the Standard for a penny a transaction as it would be a simple way of generating a hundred thousand new contactless cardholders in London. But then if I was one of the acquirers, I wouldn't care less what the issuing side of the bank was doing, would I?

ATM access [28/09/2007]

In the US ATM fees are going up, as they should be: the average number of transactions per ATM has fallen by (if my arithmetic is correct) about two-thirds over the last decade. Therefore the cost per transaction should have gone up quite a bit. Bank of America's decision to raise the cost of an ATM withdrawal to $3 may therefore be well calculated (because they have more deposit accounts and associated ATMs across the nation than others, so they have the strongest potential to gain rather than lose. Meanwhile, in the UK, where according to VocaLink the average number of transactions per ATM has fallen by a third in the last five years, there are going to be more "free" ATMs: 600 more, in fact. The government, via the Treasury, has struck a deal with banks and cash machine operators to increase free access to cash. Ed Balls said:

"The free cash machines..."

I didn't read any further, because they're not free, of course. They are paid for by other bank customers. The deal is that to persuade the cash machine operators to set up and maintain cash machines free-of-charge, banks and building societies agreed to pay a 'financial inclusion premium'. This scheme, which will compensate cash machine operators for the expected lower cash machine-use in these areas, began on 1 March 2007 and will be funded through the transaction fee banks and building societies are charged when their customers use other cash machines.

One thing that ATMs in the UK don't do is to dispense fivers any more. The governor of the Bank of England, Mervyn King, was worried about this because it meant that £5 notes have become "scruffy" and the Bank was going to look at how it can encourage commercial banks to issue more £5 notes, the number of which has fallen compared with other denominations. (This was all before they had other things to worry about, like Northern Rock, for example). Mervyn said the bank had £1bn worth of £5 notes in its vault but commercial banks did not want them. They find it cheaper to issue £10 and £20 notes and so the shortage of new fivers means that the ones in circulation are "noticeably soiled and scruffy". The British Bankers Association chief executive Angela Knight pointed out that £100 was the average amount taken out of ATMs at one visit. I say stop wasting money on fivers and twenties and above and just standardise on tens. Much cheaper all round.

Hammer of the gods [15/10/2007]

I read in my *Daily Telegraph* that there has been a postal strike in the UK I can't say that I noticed, because I never send letters anymore and never receive any except for junk mail and the occasional utility bill (which, since I pay all utility bills by direct debit, I rarely look at anyway). I'm from the same mould as the terrific US stand-up Jim Gaffigan: if I did actually see a hand-addressed envelope drop onto the doormat I'd assume that someone had been kidnapped. But I digress. I further read in the very same newspaper that in an attempt to waste an impressive amount of public money, the Department for Work & Pensions (the DWP) sent out 400,000 pension cheques last week by courier because of the strike. I was really shocked: I had no idea that they sent out cheques at all, let alone sent them out by courier when they would otherwise be delayed. Surely it should be a condition of receiving pension cheques that you get yourself a bank account and end the anachronistic printing, posting, depositing and clearing of bits of paper. If I sound more intemperate than usual about allowing this quaint Georgian payment mechanism to persist, it's because I'm writing this in Iceland.

Ah, Iceland. For a digital money nerd like me this is the best place in the world. Not because of the glaciers, volcanoes, whales, history -- the story of Jorgen Jorgenson, the "English Dane", who became King of Iceland (for a few days), is definitely one that couldn't be made up -- heritage, sagas and sub-zero vodka bars (even the chairs were made out of ice). No, I love it here because Iceland is the most cashless country on Earth. I didn't take any cash at all with me -- in fact, I'd forgotten all about cash until I started typing this article -- and never needed any. Cards work everywhere, from taxis to bars. A miniscule seven percent of retail POS transactions are cash (it's more than seventy percent back home) and there is every possibility that contactless cards and contactless phones will soon mop up that last fraction.

If people don't pay by card they pay by e-bill. There's only one processor and all the banks are onboard. If a retailer -- or another person -- pushes an e-bill at you, then you will see it no matter which of your online banking accounts you use. When you log in, there are your bills waiting for payment. Once you've OK'd the bill, they get their money. Simple, cheap. I've always been enthusiastic about pushed e-billing because it means that the retailers don't have to deal with the payment details.

It seems to me that there is every possibility that Iceland might become the first cashless society. I mean wholly cashless, with no notes or coins at all. At this point, retailers could get rid of their tills and banks could shut down their ATMs.

It's really interesting to speculate on what might then happen. I would love to plan a survey -- perhaps with an anthropologist and a sociologist -- for the time when the last Icelandic banknote is folded away, because none of us really know how a cashless society will differ from current society. It's certainly fun to speculate though.

I don't care too much for money... [10/11/2007]

Ah, a title that's amusing on so many levels means that this tragic (in the sense of inevitable) post must be written. I have no choice. It's all because *iPhone* fever swept the nation last night. People had been queuing outside Apple's flagship Regent Street store for some time. At precisely 6.02pm, the hordes were empowered to exchange wonga for widget. The guy who was first in the queue, after spending time in the freezing cold and lashing rain, proudly grabbed his trophy telecommunicator and ran down the stairs to the checkout. But he couldn't pay, because the Apple store doesn't take cash. So the guy who was second in line actually became the first person in Britain to buy an iPhone. Seems like cash can be something of a disadvantage in a high-tech economy as some bankers across the Irish Sea have noticed.

On the subject of outmoded means of exchange and what to do about them, Forum friend and e-money guru Leo Van Hove draws my attention to an outstanding bank submission to the Irish Department of Finance. National Irish Bank made a pre-budget submission, urging the government to fast track reform of the payments system in Ireland. Their proposal advocates the phasing out of cheques, and the greater use of electronic forms of payment including direct debits, debit cards and credit cards. According to Kevin Gallen, the Deputy Chief Executive of National Irish Bank,

"Ireland currently operates a highly inefficient mode of payments, which is costing the economy an estimated €750m every year. This is an unnecessary burden on exporters and households, which is adversely impacting on our competitiveness as an economy. Further, our heavy reliance on cash and cheques has a non-economic cost, in terms of both the environment and security."

According to the European Central Bank (ECB), annual cash withdrawals per consumer at Irish ATMs are well above the European average and cheques account for a quarter of all payments. So the bank suggests that the government announce an "E-Day" on 1st November 2008, after which:

1. The Government should stop issuing or accepting cheques.

2. The Law Reform Commission should investigate the issues involved in making electronic money a form of legal tender by 2010 in order to give people the confidence that if they have to make a payment, they can do so by debit or credit card.

3. The taxi regulator should make it compulsory for all taxis and hackneys to accept payment by debit or credit cards by the 1st of November 2008.

4. The Government should levy tax on the inefficient forms of payment instead of on the efficient forms.

Sensible policies for a better Ireland, and it's not just technologists like me who think so. Ronnie O'Toole, Chief Economist of National Irish Bank, commented,

"Reforming our payments system is an opportunity to upgrade our technology, and improve the cost-competitiveness of our economy. It is a win-win situation which needs strong leadership from the government to push through."

Horses for courses [02/01/2008]

I wonder if 2008 will be the year of the contactless card? Trevor Pavey, Contactless Payments Manager at Texas Instruments has a nice turn of phrase: he says that contactless payments this year will be about three M's: merchants, mobile payments and multi-applications. That sounds plausible, but I'm sure that in the immediate future it is the merchant take-up that is the dominant driver. While the roll-out of contactless payment cards around the world has been steady, it hasn't been a tsunami. One reason might be that lack of customer awareness is impeding the usage and adoption of contactless payment systems. According to the research cited (by Aberdeen), 63% of Best-in-Class companies that have already adopted contactless payments at retail locations are responding to the challenge of customer awareness by defining a set of return-on-investment (ROI) objectives and goals surrounding contactless implementation. I'm not entirely sure what that means, but I think I understand the big picture they outline: two-fifths of the Best-in-Class companies have implemented a contactless solution, and another two-fifths are considering implementation, which means that only a fifth are not looking at it for the time being. Of those who have implemented contactless technology, 91% have improved their total number of transactions, and ALL (my emphasis) have 80% or more of their customers extremely satisfied. Those seem like encouraging figures to me even if there is a lack of awareness.

Clearly some consumers are aware of contactless, because forty-nine percent of the world's consumers report they are likely to use a contactless card if their financial institution provides it, and 47% of that group cite convenience as the main reason, a KRC Research survey (across 13 countries and including 7,000 respondents) commissioned by MasterCard Worldwide suggests. The results indicate consumers' preference for convenient payment methods, says Cathleen Conforti, MasterCard senior vice president and global PayPass product manager, who goes on to say

"It's not surprising to see the high figures because [consumers] see contactless as a more convenient method."

As of last month, MasterCard issuers had distributed more than 20 million PayPass-enabled cards and other devices, and more than 80,000 merchant locations worldwide were accepting PayPass, according to MasterCard.

There's no reason, I think, for consumers to be going crazy about contactless across the board. But in some retail sectors, I'm surprised that penetration hasn't been quicker. One that springs to mind (because I just had to pay TEN QUID by credit card to park at my local train station) is car parking. Car parking is an obvious candidate for conversion to contactless payments, and the announcement by Affiliated Computer Services (ACS) that its airport parking applications in North America will begin accepting MasterCard PayPass contactless payments is therefore welcome. ACS is a leader in large airport parking systems, with more than 20 current installations at America's busiest airports, so it will be a useful barometer. If I could pay by contactless at the car park, especially without getting out of my car, I would count that as a major convenience. The car park operator wins too: when I'm paying with card (as opposed to the coins I've collected from various orifices in my car) then I might buy 4 hours just to be on the safe side instead of 3. As MasterCard figures show, not only does contactless accelerate transaction times (it's faster than cash) but consumer spending increases 28% to 42%.

Not everyone is convinced. In that same article, Steve Rathgaber, president and chief operating officer of NYCE Payments Network, which bills itself as connecting more than 2,500 financial institutions with more than 280,000 ATMs and more than 1.5 million point-of-sale locations in the United States, said that PayPass was a bad idea.

"Just because the technology is there, it doesn't make it a good product."

he said. Well, yes. But I'm not sure I agree with his specific reasoning about contactless: to consumers, new technology may be more confusing and less productive than older technology. I'm sure that someone said the same thing about ATMs but if consumers are confused about contactless technology then someone hasn't been responding to the challenges of customer awareness by defining a set of return-on-investment (ROI) objectives and goals, right?

Retail weak [25/01/2008]

The drive by UK banks to "replace cash usage with cards" came under heavy attack from the British Retail Consortium (BRC). In a strongly worded statement toward the end of last year, the trade association accused card companies of exaggerating the extent to which cards have replaced cash. A BRC survey of 10,000 stores, which together account for a third of UK retail sales, showed that cash is still the most popular payment method, accounting for 54 percent of all UK transactions by volume and 32 per cent by value. Their spokesperson said

"The card companies, in their publicity campaigns for their products, are giving the impression that cash is on the way out... For example, they are trying to present contactless cards as the 'new cash,' because contactless transactions below £10 do not require a PIN. "

Well, whether card companies are giving the impression that cash is on the way out or not, European cash payments are declining. They now account for only a third of total European household expenditure, according to Datamonitor. The value of cash payments in Europe was €1,787 billion (US$2,651 billion) in 2006, accounting for 34 percent of total household expenditure, down from 38 percent in 2002. And, as APACS pointed out at the time, the vast majority of cash transactions are under £5, whilst the average credit card transaction at a retailer is over £50 for credit. Anyway, the BRC's point is that cash costs retailers less than cards. Their figures are that on average, a £20 cash transaction costs a retailer less than four UK pence, while a £20 credit card transaction costs at least 17 pence. I'm sure these are accurate: the costs of cash fall on consumers (and society) rather than retailers, so naturally retailers are in favour of it. There's nothing wrong with that, but it seemed a little over the top for the BRC director general Kevin Hawkins to say that

"Banks have long abused their position by imposing much higher charges on retailers for processing card payments than cash... Clearly, the banks have spotted that replacing cash with cards would mean a further boost to their profits."

The BRC says it is asking the Office of Fair Trading (OFT) "to force the banks to reduce their (card processing) charges." Surely the way to make a market work properly isn't to ask regulators to fix prices but to increase competition. If retailers feel that cards cost too much, then they should develop alternatives, shouldn't they? All they have to do is call...

How much would it cost to create an infrastructure capable of replacing cash? Both e-payment mechanisms need infrastructure, and that costs money. But let's forget the mechanism for a moment: let's just suppose that every mobile comes with e-payments built in somehow and focus on the rest of the infrastructure. Who should pay? The dynamics behind this specific debate are not limited to the UK in the example above. Just like consumers in countries in Western Europe and East Asia, Americans are also abandoning paper-based forms of payment (i.e., cash and checks) for various kinds of electronic and plastic payment models. The result is overloaded networks and processing systems. According to Chase Paymentech Pulse Index, 1.9 million online shoppers made purchases worth $104.8 million at 10 major online retailers on "Cyber Monday" 2007. Cyber Monday is the first Monday. Those numbers are up 32.5% and 40.6%, respectively, over the same day last year. Network traffic is growing the same way. Visa USA, the world's largest credit card network, is seeing 15% per annum transaction growth. This is not only in credit cards but debit cards and prepaid instruments. Debit and prepaid cards represented 56% of the volume of non-cash payments in 2006, and are growing at 19% a year. It is reasonable to assume that as contactless begins to eat into cash, the volume of low-value transactions will begin to climb as well. Visa, which has seen its traffic volume rise to nearly 7,000 messages per second (a "message" can include 10 or more individual transactions), expect that volume to reach 30,000 or 40,000 in coming years, which I think is both truly astounding figure and also a testament to the technology.

It makes you wonder what kind of volumes the systems would have to deal with in order to make serious inroads into cash. At first, it would seem like a lot, because the volumes would go up tenfold at least (except in Iceland, where more than 90% of retail payments are already electronic) but when you factor in Moore's Law and the typical replacement cycles for retailer and back-office systems, it doesn't seem such a mountain to climb. In fact, I'd go further. The time when e-payment infrastructure can handle the replacement of cash is not even a generation away.

Cashlessness and futures [15/02/2008]

Chris Skinner was talking about cashlessness over at *FinanSer* but says that we're not going in the direction. In fact,

"instead we have rising levels of cash in the economy"[16]

I don't think that's true, or at least true everywhere. In Iceland, 93% of all retail transactions are non-cash. Recent data by the Bank of Japan showed that the number of coins in circulation dropped 0.25 percent to ¥91.45 billion in June, the largest year-on-year decline ever, due largely to the spread of e-money. In Hong Kong, the Octopus transit card has replaced 1% of the cash in circulation. In Singapore, the government has been considering Singapore Electronic Legal Tender (SELT). In Japan, unlike all other developed countries, the number of coins in circulation has started to fall (because of mobile phone-based payments). In Kenya, the new mobile payment system M-PESA has more than a million customers. In the UK, debit cards have overtaken credit cards and cheques will certainly vanish in our lifetimes. It seems as if the trend toward electronic payments is accelerating around the world.

How far will this trend go? Since the social cost of cash is high, and the associated transaction costs fall disproportionately on the poor, we might all be better off once the shift to e-payment (m-payment, actually, for most people in most of the world) is complete. But we need to explore to be sure: there are some aspects of cash (such as anonymity) that are valued and we need to understand how and why some characteristics might need to be preserved. Is a cashless economy realistic? Or desirable? How might such an economy emerge and is it possible to imagine the impact of the end of notes and coins?

---

[16] But cash is better than cashless, The FinanSer

Is the use of cash stable or falling? [25/02/2008]

Spurred on by recent discussions about whether the use of cash is actually falling, whether it might stabilise at a plateau or continue to fall (if it is, indeed, still falling) I decided to take a look at the US figures in more detail. Now, the "headline" figures certainly seem to support the theory that cash is losing market share:

"Last year the number of ATMs in the United States fell 9 percent, the first big drop since the devices were introduced in the 1970s. The percentage of cash-payment transactions in the United States also is falling."[17]

Although the percentage of cash transactions is falling, US currency in circulation is still going up. US currency in circulation was $784 billion in 2006. Mind you, at least half of that is held outside the US (mostly under mattresses). That suggests that less than $400 billion in currency supports a $13 trillion economy. In 1970, the economy's relative need for cash was almost twice as high. As Robert Samuelson says...

"We have crossed a cultural as well as an economic threshold when plastic and money are synonyms and the crime of choice is identity theft, not bank robbery."[18]

But as Samuelson also notes in that article, almost all of the bills printed by the Feds last year were to replace worn notes, not to expand the stock. So what is the actual situation with regard to cash usage? Since in the US, as in Europe, the volume of notes in circulation is climbing but a large portion of the note stock is being used as a store of value rather than as a means of exchange, we probably cannot use M0 as a measure. A useful contribution to the debate comes from a research paper from the Federal Reserve Bank, Cleveland, which looks at some proxy measures to determine whether cash usage is falling or not. One measure, which strikes me as being potentially very accurate, is the number of worn banknotes being take out of circulation and destroyed. If notes are being stuffed into mattresses, this figure will fall. If notes are being used in transactions, this figure will rise. Well, according to the Feds this proxy provides evidence consistent with other estimates that the use of cash in the US actually peaked more than a decade ago, in the mid-1990s, and has

---

[17] Withdrawing from the ATM habit, *The Boston Globe*

[18] A Quiet Revolution In Money, *washingtonpost.com*, Robert J. Samuelson

The Digital Money Reader 2008

been falling since. In fact, using this proxy across 16 developed countries, they found that cash use was falling in 13 of them. This is why I said previously that the amount of notes and coins in circulation may not be a reasonable measure of cash usage.

Does the fall in the number of ATMs in the US foretell the end of ATMs or does it mean that inventive manufacturers and service providers will have to work harder to make ATMs do some new things?

Chapter 9: Legal and Regulatory

Payments is a regulated business, so it is important to understand the legal and regulatory trends as much as to understand the technology and business trends.

The prepaid backlash [23/02/2007]

I once decided that I wanted to move to New Zealand after I saw an excerpt from an NZ "most wanted" kind of programme where the lead crime was the theft of some sheepskin car seat covers. But perhaps more criminals will be attracted to NZ by the latest threat to civilisation as we know it, the prepaid card. Since last November, NZ Post has been distributing what sounds like an excellent product, pretty similar to prepaid Visa cards distributed by the post offices in Italy. The prepaid Visa card lets anyone make anonymous purchases over the web and is encouraging more people to shop online, but "fears are being voiced" that the cards may be misused by children and could aid criminals. They didn't mention terrorists.

NZ Post has marketed the card primarily as an alternative to gift vouchers or giving cash, branding it as the *Prezzy Card*. Customers key in the number and expiry date on the card when buying online and type "prezzy card holder" into the name field, if required. NZ Post has so far sold 40,000 Prezzy Cards and more than 10 per cent of the transactions have been online purchases, Mr Jamieson says. One appeal of the disposable card is that customers need not disclose their credit card or bank account details when buying online, and the most any customer could lose through fraud would be the outstanding balance on their card.

The card has also been taken up by kids to pay for subscriptions to online games. If grandma and granddad give you old fashioned cash for your birthday, what use is that? You can't use it for anything important, like World of Warcraft. Why not give mum and dad a credit card linked to the kids Prezzy Card, with cashback in World of Warcraft gold instead of boring NZ dollars. I want one for my kids: I don't want them giving credit card numbers or their real names out on the Internet.

The moaning about prepaid cards is, however, only one front in the backlash against e-cash. The use of mobiles to make payments is clearly a boon to terrorists (or, at least, terrorists who have never heard of 500 euro notes) as Rachel Ehrenfeld, founder of the *Terror Finance Blog* has noted. She calls the hook-up between the GSMA and MasterCard a "terrorist dream". David Nordell, another finance terror blogger, says, "Person-to-person transfers via mobile phones will be almost anonymous, and completely uncontrollable unless the regulators intervene and block these new services until ways are devised to track the flow of funds." I'm not, however, sure that Mr. Bin Laden will be moving his account to his local GSM operator. If I'm a known terrorist suspect and I use, let's say, text messaging to transfer money to another terrorist colleague, then not only will the authorities know where I am, they will know where my colleague is as well (since he will have to switch on his phone to get the text message). In real time. And they will also have a handy record of transfers and movements.

Distributing liabilities [24/05/2007]

Steve Mott, whose opinions I always value, wrote an article arguing that so far as US payment cards are concerned, security went wrong many years ago when the industry decided not to go to PIN. Of course, outside the US the migration to "chip and PIN" is steady if not spectacular. But it's not making a big difference overall, because fraud is migrating to remote channels. He says this is testing "the resources and will of an industry still reluctant to abandon the gravy train of fees and interchange to commit to safer, better, and cheaper alternative payments". He goes on to point out that the payment card industry spends about a dollar in prevention for every $10 they lose in fraud, which he compares to the health care industry that has three times as much fraud but spends less than a tenth as much on fraud prevention. My reaction to reading this was to think how the payment card industry might spend its anti-fraud budgets more effectively, but I don't think that was the main point. The main point was that we're not doing very well against fraud at a time when we're introducing contactless payments and trying to shift transactions online. Perhaps one of the reasons is that by offering zero liability to consumers -- no matter how reckless they might be -- "a generation of consumers has been trained to disregard safe practices for use of financial accounts". Steve says that...

"it's time to throw out the blanket zero-liability paradigm and get legitimate, responsible consumers to put some skin in the security game, too. The good ones appear to be ready to do what's needed to protect themselves. Consumers who can't should get restricted account access. Those who won't should bear the specific costs of their misbehavior instead of loading their burden on the backs of the vast majority of responsible transactors."

Interesting, and different to my plan to make it both the issuers and customers' problem by changing the law so it's not illegal to use someone else's card. My plan delivers zero fraud, instantly.

Steve makes, as always, a lot of sense. But as Chris Skinner noted, when he was discussing the UK government's "Get Safe Online" initiative, only 24% of UK online consumers think they should be primarily responsible for their own online safety. In other words, 76% think they're not responsible for their own safety when shopping, banking or doing stuff online. Zero liability has, indeed, created a kind of moral hazard: products that were never meant to be used online are being shoehorned into channels where they are less than wholly safe, where they are being used by consumers (like me) who don't care about security because they are indemnified against loss. Hhhmmmm.

At the moment, neither the banks, the consumer nor the police are sufficiently incentivized to stop identity theft, so who is? The merchant. In the case of CNP, it's the merchants who are losing the money, but even so the take up of anti-fraud 3D Secure technology has been rather limited: apart from anything else, the merchants themselves don't want to implement it for fear they will lose more from basket abandonment than fraud.

There's a good article about the fraud/lost sale trade-off in this month's *Digital Transactions*, by the way.

The glorious five year plan [18/06/2007]

You may not have noticed, but the European Parliament finally adopted the Payment Services Directive (PSD). The text of the PSD will now be forwarded to the EU Council for final adoption. The Member States should then transpose the Directive as early as possible, and by 1 November 2009 at the latest, into national law. So if all goes well, in a couple of year's time, I'll be able to use my debit card in Ireland (as I did last week) and my credit card in The Netherlands (as I did a couple of weeks ago). Hhhmmm. Oh well, at least I'll now be able to give my bank account details to companies in Romania so that they can direct debit my current account...

While SEPA is the cause of considerable activity in the business world -- such as the announcement by UK payment services companies Voca and the LINK Interchange Network that they will merge to form a company that will handle 8 billion payment transactions per annum -- I wonder what it will mean to the average consumer. A very small proportion of European retail payments are cross-border, so for the typical European consumer, it will have no impact whatsoever. For the typical merchant, it may well mean higher costs. For the typical bank, it definitely means higher costs. The European Savings Banks Group (ESBG) -- an international banking association representing about one third of the retail banking market in Europe -- has welcomed the PSD, but warns that delays in approving the text could yet undermine the legitimacy of the new SEPA-inspired payment instruments. In a slightly predictable move, the group says that

"the PSD might weaken public confidence in electronic payments by opening the doors to a new category of non-bank 'payment institutions'"

I do agree with them about one thing though: while the PSD increases costs for providers of electronic payment services it doesn't do anything about cash, which is

"the most expensive means of payment for society as a whole."

Education policy [10/07/2007]

As was discussed here absolutely ages ago, something has gone fundamentally wrong with the payment schemes efforts to cut card-not-present fraud on the Internet by introducing 3D Secure (in the form of *Verified by Visa* and MasterCard *SecureCode*) to the masses. It's this: reasonably intelligent customers who are concerned about the security of their Internet payment transactions find it impossible to distinguish 3D Secure dialogues from phishing attacks. They can't tell whether the request they get when shopping to register their card with Visa or MasterCard is a scam, or for real! So what are consumers to do? They can't tell the difference between a site that's doing what it should and a phishing attack, they see crashes when they visit financial services organisations websites (which must undermine confidence) and even if they take the trouble to understand SSL and certificates, they are presented with meaningless gibberish from companies they have never heard of (what does "Verisign" mean to my Dad?).

This is a really interesting case study and I want to learn as much as possible from it. Now, I can see why consumers don't care about 3DS. After all, their Internet card payments are protected: if someone uses my credit card number on the web somewhere, I don't much care because my issuer will refund the money (I have never had a problem with this with any of my issuers) and send me a new card if necessary. It doesn't cost me anything. This is one of the reasons why I only ever use my credit card to buy stuff online and simply cannot understand why anyone ever uses a debit card -- or even more unbelievably, a cheque -- to buy anything, let alone anything online. All 3DS means to me as a consumer is hassle. But to the merchant 3DS is more straightforward and hence the current situation is more puzzling: 3DS to a merchant ought to be a no-brainer because if they offer 3DS then they are covered against chargebacks for all transactions, not just the 3DS ones. So it would seem rational to me that merchants should provide incentives to get me (the customer) to use 3DS. But they don't. They seem to be losing a lot of money to fraud, yet more than half say they've no intention of implementing 3DS because it's too complicated for consumers. I know that online merchants are concerned that additional clicks lead to abandoned carts but is the drop off rate so high? And if it is, what could be done to educate consumers more effectively to continue with 3DS authentication and not give up and click away? Or, and I hate to say it, should Visa and MasterCard sit down and rethink the whole approach?

Some central issues [06/08/2007]

A number of people are pointing at an article (published by *IDATE*, Institut de l'Audiovisuel et des Télécommunications en Europe) by Forum friend and leading European payments scholar Leo van Hove.

In essence, the article states that central banks should place greater emphasis on improving the efficiency of retail payments and less on protecting their own self interest. I've been fortunate enough to have had sometime over the weekend to read Leo's article. I focused on the first section about the social cost of cash and some associated issues. If you're the sort of person who reads blogs on digital money (!) you really should read it all.

Payment instruments are not ordinary products. Hence, the market for payment instruments is not an ordinary market. For one thing, the demand for payment instruments is a derived demand: consumers don't want to buy payment instruments, they want to buy other goods and services and are required to use payment instruments to do so. One of the most obvious implications stemming from this observation is that there is a low price elasticity: the consumer demand for goods and services does not depend greatly on the cost of the payment instruments. Another observation is that (I've no idea if this is a real economic concept or not) there is a low "satisfaction elasticity": if the payment service does a great job, the consumer barely notices. A final observation is that there are very high network externalities, well-recognized by all players in the payment space, because of the nature of the consumer and merchant acceptance (i.e., the good old chicken and egg issue). Meanwhile on the supply side, the barriers to entry are significant. It is simply not the case that anyone can start offering new payment instruments, as distinct from payments processing services. Regulators take both consumer protection and financial stability quite seriously. This is not to say that regulators do not recognize that it might be an overall benefit to have more competition in the payment space. In Europe this recognition translated first into the Electronic Money Directive (EMD) and then the Payments Services Directive (PSD) as part of the SEPA drive.

With this background, let's think about the competition between cash and electronic payment instruments. Leo's point is that there is an odd competition between private and public players on the supply side. Both commercial banks and the central banks are active in the market: the banks issue payment cards, the central banks issue cash. We all understand the basic dynamics for the commercial banks on the supply side. In Europe banks lose a great deal of money on cash and cheque handling, roughly break even on debit cards (a McKinsey study in the Netherlands found that Dutch banks lose 8 euro cents per transaction) and make money on credit card transactions. Overall there is a heavy cross-subsidisation of cash. Setting to one side the issue of whether some form of electronic payment system might be a public good and should actually be provided by the central banks (one might, for example, envisage the European Central Bank issuing a European debit card that worked the same way as the Capital One non-account linked debit card), Leo focuses on the apparent tension between a central bank's duty to ensure efficient payments systems and its operational activities in providing the least efficient payment system of all.

We've agreed that the market for payment instruments is very different from other markets. So different, in fact, that "market" is probably an inappropriate description. This issue is a basic structural problem: central banks are charged with improving the efficiency of the payment system while being responsible for the most inefficient mechanism. Inefficient here means, just to be clear, "has highest social cost". Note that the social cost of a payment instrument is the total of the resources that society as a whole consumes in using the service (the sum of the private costs to all stakeholders less transfer payments). The social costs of payments systems have only recently been studied to any degree of accuracy by, for example, the Dutch and Belgian central banks (who found the social cost to be 0.65% and 0.74% of GDP respectively). In both of these countries, cash accounts for three quarters of the total social cost. In other words, each family in the Netherlands pays about 300 euros per annum to use cash. Cash is not free.

In attempting to lower these social costs, the e-purse was (more than a decade ago) seen as being a reasonable way forward. There is some justification to this argument on economic grounds because e-purse transactions (taken by me to mean offline, pre-authorised or prepaid transactions) have a very low marginal cost. The figures that Leo brings to bear show the marginal social cost of an e-purse payment in the Netherlands is only 3 euro cents, whereas the marginal social cost of a cash payment is 11 euro cents. The low marginal costs of e-purse transactions mean that society as a whole would clearly be better off by substituting cash payments with e-purse payments. Yet as we all know, this argument founders on the high cost of introducing a new e-purse scheme, primarily on the acquiring side. As has been discussed before, for electronic payments to make a real dent in cash payments they need to have at least an order of magnitude more acceptance points and this investment is very difficult to reconcile with the private interests of banks or merchants in the short term. While it's not the subject of this discussion, this is of course one of the reasons why the mobile phone is such a significant device in the evolution of retail payments. It is not because the phone can be used on the issuing side to deliver new payment instruments (or mobile versions of existing payment instruments) but because it can be used on the acquiring side to accept electronic payments.

But back to the tension. Central banks derive their revenue from the seigniorage on notes and coins. Hence a reduction in the notes and coins means a reduction in central bank income. If you take a look at the UK, where the note issuing department of the Bank of England is undoubtedly the most profitable nationalised industry in history, under legislation going back to 1844 the entire profit of the note issue is given over to the Treasury (cash is indeed a "stealth tax"). Interestingly, in the eurozone things are a little different. The European Central Bank keeps 8% of the seigniorage loot for itself and divides the rest up between eurozone members according to (of course) a complicated Euro-formula which, incidentally, is unrelated to usage and instead based on total population and GDP.

Leo sets out these basic facts and figures with admirable clarity before moving on to discuss the specific policy issues that are on the horizon. The core of the argument around cash is that all of us end up footing the bill, even those of us who choose more efficient payment mechanisms. Hence in economic terms, a shift to cost-based pricing is desirable. This does not mean pricing at cost. What it does mean is that policy makers should recognise that price is an important element of communication. If consumers see the relative costs, they can make more efficient choices. The problem in the case of cash is obvious: any attempt to price it properly results in public uproar and political interference. This happened in Belgium a couple of years when one of the banks decided to start charging 6 euro cents for some cash withdrawals whereupon there was immediate public outcry and the Minister for Consumer Affairs threatened to bring in legislation to regulate the pricing of cash withdrawals. To my mind this demonstrates clearly how politicians do not know how to serve consumer interests properly, but that's just my opinion. Studies in other European markets show that unlike other retail point of sale payments, the price elasticity associated with cash withdrawals is quite high, so cost-based pricing of ATM withdrawals would significantly reduce cash payments and boost debit card use. One of the surveys referenced suggests that in Europe as a whole the market share of cash would fall from 96% to 81% under such a pricing structure and debit cards would jump from 4% to 19% of retail payments by volume.

Now, actually, some central banks have already made it clear that they would be happy to see seigniorage income fall in return for a more efficient payment system which is better for the economy as a whole. The Norwegian Central Bank, to pick one example, has consistently promoted the principle that the party that chooses the payment service should pay for it in a cost-based structure with the natural result that cash and cheque usage suffers. The ECB itself has pointed in the same direction. Gertrude Tumpel-Gugerell, the member of the Executive Board of the ECB responsible for payments systems and market infrastructure (Ms. SEPA), has said

"I would expect banks to apply pricing methods that better reflect the efficiency of the respective instrument. Consumers may choose inefficient payment instruments, but they should pay the true price of the instruments and bank should not subsidise inefficient payment instruments by making efficient instruments more expensive."

The dynamics of a potential transition away from cash will undoubtedly shape the roadmap. The average cost of a cash transaction increases substantially as the number of transactions drops so in a country that has high non-cash usage, the cost of cash escalates. The most cashless country in Europe is Iceland and the average social cost of a cash transaction in Iceland is 3.1 euros, more than five times more than the average social cost of a cash transaction in Belgium. Therefore, as the usage of cash falls, the cost of cash will increase, hastening its demise.

The recommendations from this fascinating review of the situation in Europe are straightforward. Policy makers should foster cost-based pricing and create a legal environment that makes it possible for banks to use it. Meanwhile, of course, any government that introduced charges on cash would be committing electoral suicide and the impossibility of explaining economic concepts such as social cost and net welfare to the general public are insurmountable. Where next?

More regulation [14/09/2007]

The European Central Bank, which has already said that it would like banks to set up a debit card scheme to challenge the dominance of Maestro in the eurozone and proposed a new cross-border legal framework to oversee all card payment schemes operating in that zone, is very keen on new regulation to improve the state of the European payments market. One of the ECB's points is that they want to create a level playing field of payments. This is a good idea: so is there a single or simple action that could be taken to do this?

As Chris Skinner noted, there's an analysis of the most recent SEPA progress report over at Linkdump on Payments. It's well worth reading, but in case you haven't the time to pop over there I'll just highlight one quote from the analysis:

"The ECB don't apply their own one-SEPA-size fits all-reasoning to their own product: cash. In the cash area they go out of their way to explain that they are unable to harmonize cash rules in Europe."

If there is going to be a level playing field, then lightening the regulatory burden on e-cash might be an obvious place to begin. One source of costs is the requirement to verify the identity of e-cash users. There is a simplified due diligence procedure for a limited set of circumstances:

1. If the device cannot be recharged, the maximum amount stored in the device is no more than 150 euro; or
2. If the device can be recharged, a limit of 2,500 euro is imposed on the total amount transacted in a calendar year, except when an amount of 1,000 euro or more is redeemed in that same calendar year by the bearer.
3. Where e-money purses cannot be recharged, and the total purse limit does not exceed €150, verification of identity does not need to be undertaken.

These limits seem low to me. I think the limit should have some symbolic value: since the largest denomination banknote is 500 euros, that should be the limit. If a purse can store more than 500 euros then KYC/AML applies, if it can store less than 500 euros then KYC/AML should not. This reasonable compromise would stimulate the prepaid market and provide for a much lower cost of operation, enabling new entrants (and therefore more competition) to the e-purse, m-purse and whatever else purse market. This, in turn, I am sure would lower transaction costs across a swathe of the online marketplace and therefore stimulate further growth.

More on the cash menace [21/09/2007]

There was a story in the Wall Street Journal today about money laundering, talking about how Columbian drug dealers employ "smurfs" to go round depositing small amounts (a few thousand here, a few thousand there) of dollars from drug sales into banks in the US so that their Mr. Bigs can then withdraw cash in pesos in Columbia. By coincidence, I happened to be at a World Online Gambling Law seminar today -- along with a couple of our clients -- and learned a lot about the topic. Not from a "how to" perspective, of course, but more from a "this is why we're imposing massive costs on the payments industry" point of view. One of the things that I learned was that the money-launderers best friend, the 500 euro note, is increasing in popularity as it strives to replace the $100 bill as the criminals' store-of-value of choice. Apparently a substantial fraction of the 500 euro notes that have been printed are no longer in circulation in the eurozone, so Latin American drug barons are making substantial interest-free loans to European central banks, just as they have made interest-free loans to Uncle Sam for years. I'm sure that crime, drug dealing, corruption and terrorism have all fallen significantly since the introduction of more stringent anti-money laundering (AML) legislation, although I don't have any figures to hand...

My favourite new acronym is PEP: not the Personal Equity Plan familiar to the British middle classes but a Politically-Exposed Person. It turns out that banks have to screen for PEPs because such PEPs (e.g., members of the European Parliament and deposed African strongmen) after often involved in corruption. Anyway, the money laundering regulatory framework is very complicated. As a mere technologist, they look to me more like a backdoor full employment act for lawyers rather than a rational mechanism for reducing crime, but that's a rant that doesn't belong on this blog (I'm just jealous). One of the guys there did tell me that some piece of AML (I don't remember which) cost more than $20 million for banks to implement and in its first two years in operation froze only half a million dollars in accounts. That doesn't seem like a particularly good return.

Why do I keep going on about AML regulation? Because it raises costs. And the rate of increase shows no sign of slowing. The cost of banks has risen by almost two-thirds in the last three years. In addition to raising the cost of banking, it also raises the cost of electronic payments. If it is indeed European Commission policy to get customers to use other instruments (i.e., cards) instead of cash -- as was stated in the presentation about SEPA -- then surely one obvious step toward this goal would be to lower the cost of the alternatives. You should be able to pick up a prepaid card with a maximum balance of, say, 500 euros with no form filling, passport photocopying or anything else.

As an aside, Forum friend Dominic Peachey of the Financial Services Authority was at the seminar and he made a typically experienced and perceptive observation about the extent to which regulation in the prepaid space is evidence-based. Quite. I've noted this before. There are many benefits to society that follow from increased commerce, and both physical commerce and retail e-commerce would be stimulated significantly if prepaid products were more widely available. But if the cost and complexity of prepaid products are inflated by overly broad AML, then surely the net welfare is a long way negative.

Third men [04/10/2007]

By complete coincidence I found myself reading two papers on the "third way" for European cards this morning (yes, my life really is that interesting). The first from our good friends at Payment Systems Europe (PSE), the second from our good friends at Welcome Real-time. Welcome's Pierre Boces has published a whitepaper that compares strategies for payment scheme competition. His perspective is that the existing international card schemes are so well-established that it would be better to focus on having them deliver more value to the marketplace than spending a lot of money creating a new "third way" euroscheme (whether under the EAPS or something else). Peter Jones from PSE also points out that creating a new "third way" euroscheme will involve considerable effort and expenditure and puts forward another alternative: hook up the ATM networks and then extend them to POS. As Peter points out, many of the domestic debit schemes that are vanishing because of SEPA started life at ATM networks anyway.

Perhaps it not really worth worrying about, because no-one is bothering with SEPA anyway. According to the EFMA, ABN AMRO and *Capgemini World Payments Report*, which looked at SEPA preparations in 13 countries, it is "unlikely" that a critical mass of SEPA payment instruments will be achieved by 2011. They are calling for regulators to provide incentives in order to mobilise public sector companies and corporates to migrate to SEPA payment instruments, which I can't comment on, but also point out that the SEPA implementation is all about interbank standards that won't make much difference to those corporates. In their case, who cares if payments are pan-European if everything else isn't: they want pan-European e-invoicing standards and the like otherwise they can't cost justify the not inconsiderable investment.

Some banks are pushing on, however, and looking for ways to make their SEPA expenditure pay something back. Deutsche Bank is an example. They have said that they will offer a "common price" for any payment transfer within the eurozone, effectively treating all payments the same and removing the distinction between high value and low-value payments. They see this as a carrot to persuade corporates to move on adopting SEPA. To me, saving money on payments seems like a good idea, but just as in the retail case, will it be enough to simply provide the payment instrument in the future, or should banks focus on providing a payment service that wraps the instrument with a variety of value-added services?

Sectioned [19/11/2007]

One of the reasons why I always -- and I mean always -- use one of my credit cards both online and offline (and remain mystified about the growth in debit card usage) is because of the Consumer Credit Act (1974). In particular, it's because of Section 75 of that Act. For those of you unfamiliar with the details of our credit regulations, "s.75" is the part of the Act that says to me as a consumer that (in essence) if shit happens, it's the bank's problem and not mine. So if I buy a holiday from a travel agent who subsequently goes bust, I get my money back. If I buy a dishwasher from a website and the dishwasher doesn't show up, I get my money back. This isn't a universal right (it's limited to transactions between £100 and £30,000), but it covers most of the important transactions I ever make. Naturally, banks have been complaining about it, as I would if I was a bank since s.75 has an element of moral hazard about it: as a consumer, there's no need for me to take any care in checking out the web merchant I'm dealing with because I'm not liable.

The banks have been in court about this, trying to get the liability restricted on a couple of points. I'm not a lawyer, so please don't imagine that my relaying of these points is in any way accurate, but they were something to do with overseas transactions and something to do with "four party" transactions (i.e., that the acquirer has the contract with the merchant, not the issuer). They lost on both points and were refused leave to appeal on the second point. So they appealed the overseas transactions point to the highest court, the House of Lords. Well, the House of Lords recently found against them and confirmed that credit card users have the right to compensation for defective goods bought overseas. Carl Belgrove, Senior Policy Advocate at the National Consumer Council (NCC), welcomed the ruling:

"The House of Lords judgement is great news for consumers. People in the UK are heavy credit card users and with more of us travelling abroad - coupled with buying products online from all over the world – Section 75 provides an extra safeguard and boosts consumer confidence."

Lloyds TSB, one of the issuers contesting the case, said

"We are disappointed with the decision as we have long believed that Section 75 has no validity in relation to foreign credit card transactions. However, given that the House of Lords has confirmed the Court of Appeal ruling, we will continue our policy of paying valid claims for overseas transactions."

This seems a pretty reasonable response, so there's basically no change. That's not why I wanted to highlight the case, though. What caught my eye was the comment of one of the judges. Lord Hope made it clear the customer has no responsibility for checking out retailers, saying that

"The debtor is entitled to assume that he can trust suppliers who are authorised to accept his credit card."

Here he is surely on the right track, irrespective of how the payment card world actually works. As competition increases and the networking side of payments becomes steadily commoditised, it is the trust and reputation elements of a transaction that remain more difficult for potential new competitors to tackle and therefore the more valuable elements. After all, anyone can connect up a retailer and a bank. But how far does this trust extend?

I suppose the other impact of the ruling, looking forward, might be that acquirers have to do more work to screen retailers and are allowed to keep more of the merchant service charge for themselves in return for accepting some of the liability. There's definite logic behind the banks' position: the acquiring bank has the commercial relationship with the retailer, the issuer does not.

Greens back [28/11/2007]

Payments, just like every other business, are acquiring a green tinge as the marketing folk get to grips with the low carbon economy. There have been some efforts before -- some of you may remember that *Visa Swap* earlier in the year -- and I'm sure there will be more of these (rather limited) initiatives to come. It's not transparently obvious to me that this sort of thing makes much of a difference to consumer behaviour but I'm sure every little helps. Consumer research from PricewaterhouseCoopers found that more than half of respondents would be likely to replace their existing credit card with a 'green' credit card if it helped them tackle their carbon footprint and two in five said they would give up an existing loyalty programme or cash reward card in favour of a green alternative. I know consumers' revealed preferences may be at variance with their environmental aspirations but you can see the trend building. Surely, a truly green credit card would be one that allowed you to buy organic tomatoes but not a flight to Spain. We haven't got that far yet, but Barclays has launched a carbon-offset corporate card. Barclaycard Business manages the process on behalf of corporate customers by providing them with commission-free access to the Certified Emission Reduction Market via Barclays Capital's Emissions Trading Desk. So Barclaycard tell you how much your employees have been spending on air travel and then you can buy carbon offsets to match them and assuage your environmental guilt at allowing them to fly so much.

There are wider industry initiatives as well. In the US, NACHA has formed a "green coalition" (with, amongst others, Bank of America, CheckFree, Citibank, Wells Fargo and so on) to educate consumers about the positive environmental impacts of choosing e-bills, e-statements and e-payments over the paper versions and I'm happy to try and find ways to spread their message. Generally speaking, I don't want paper anything and the sooner shops begin sending receipts to my phone or my e-mail account the better, so being green by going with the grain sounds good. Again in the US, I think it is a very good sign that the Fed was prepared to reconsider how instructions such as Regulation E (and presumably in the future Regulation Z as well) should be reconstituted for the e-payments age. Earlier in the year, they announced an exception for transactions of $15 or less from

Regulation E's requirement that paper receipts be made available to consumers for transactions initiated at an electronic terminal.

NFC phones could make us even greener, because phones could eliminate paper receipts for many transactions, not just the ones under $15. At the moment, NFC phones simply emulate cards, and that makes sense because banks and operators want to roll them out without needing changes to the existing infrastructure. Looking forward, though, that's not enough to open up the POS transaction to the kind of value-adding services that are being envisaged. A simple change to the payment protocol could flag to the POS that it's a phone not a card and therefore -- as an obvious example -- can receive a receipt electronically. It shouldn't take much to devise an appropriate XML coding (there may be a suitable one buried in the IOTP standard somewhere).

This might be an interesting angle to try in one of the current set of NFC pilots. Since a variety of pilots have already established that using NFC phones as "cards" seems to work, perhaps some of the bank and retailers could consider having a looking at this in one of the trials getting underway. There are quite a few to choose from. One of the recently announced trials is the "Payez Mobile" one involving 1,000 people in Strasbourg and Caen. This is worth following as it involves all three French mobile operators, six major banks, three handset suppliers (Motorola, LG and Sagem) and both Visa and MasterCard, so it should provide some useful lessons about interoperability. I was surprised by this comment in the announcement though. Jérôme Sion, director for mobile contactless activities at Gemalto (and a very nice chap) said:

"I don't think it will replace cash... Just as checks didn't replace cash, and bank cards didn't replace checks, you will still have cash along with the contactless phone."

But bank cards have replaced cheques in the UK, just not in France, so we are already greener than they are.

Euros centric [01/02/2008]

I went along to a seminar, kindly hosted by Barclays, to take part in a discussion organised by the Centre for European Reform on the future of retail banking in Europe. David Shirreff, the Frankfurt business correspondent for The Economist, has written a pamphlet for the Centre called "European Retail Banking: Will there ever be a single market?". David's key points are that in smaller countries markets have opened up, but in larger countries (e.g., Germany) there has been resistance to change; that the Commission should use competition powers to take on vested interests but stick with a light touch; and, most controversially, that regulators should create a framework in which each business within a bank (and I guess this would include payments) should have its own capital and profit and loss account to increase the scope for cross-border mergers and acquisitions below the mega-merger level. I am absolutely not qualified to comment on whether this makes sense or not, but I thought that Digital Money devotees might be interested in the discussions that followed (I've not attributed any of the comments, in case I misunderstood them in some way, and I've tried to focus down on the relevant part of the discussion).

First of all, as a backdrop, it must be pointed out that over the past ten years, the largest European banks have doubled their cross-border business within Europe (from a sixth to a third) while their cross-border business outside Europe has remained static (at a quarter). So clearly, as per the Barclays - RBS - ABN AMRO story, there is more competition in European banking than there used to be. But a general criticism of the current situation is that a free market in capital and labour needs pan-European solutions, but the operations of retail banks in different countries are not, in fact, connected (other than on the balance sheet), which makes the banking sector quite inefficient. Yet it has not been that easy for new entrants to set up in each other's countries -- for a whole variety of reasons -- and share prices have been high so it's been hard to "buy your way in". In the case of British banks, they did try to become more pan-European a decade ago but that push didn't generate huge results, so they focussed on expanding their domestic businesses instead.

The current supervisory structure is not geared up to managing pan-European banking structures. Now, setting aside the issue as to whether some, any or all banks should be pan-European -- in the US "single market" this is not the case -- let's assume that the goal is seamless pan-European service for customers and see how things are going. For most people (since most Danish consumers are not at this instant particularly clamouring to take out mortgages from Latvian banks) this comes down to their day-to-day interface with the pan-European banking system: payments. Now payments, which are crucial to a single market, has already moved forward, because of SEPA and the PSD.

The focus on payments is good, because it directly affects businesses ability to operate across Europe, but it must be recognised that payments are not banking and that there are much wider banking issues that need to be addressed in order to get real pan-European competition. There was an interesting discussion, that didn't really get going until the end, about what the goal of European policy is: one of the attendees put it rather well, asking whether consumers on the whole actually want cross-border banking or do they really just want more effective and efficient remittances? Having had time to reflect on this, I wonder if it isn't a rather accurate summary of the requirements outside the finance world.

There was a discussion about capital requirements: Basel II has come too late to help in current circumstances. Although I can't say I understood the nuances, there were some comments that there is a danger in this kind of framework because regulators become drawn into the process of risk management (see, ad nauseum, Northern Rock). Inevitably, because the discussion took place shortly after the news that a French barrow boy had done a Leeson, I was straining to understand the issues around the core of risk management because it links to our business in the more technology-centric risk analysis sense. This is where David's suggestions about the separate P&L for the "narrow banking" business and the wider investment banking business was discussed: I must report that there didn't seem to be much enthusiasm for what sounded to me like an idea worth at least some consideration.

In his pamphlet, David says that

"European lawmakers need to decide what types of business they want to be done by bank, and what types by non-bank competitors."

I agree wholeheartedly. In our space, payments, it seems transparently obvious that more competition -- rather than more regulation -- is the best way to drive innovation forward and deliver needed services to the market. As was pointed out in the discussion, though, in modern business there is no best model that regulators could aim for, so their aim should be to create the conditions for a more competitive environment, not to determine a priori of what that more competitive environment might be, then regulate it into existence. Just to tack on my own opinion: one of the speakers (it may have been Christine Farnish from Barclays) said that one the biggest barriers to overcome is actually the inertia of customers, and I'm sure this is true. People moan about banks all the time, but they don't change their accounts: more movement at this level would surely be the way to open up new competitive spaces in the market.

Finally, what I thought was the most relevant part of the discussion to this blog was not part of the regulatory or SEPA discussion, but a point made in passing by one of the senior bankers present. He said that there's a problem with a lack of innovation in retail banking because of opportunity costs: in other words, legal and regulatory change absorbs so much of European banks' resources that they are (as he put it) "off the pace" compared to the rest of the world (examples such as current account mortgages and mobile phone payments were used to illustrate the point). This is clearly correct, and needs to be added as a factor in future discussions about innovation.

Incidentally, I must declare a connection here: David Shireff's father Donald was my economics teacher 30+ years ago, and one of the best teachers I ever had.

Chapter 10: Fraud

Eradicating fraud is an unrealistic goal for a payment system, but getting it down to a manageable level is central to the operation of payment systems. These posts explore some of the payment frauds that have taken place in the last year in order to uncover valuable pointers for the design of future payment systems.

Risk and reputation [29/01/2007]

One of the most difficult things to assess as part of the risk analysis for a new electronic payment product is reputational damage. Not only is it hard to quantify, it's hard to rank the reputational risk due to payment products alongside other reputational risks. There are quite a lot of these if you're a bank. I used to read newspapers more often but now I only read the newspaper once a week when I get the Telegraph on a Saturday. It happens to have a number of stories around this topic today. The one I'm curious about is...

It's not the story that the top five banks in the UK are about to declare a total of £37 billion in profits for the last financial year.

Nor is it the story of the student opening his first bank account. He paid in £41 to cover the cost of a direct debit for insurance. The direct debit actually turned out to be £42 so the student was charged an additional £38 by the bank. He didn't know this so when his insurance company told him that the debit had been refused, he paid in the missing pound and asked them to try again. But now, of course, his account only has £4 in it, so when the insurance company try to debit, they are again refused and the student is charged another £38.

Nor is it the story about the woman who called her bank to tell them that her husband had died. She then got a letter from the bank asking her to repay her son's overdraft. This caused some family upset because she didn't even know that her son had an overdraft. Her son then discovered that the bank had notified credit reference agencies of his death. You can see how embarrassing this was going to be: You go into a shop to get a mobile phone and you're told 'Sorry, you can't have a pay monthly mobile phone because you're dead.' The bank had, of course, mixed up the dead father and the not- dead son.

No, the story that was most interesting was the story about the person whose credit card statement turned up with two charges in India. When they rang the bank to complain, they were told that their signature must have been forged, clearly implying a retail (not ATM) transaction. It then transpired that the transactions were PIN not signature. The person had the card in their possession in the UK the entire time. The card never went to India. And the person said that they never disclosed their PIN to anyone either. The issuer gave the money back together with an additional ex-gratia payment for charity because it took so long to sort out, but I'm very curious as to how a retail PIN transaction could have taken place in India when the card was in the UK. Anyone reading this in the newspaper would have -- incorrectly, I'm sure -- deduced that the bank in question was issuing chip and PIN cards that could be counterfeited. They would then, presumably, make a mental note to use a different bank next time they wanted a credit card. How does a bank factor this kind of reputational risk into technology investment decisions?

My point is that at a time when credit card fraud is, say, 7 points and bad debt is 700 points, it's easy to push fraud down the priority list and stop listening to people like us who think that technology should be used to improve security. But would the net income lost to the issuer because of customers going elsewhere be more or less than the seven basis points lost to fraud? That's one of the questions I'm going to be asking at the card fraud conference in London today.

Incidentally, there was also a story about a person trying to send £250 to a family member in Australia. They had such faith in the international money transmission network that they put cash inside a card and posted it, but it never arrived. They can't get their money back from the Post Office because it turns out that it's illegal to post bank notes in letters in Australia. Who knew?

Comforting phone call [16/03/2007]

There are some strange things going on in the world of chip and PIN. First of all, the Scottish Grocers' Federation (SGF) Retail Crime Survey for 2006 shows that card fraud in Scotland's convenience stores has gone up by 54% since the introduction of chip and PIN, an increase for which they can provide no explanation, which is even odder considering that card fraud is continuing to fall at other kinds of retailers. I'm really, really curious to know if anyone has any theories. Second of all, the issuer of one of my UK credit cards called...

I know it was them, because I wasn't in and they left a message on my answering machine: this is the security department of bank X, we'd just like to confirm a couple of transactions as a standard anti-fraud check, or words to that effect. I called back using a number I know to be them (because I got it from my last statement). So it wasn't phishing. One of the transactions was a PayPal payment earlier today. Yes, that was me. I use PayPal several times every week, so it wasn't obvious why this particular twenty pound transaction should attract attention, but OK, I know they're just looking out for me and I don't mind at all (in fact, it's reassuring). But the second transaction was a chip and PIN payment at my local supermarket last Sunday morning.

Now there was nothing wrong with the transaction, as I was happy to reassure them. But after I hung up the phone, I started to wonder: why would the artificial intelligence neural network database driven heuristic anti-fraud software flag up a chip and PIN transaction where the correct PIN had been entered? Unless the said system either a) doesn't know which transactions are chip and PIN and which transactions are stripe or b) knows which transactions are chip and PIN but is concerned about chip and PIN clones. Being a payments nerd, I'm curious: has anyone else had a similar call recently?

Anti-fraud people in favour of untraceable cash? [23/03/2007]

There's a letter in The Economist concerning their recent story on cashlessness. It comes from someone who works in a bank fraud department and they paint an apocalyptic picture: "The potential for digital piracy of cash soon dwarfing the piracy of digital content is very real... Not only will the value of national currencies be undermined, but they will also be open to manipulation when effectively privatised and under corporate control. If digital money becomes standard, those insisting on paying with cash will be penalised. I am currently charged a 'non-Direct Debit fee' each time I pay my cable bill over the phone – speaking with an automated voice, no less – because I refuse the 'convenience' of Direct Debit. My local lunch restaurant no longer accepts debit or credit card payments under £10 because the banking fees are too high. Cash works just fine." Now I'm confused: as a law-abiding, tax-paying citizen (well, subject), should I be for cash or against it?

Now, setting aside for one moment the privatisation of national currencies and whether it might be a good thing or a bad thing -- I promise to return to this issue on the blog sometime -- is this person right that the risk of electronic cash is just too great? Is sticking with the cash the only way to avoid national calamity? Is the risk of e-payment just too great? The folks over at Terror Finance seem to agree. They think that a combination of mobile phones and electronic cash is asking for destruction....

This is how it works: You buy a stored value card for X amount of dollars and a prepaid mobile phone. Next, you register with the m-payment service provider using a free anonymous e-mail account, your prepaid mobile phone number and the money on the stored value card. Using your mobile phone, you log on to the m-payment service provider and give them the number of the mobile phone to which you wish to transfer the funds from your stored value card. The m-payment service provider sends a message to the receiver's phone number asking where to transfer the money. The recipient can request the transfer to his stored value card and withdraw the funds from any ATM.

They go on to say that "Since the Near Field Communication security technology (which is the basis of the m-payment system) features sophisticated encryption, it represents a formidable impediment to law enforcers and intelligence services trying to detect suspicious money transactions". I think this is based on an incomplete understanding of e-cash, mobile payments and NFC but other than that I suppose it's a fair point.

But here is what is most puzzling, something that I've remarked on before. They say that "The challenge is compounded by the fact that the m-payment process can leave little to no audit trail; perhaps, two mobile-phone numbers; the amount; and short and simple instructions on transmission and reception". So law enforcement officials have only the mobile phones numbers (therefore the locations) of the perps? I'm no expert on international money laundering, but that sounds like a bit of a head start to me.

All sorts of payment frauds are growing [25/06/2007]

Not all of the payment fraud in the world is payment card fraud. A survey of more than 3,000 corporate treasury officials raised the alarm about cheque and electronic payment fraud.

"Payments fraud last year was pervasive and increasing"

says a report from the Association for Payments Professionals. The Association for Finance Professionals (AFP) did another survey and found that 72% of its 414 respondents had been victims of actual or attempted fraud in 2006, up from 68% in a 2005 survey. But here's the good news: electronic payments turn out to be significantly safer than paper (cheques processed as images are also much safer than paper cheques) even though ACH and payment card networks are subject to increasing fraud attacks, particularly in transactions on the Internet and over the phone. Nearly all respondents said they had been the target of actual or attempted check fraud in 2006, while 35% reported fraud activity in ACH debits. Seventeen percent said they had seen attempted or actual fraud with consumer credit cards. Of those who reported fraud activity with cards, consumer credit cards accounted for by far the most response (82%), with signature debit cards registering 18%, stored-value cards 7%, and PIN debit cards 4%. Of those respondents that accept consumer payments via the phone or over the Internet and also reported ACH fraud, some 44% said they received fraudulent ACH instructions from their Internet channel; 45% said the same about the phone channel. Similarly, the organizations responding to the AFP survey are sustaining fraud losses from card-not-present transactions. Liability for these transactions is cited by 64% of those respondents that sustained losses because of card fraud as the primary reason for the loss. Delays in filing chargebacks comes in second, at 25%.

"Organizations that suffer financial losses from card payments do so primarily because they are 'card-not-present' merchants"

notes the report, although it might have gone on to say that they are CNP merchants that have not signed up to 3D Secure. Interestingly, in light of a recent string of hacker intrusions into merchant databases, none of the respondents reported fraud stemming from a card-data breach. But then, as has been discussed on Digital Identity, there is a clear correlation between the size of the breach and the likelihood of fraud (and the type of data). If a neighbour steals your card from the post, there is pretty likely to be a subsequent fraud. If some government department tells the entire world your personal details, there may be a few frauds, but not that many.

While not all payment fraud is card fraud, there's still plenty of card fraud. In the payment world, in the UK, we have driven fraud online but the banks will be making a serious attempt to mitigate this with another improvement to online security is on its way later this year. The MasterCard CAP (Card Authentication Programme) and Visa DPA (Dynamic Passcode Authentication) programmes use a handheld security device in combination with an EMV card. The combination will generate a unique, once-only security code for each online transaction. These schemes should ensure that only the rightful owner of the card can use it online, because it won't work unless the correct PIN is entered. They won't really help that much against phishing unless they are used in signing mode, which is a bit of a pain for customers, but every little helps. Barclays said they will begin to roll-out such devices shortly and RBS is issuing similar devices already, but they are already widespread in other places. Croatia-based Privredna Banka Zagreb has distributed handheld smart card readers to all its Internet and telephone banking customers, which they would use along with MasterCard-branded EMV debit cards. The bank plans to have 40,000 customers using the card readers by the end of this year.

So, the big question is will card fraud in the UK be up or down this time next year. My guess is up. In Croatia? Don't know, but would be genuinely interested to hear from a Croatian reader to see how it's going over there.

Security reporters [02/07/2007]

With contactless payment systems continuing to expand, I see another report from the US concerning fears that the wireless technology behind those systems is not secure enough for widespread adoption, despite assurances from Visa, MasterCard, and other major players. Aneace pointed to a similar discussion in May, except that this time it was the retailers who were saying that

"Once the US overcomes its security issues with contactless payments and assures the public of the safety of using them, this technology will explode."

But what are these stories about (and what do they mean)? A typical example is a story about cards transmitting cardholders' names and numbers in the clear that is illustrated with a picture of a card that doesn't. But look at the heart of that story. According to a study by researchers at the University of Massachusetts and at security companies RSA and Innealta, many contactless cards will transmit your name, the credit card's number, and its expiration date (but not the CVV) unencrypted to anyone nearby with an RFID scanner. This is true, but I'd put a different spin on it: researchers have discovered that these cards comply with their specifications and do exactly what they are supposed to do.

Now, of course it makes no real sense for the cards to transmit the card holder's name. That's true. But it also makes no sense for standard chip and PIN cards to transmit the card holder's name either. It's just legacy thinking, another example of the transition to a new technology that is merely, in its first generation, used to simulate the old technology. In fact, as my colleague Tony Pickup has previously recommended, there's also no reason why the chip and PIN cards should deliver the same number over different channels. Why does, for example, my debit card give up the same PAN to a POS terminal as to an ATM? All this means is that PANs stolen from POS terminals can be used to make bogus ATM transactions. Let's start designing fraud out, we're all agreed on that.

But back to the impending security catastrophe that the journalists are warning us about. It's what these stories mean that continues to bother me. They suggest that card issuers will put cards into the market that will increase their risk. If this were true, what would be the explanation? That card issuers are dumb? That banks don't have any security experts? That suppliers are misleading banks? I'm really keen to know.

More post-modern policing [03/07/2007]

There's been a bit of a fuss in the media here about card fraud. I paraphrase, but essentially the police are too busy to investigate credit card fraud so it's been agreed that it's up to the banks to sort it out. This is being reported (incorrectly) as card fraud being decriminalised and the newspapers say that the Home Office is failing to take credit card fraud seriously. In essence, under some guidelines which came into force in April, it is now the responsibility of banks to decide which offences to pass on for investigation. Critics suggested the move is being made to reduce crime figures and "demanded a rethink". Now, I have to say that I've often argued for this policy: it's a bank problem and it should be up to banks to take the lead in sorting it out (and paying for it). But you can see how the spin could have been managed better: perhaps labelling the policing of card fraud as post-modern rather than as low priority.

This led me to think about other ways in which modern payments subject to post-modern regulation and I remembered an interesting example from a couple of weeks ago. Someone wrote to The Daily Telegraph to sort out a payments problem. The person had asked one of the UK's largest insurance companies to transfer some money to one of the UK's largest banks. After six weeks the money hadn't arrived and when the customer checked, it turned out that the insurance company had sent it by cheque and, somewhat predictably, the cheque had been stolen and cashed by an identity thief. Here's the cute part: the newspaper columnist says

"The police then suggested you wrote to this column"

After the newspaper spoke to the insurance company, they insisted they were not legally liable but agreed to pay back the £7,649 as a goodwill gesture. So, essentially, reporting the crime to the police was a waste of time but complaining to a newspaper got the money back. The details of the story aren't that relevant, but it left me thinking "why in the year 2007 would a large insurance company pay a large bank several thousand pounds using a CHEQUE"? How is the payments system working for the economy if it supports these kinds of choices? Why are you even allowed to write a cheque for more than a few hundred euros anyway? Surely one of Britain's largest banks has its own International Bank Account Number (IBAN) sorted out by now?

Chip and PIN mythbusters [12/10/2007]

Chip and PIN has been back in the news again. This time, it's reported that large numbers of cash withdrawals are being made using cards without a security chip and it is the banks themselves that are allowing it to happen. The newspaper story says that there are more than 140m cards in circulation and every day more than 7m withdrawals are made at cash machines across the UK, which is true. It goes on to say that if banks rejected every card with a slight fault in its chip they would be inundated with complaints from furious customers -- which is true, of course -- and therefore fraudsters using cloned bank cards that have no chip can still get their hands on other people's cash and it gives the lie to industry claims that the system is totally secure. Wow, that sounds terrible: there's a flaw in chip and PIN. Let's find out more...

I love the programme Mythbusters on the Discovery channel and watch it with my boys. I admire the way that they conduct experiments themselves, building from scratch and not relying on other people's opinions. Hence, when my new Barclays chip and PIN card arrived a couple of days before the old one expired, I decided to do my own chip and PIN experiment to see if this story is true. I took the chip out of my card and went off to try it out stripe-wise. I put it in a Nationwide ATM: transaction not authorised after PIN entry. I put it in an in-store ATM: transaction not authorised after PIN entry. I tried to pay with it in a supermarket and the card was rejected even before PIN entry. Well done to Barclays, who were clearly rejecting cards with a chip service code but stripe read. So clearly, the fraud here is not as simple as making magnetic stripe counterfeits and then using them in UK ATMs.

In fact, the main problem is that UK magnetic stripe counterfeits are being used in foreign ATMs.

So there is a genuine issue and we ought to consider what is to be done? There are few people around who know more about the issue than the head our banking practice Richard Allen and senior consultant Tony Pickup so I was discussing it with them earlier. The discussion was rather interesting, so I thought it might be a further experiment in corporate social networking to open up part of the discussion (with all client information and some other details removed) for blog readers...

[Anthony Pickup] The issue relates to the card scheme-agreed process which means that in the ATM environment, online PIN checking is performed for all transactions. For a number of reasons the PIN is not validated by the card -- even for chip and PIN cards -- but is sent to the card issuer for authentication. There is some techie stuff over the PINs being encrypted by the PIN entry device also at ATMs (my pet subject). Therefore to resolve the issue of magnetic stripe data cloned onto cards being used with a PIN value captured from a transaction either physically (shouldering) or electronically (compromised terminal), there are decisions to be made by the card issuer or ATM operator.

The decision that can be made by the issuer is to reject transactions. In short, they simply turn off "fall back to magnetic stripe at ATMs". The issue here is that ATM chip card readers can fail but remain operating with the magnetic stripe reader working. An issuer can pick this condition up if the data elements from the device are trusted. Another, perhaps better, solution would be for the ATM owner to reject the transaction if the service code on the magnetic stripe indicates a chip on the card and the ATM chip card reader fails to read the chip data due to either a card or a device failure. This would need to be mandated by the card schemes but would address the issue for their card issuers and ATM service providers, although it may mean the ATM owners losing a small number of legitimate transactions. This I believe would resolve the majority of the issue of fraudulent transactions, rejecting valid customer transactions and ensuring maximum ATM availability.

[Richard Allen] I'm not so sure. It is not up to the accepting party (either the retailer or the ATM owner) to make this decision -- it has to be the card issuer. The information necessary to make the "risk" decision is with the issuer, not the ATM owner. If the card issuer is willing to accept the risk, then why not allow fallback (and accept any consequent loss)? For example, I've already reported to my bank that my chip doesn't work, for some reason. They'll take two weeks to get a new card out to me, but will happily allow fallback in the meantime. On the other hand, someone else (let's say a long-standing customer working at CHYP) wants to take out £250 cash at 23:59 on a Friday night in London having only ever taken out less than £50 in a day prior to this. Clearly this fallback transaction is fraudulent (they may have visited a Shell garage two days previous). I think that only the issuer has all the information to make the right decision.

Also, who pays the loss? Clearly, if the issuer makes the risk decision, then they must accept the consequent loss -- and that's what happens now with the overseas ATM fraud Dave mentioned (which is, as an aside, the fastest rising card fraud in the UK). So, my issuer would only approve my ATM withdrawal in Buenos Aires if I called the bank to say I was going to be there (of course, in the future, when my card is in my phone, this will be a simply query to T-Mobile). If Tony goes to Thailand and doesn't tell the bank, then his ATM withdrawal will be declined. Admittedly this is not a fallback issue, but it's a magnetic stripe issue just the same and the same fraud risk. I don't think an issuer would want an ATM operator declining customers on their own. Maybe they're not likely to -- because they depend on the fees -- but the point holds. Issuers do not want their legitimate customers being inconvenienced and they are prepared to accept some losses as a consequence. Declining everything lights up the call centre and the customers go elsewhere. Declining nothing means losses. But again, it's the issuer's problem to find their ideal decline ratio to balance loss and churn.

[Anthony Pickup] Surely this is why we have schemes and rules, isn't it? It's to resolve issues like this. Personally, I think an obvious solution is to use chip cards in a more intelligent way. They are computers, not secure stripes. Since the card knows whether it's in an ATM or not, why not get the cards to give different PANs at ATM and POS (and through the contactless interface). The PAN on the card (and in the stripe) should not be the same PAN as given up to EMV POS. That way, if fraudsters compromise the POS and capture card details and PINs, they can't make cards for use in foreign magnetic stripe ATMs or UK ATMs where the ATM is doing as little processing as possible.

It was a cunning plan [24/10/2007]

It's amazing to me -- no, not amazing, more kind of quaint, reassuring and comforting -- that in this high-technology e-money world, there are crooks who still try to rob banks the old fashioned way. Not the modern way (by working for them as traders) but the old fashioned way. There are still people out there who rob banks with shotguns. And there are still people out there who make dodgy banknotes. An example being the gang of Chinese counterfeiters currently on trial in London for attempting to defraud the Bank of England of more than TWENTY EIGHT BILLION POUNDS. Yes, that's right. They tried to cheat the Bank of England out of more than FIFTY BILLION DOLLARS by swapping 360 "special-issue" £500,000 notes and 28 million £1,000 notes for lower denominations. Unfortunately, there were two tiny flaws in their master plan: the Bank of England has never issued a £500,000 note and £1,000 notes were taken out of circulation in 1943 (and there are only 63 of them not accounted for). The criminal geniuses tried to get the Bank of England to accept £1,000 notes with the signature of Jasper Holland, the chief cashier in

1963. Now, far be it from me to criticize -- I know virtually nothing about counterfeiting -- but c'mon guys. Didn't anyone think that the Bank of England might double-check if someone turns up with twenty eight billion pounds in used notes? The only way to get away with this kind of thing is to skim off a small amount from each legitimate note in circulation (like the Chancellor of the Exchequer does).

E-crime must surely be less risky, which is why it continues to grow. Phishing is now commonplace and not a day goes by without more e-mail arriving from "Royal Bank of Scotland", "Citibank" and "Merrill Lynch". In the latter case, this convincing missive arrived while I was typing the beginning of the paragraph!

"Merrill Lynch Enhanced Security Authentication: We have enhanced the Merrill Lynch Business Center security access to further safeguard access to your account information. Click on the hyperlink below and follow the prompts to answer and record answers to five personalized security questions. We may, in the future, ask you for answers to these questions when you log into the Business Center to ensure that only you are accessing your account information. By clicking the link below and/or by using the Merrill Lynch Business Center website ("site"), you: Login by clicking here: https://wcma.businesscenter.ml.com/ [deleted URL for security purposes: 8yvcv.com] I. Represent and warrant that you are authorized to accept the Merrill Lynch Business Center Terms Conditions [deleted URL for security purposes: 8yvcv.com] and use the site on behalf of yourself and your employer and in doing so you are acting within the scope of your duties and II. Accept the Merrill Lynch Business Center Terms Conditions [deleted URL for security purposes: 8yvcv.com] on behalf of yourself, agree to be bound by them."

Pretty convincing, I'm sure you'll agree. I almost clicked on it myself, but didn't because I don't have a Merrill Lynch account. But some people do, and some of them will click on it. The phishers rely on familiarity to acquire sensitive information, such as usernames, passwords, and financial data, by masquerading as a familiar or nationally recognized bank, credit card company or even an online auction site. A McAfee Avert Labs report showed the number of phishing websites increased by 784 percent in the first half of 2007. Social network sites are also a new target for the fraudsters: in December of 2006, cyber criminals targeted *MySpace* and used a worm to convert legitimate links to those to lure consumers to a phishing site designed specifically to obtain personal information. Until we begin to assemble a proper digital identity infrastructure, I can't see much changing here to be honest.

So "real" world money isn't safe and online money isn't safe either. In fact, fraudsters happily straddle both worlds, compromising physical point-of-sale terminals to collect and store the data on cards and then whisk it around the world to manufacture bogus cards for use in POS and at ATMs or in card-not-present environments. Avivah Litan of Gartner says

"It's almost more dangerous to go to the gas station than it is online."

That's if you can find a gas station that still takes cards, of course. She also said that of 160 data breaches investigated for one major credit card brand, 128 were card present (hence all the efforts to strengthen the Payment Card Industry Data Security Standard (PCI-DSS)). It doesn't look as if there will be much improvement either: Gartner predicts that only a third of POS software will be PCI-DSS compliant by 2009. But even when the POS software is fully PCI-DSS compliant, the problem of criminals tampering with POS terminals will still grow. So long as people are being asked to put their PINs into a device they cannot trust, criminals will target that process as the weak link in the card security chain.

Payment and tender [29/10/2007]

We've previously discussed the Snap Cafe in Washington, an establishment of some note to Digital Money debaters because the owner stopped taking cash. As I recall, there was some discussion about whether it is legal to do this, since Federal Reserve Notes (i.e., greenbacks) are legal tender in the USA so the cafe owner could not refuse them. I came across some interesting clarification in a paper from New Zealand. It's called Payments and the concept of legal tender by Nick McBride, Legal Counsel, Reserve Bank of New Zealand. The paper describes what happened last year, when the coins in New Zealand changed. The new coins were introduced on 1st July 2006. For a period of three months, the old coins were circulating in parallel with the new, but some retailers put up signs saying that they wouldn't accept the old coins. This, presumably, was because they didn't want the hassle of having to bag them all up and take them to the bank to swap for new coins. So could they refuse to take the old coins in payment even though they were legal tender? The answer is yes (sort of).

As was observed in the discussion of the Snap Cafe, you cannot force a retailer to accept cash. If, however, you buy something from them and there is no contractual barrier to the use of cash, and you offer legal tender in payment, and they refuse it, then they cannot enforce the debt in court. So if you incur a debt, you can discharge it with legal tender, but you cannot be forced to incur the debt in the first place, if you see what I mean. This came up again today: a Techdirt story about Apple refusing to accept cash for iPhones and insisting on credit cards conveniently had a link to the relevant US Treasury page[19].

Incidentally, I heard on BBC radio that it now costs the US mint approximately 1.7 cents to make a penny and an astonishing 10 cents to make a nickel. This isn't (entirely) because it's a government-run industry but because of the metal content of the coins. UK "copper" coins are actually steel with copper plating and so safe from melting down for the time being (but the face value of the pre-1992 copper coins is below the scrap value). No-one here will be melting down coins to make more valuable razor blades (as they do in Bangladesh) just yet!

Safe and sound [03/01/2008]

As the whole TJX matter trundles toward a settlement, it does serve to remind us that cost is not the only area for dispute between banks and retailers at the moment. There's also security. In the US, the National Retail Federation (NRF) has already launched a campaign to get credit card companies to permit retailers to not store credit card numbers and have the details stored by the issuers instead (so, perhaps, the merchant has some sort of reference number that gives them access to the data for transaction purposes). The NRF say

"It makes more sense for credit card companies to protect their data from thieves by keeping it in a relatively few secure locations than to expect millions of merchants scattered across the nation to lock up their data for them."

This seems fair enough. But would it solve the problem or it would it just mean that a data breach would result in more (and more accurate) data being stolen? Either way, it seems unlikely that it would mean no more breaches at all even if the House of Commons Justice Committee gets its wish and to criminalise data breaches.

---

[19] http://www.ustreas.gov/education/faq/currency/legal-tender.shtml#q1

This is a stonewall prediction, because absolute security costs infinite amounts of money, which neither banks nor retailers have. Anyway, even if systems are built securely, people always make mistakes. Last month, a Georgia man was notified that he had a negative balance of $211 trillion at his Wachovia bank account. His overdraft makes the US national debt, which is only slightly over $9 trillion, seem like small change. Luckily for him, Wachovia reports that the balance was caused by "an isolated banking error", and that of course he would not have to pay any overdraft charges. Apparently the error was that his account number was entered in place of his balance. Like the $218 trillion phone bill we saw in 2006, why are errors of this magnitude not caught by some sort of bounds checking algorithm in the bank's software? Furthermore, if an error this size gets through all of the checks and balances, then what other, less noticeable errors are falling through the cracks every day?

I hate to sound like an old fart, but in my day I'd like to think that this wouldn't have happened -- I blame object-oriented web 2.0 C doubleplus-good or whatever it is the kids use today. It's been many years since I wrote any code, but I would have thought that an occasional bounds check might be appropriate from time to time, wouldn't you? Don't the banks have some ready reckoner for this, such as "if a personal overdraft is greater than 25 times the TOTAL NATIONAL DEBT, then double check it?" or something like that.

Don't worry, it still works fine [10/01/2008]

There are lots of fraud stories around today, including the one about the fraudster who managed to con high street bank Barclays out of £10,000 in a credit card scam by posing as the bank's own chairman, Marcus Agius. It seems as if the card fraud meme has been spreading. I don't know if you saw the wonderful story in The Guardian back in December, but it was about the English town of Letchworth (the world's first garden city) and the essence of the story was that card fraud is so out-of-control that a kind of panic has set in. I won't reproduce all of the details here, but I wanted to pull out a few key quotes from the story in order to make a couple of points and to reflect on the conclusion of the story, which is that whole communities are losing faith in payment cards and are turning back to cash-only transactions. The meme has been spreading through various channels and there are more and more stories about the failure of chip and PIN (i.e., failure to eliminate fraud), the rise in ATM fraud, CNP fraud and so forth. But I'm getting ahead. In the Letchworth story, the reporter found many people "boycotting" outdoor cash machines, and, in some cases, abandoning the use of payment cards at retail POS.

"Shoppers at the Shell petrol station told us they will never use their bank cards to pay for fuel again, after witnessing the chaos caused to friends who have had bank accounts plundered by fraudsters. Outdoor ATMs are strangely quiet, while inside banks there are queues of customers taking out cash."

The story says -- and I'm not questioning it -- that in the town (of 33,000 people) virtually everyone the reporter met had either been the victim of card fraud or they knew of someone who has had money illegally taken from their bank account. Usually the illegal withdrawals take place in Australia. This is a novel twist (it's usually Italy or Bulgaria) suggesting a specific gang at work. Several people said they were now only using cash. Almost all said they would no longer use cash machines unless they were inside the bank. One specific problem identified was the petrol station. Card-reading equipment at the Shell garage, on the main road in and out of the town, was compromised. Another was the bank. An ATM at a bank branch had a skimming device fitted. The local paper reported the stories with additional coverage when it emerged the problem had spread to another Shell garage in nearby Hitchin. I'm not trivialising the issues: the stories involve real people, such as

"Hilary Gibson defaulted on her mortgage because thieves stole the £700 she had deposited to cover the payment the following day. Leisa Virgo from Hitchin was another victim. When the bank called to check a payment, she immediately cancelled the card - but not before £300 had been withdrawn."

Hertfordshire police also reported that CCTV monitoring had foiled another attempt to install a skimming device at another ATM and four people were arrested. Nevertheless, residents such as Peter Merrigan are concerned:

"To be honest, I have stopped using bank cards... I now prefer to go into the bank and get out my money the old-fashioned way - I certainly wouldn't use a cash machine."

The reporter found the ATM outside the Barclays branch with wires hanging out. It had clearly been attacked. The staff were sanguine:

"Don't worry, it still works fine."

I'm not sure that the residents have been doing their risk analysis homework, because (and here I agree with the APACS spokesman) carrying around wads of notes is (I'm sure) more likely to lead to loss than carrying around a card: if I lose a tenner, it's gone for good, but if my card is skimmed I'll get the cash back from the bank. Sorted. Since I never, ever, use my debit card except at ATMs, I feel fairly comfortable. But then I don't live in Bicester, where fraudsters tried to attach a skimming device to every ATM in the town, or Houghton on the Hill, where the local garage was compromised so that everyone's card details were stolen.

Note that the frauds discussed in that article, and discussed here at the Forum more than once, are not chip and PIN frauds. They are PIN frauds. They rely on the fact that you can put a bent card (with a cloned stripe but absent the non-copyable chip) into a foreign ATM and it will work. That is not to say that one day chip and PIN fraud might occur, but when banks roll out DDA (i.e., asymmetric) cards instead of the SDA (i.e., symmetric cryptography) cards used in the UK today, the likelihood is slim. I'm not putting on rose-tinted glasses here. There are some issues with SDA chips that need to be resolved because a flawed method of cheaply cloning cards without knowing the PIN does exist. It involves copying the rest of the chip's data to a another card, nicknamed a "yes card" because whatever PIN you put in the terminal, the (bent) card will say "yes, that's the right PIN" and then give up the copied data. In theory, this is only a problem in offline terminals, because in an online transaction the bank host is supposed to verify the transaction cryptogram which depends on the security key (this is never given up by the original card, so it's not present in the copied chip). This cannot be the mechanism behind the fraudster's rampage through middle England, though, because (as Mike Bond observes in the article) all ATM transactions are online and, in any case, ATMs don't send the PIN to the card for checking but send it back to the bank host.

The problem with foreign ATMs, on the other hand, is real because they allow "fallback" so that a chip card without a chip can still be used as a magnetic stripe card. I was wondering if, in current circumstances, merely using a chip and PIN card in a foreign non-chip ATM might be enough to trigger anti-fraud alarms, despite the fact that it would inevitably inconvenience customers (e.g., me, because I travel a lot and use ATMs because I'm too lazy to get foreign currency sorted out in advance) and it looks as if this is now the case:

"The "unusual" activity turned out to be cash withdrawals I had made from ATMs in the US."

There's one simple step that the UK banks could take, isn't there? If I could log on to my home banking and switch my debit card on and off for non-UK ATM transactions, that would make a significant dent in the problem. Most of the time, my card would be "off" and all transactions from foreign ATMs automatically rejected. When I'm going overseas, I simply turn it "on" until I get back. I'm sure this plan is too simple to work: how about you?

Note to foreign readers: in the English vernacular, "bent" means fake or counterfeit. Hence, "bent as nine bob note".

Don't panic! [26/02/2008]

Just a note to assure everyone that the sky isn't falling in, despite the rash of press reports about contactless payment card security over the last few days. A number of articles have pointed to Adam Laurie's recent demonstration that American Express ExpressPay chips work exactly as per their specification and in line with the relevant international standards:

"As part of his presentation Wednesday, Laurie asked for someone from the audience to volunteer a smart card. Without taking the card out of the volunteer's wallet, Laurie both read and displayed its contents on the presentation screen -- the person's name, account number, and expiration clearly visible. As a disclaimer, Laurie said he spoke to American Express, the company that issued the volunteer's card. Laurie said that American Express told him: "We are comfortable with the security of our product." Laurie added that the company told him the number he displayed on the presentation screen was not the account number printed on the card, which Laurie proved by opening the wallet and comparing. However, Laurie noted that the captured account number could still be used for online transactions."[20]

Adam is a great guy and he does excellent work, but on this one he's wrong. You cannot use the alias PAN (i.e., the PAN given up via the contactless interface, not the one printed on the card) in anything except a contactless transaction and you cannot use it to make a bent contactless card because you need the Amex security keys in order to

---

[20] The hands-free way to steal a credit card, *CNET News.com*

generate the right digital signature. If you attempt to use the alias PAN in an online transaction, the Amex host will decline it.

I hate to add my usual rant about the reporting of contactless security issues, but it does annoy me that some of the media reports have a tone to them that sort of asks how come Amex (and by extension, their consultants!) are so dumb that they design and build a new payment scheme that can be trivially defeated? The assumption that card issuers know nothing about security is, frankly, slightly offensive.

Once again, it's "PIN fraud" not "chip and PIN fraud" [27/02/2008]

Well that was dull. I got all excited about this...

> *"Whatever you buy in the shops, you probably pay with a chip and pin card, tonight Newsnight has exclusive evidence that they are vulnerable to fraudsters. The implications could be huge for millions of shoppers. We'll be asking what are the banks going to do about it?"*[21]

But it turned out not to be an exciting breach of chip and PIN security, using (for example) liquid nitrogen to extract keys or something similar, leading to "chip and PIN" fraud, but "PIN fraud" as usual. The allegation -- which is, as far as I know, wholly true -- is that track 2 data and PINs are being stolen from compromised terminals and then used to create counterfeit magnetic stripe cards. Sandra Quinn from APACS, who was being tortured by Paxo (it's a peculiarly British bloodsport), said -- again, wholly true -- that ICVV has been introduced from 1st January 2008 to mitigate this particular fraud. For the uninitiated, ICVV replaces the CVV in the Track 2 (equivalent) data stored in the EMV chip. Thus, if a bank host sees a magnetic stripe transaction with the ICVV in it, they know it's a counterfeit stripe. The ICVV varies from CVV by replacing the PAN Sequence Number with 99 instead of the actual value when deriving the code.

I must point out, in the spirit of shared openness and truth seeking, that we just checked the three cards we could find in our office that were issued after 1st January 2008 and we found that the Barclaycard

---

[21] Tuesday, 26 February, 2008, Talk about Newsnight, BBC NEWS

and the Nationwide card do have ICVV, the other unnamed large UK issuer's card doesn't have ICVV. So, on balance, Sandra wins!

The guys at Cambridge (who were featured in the programme -- I'll see if I can grab them for a podcast next time I'm in Cambridge) made a number of good points (asking, for example, why cardholder data is sent between cards and terminals in the clear) but in essence it's the same story that we've been tracking here for years. Not that I'm in any way dismissing the real problems that it means for members of the public whose cards details are compromised in nobbled terminals. And Ross' key point that PINs used to be only used in controlled environments (ATMs) but are now used everywhere and are therefore easier to steal is, of course, unanswerable. The solution is to stop using magnetic stripes, of course, but that looks some way off!

Following on from the programme and yesterday's blog posts, I was once again thinking about the difference between tamper-resistant and tamper-evident. As far as I am aware -- but I'd be delighted to receive more information on this topic -- there is no requirement for EMV POS terminals to be tamper-resistant but they are supposed to be tamper-evident. The always-worth-reading Nick Szabo had a good post talking about tamper-evident technology. He wasn't talking about smart cards that blow up when you probe them, but the ancient Sumerian equivalent. Along with the tamper evident clay (once you'd baked it, no-one could change it), they developed a kind of virtual tamper evidence. It took the form of two sets of numbers. On the front of the tablet, each group of commodities would be recorded separately. The example Nick gives is that on the front of a tablet would be recorded 120 pots of wheat, 90 pots of barley, and 55 goats. On the reverse would simply be recorded "265", the total (without categories). The scribe, or an auditor, would then verify that the sum was correct. If not, an error or fraud had occurred. Note the similarity to tamper evident seals -- if a seal is broken, this meant that error or fraud had occurred. The breaker of the seals, or the scribe who recorded the wrong numbers, or the debtor who paid the wrong amounts of commodities would be called on the carpet to answer for his or her discrepancy. So there we go: clay seals for all Shell garages and the problem is sorted!

Chapter 11: History and Perspectives

Those who fail to understand history are, as we are all tired of hearing, condemned to repeat. Besides, history is interesting.

The new frontier (for crime) [05/02/2007]

Society's response to new technologies always seems to be the same: assume the worst and plan for the sky to fall in. There was a super edition of the BBC's The Long View recently, showing how fears over the dangers of computer games were essentially the same concerns that were raised in Georgian England around the invention of the novel. Samuel Richardson's novel 'Pamela' took the public imagination by storm. For the first time readers were entering a hyper-realistic world -- one where a servant girl was being pursued by her master -- and there were concerns from the l33t that the line between reality and fiction would be blurred and confusing to ordinary people (e.g., you and me). Similarly, as I noted in an article for The Guardian back in 2000, the invention of the bicycle meant concerns about poor people cycling into rich areas and committing crimes as well as vision of bicycling Huns sweeping across Europe. Nothing changes! Whatever new technology comes along, we project existing fears on to it before we begin to explore the possibilities. Virtual worlds, for example.

I found an article pointing out that the virtual worlds that we are fascinated with as sandboxes for digital money experiments could be used by money launderers to move illicit cash and convert that cash into "real" money. The article further notes that banks may be guilty of money laundering if they "facilitate" deposits or payments in these virtual worlds, because there is no due diligence on players. I wonder what will happen to the population of World of Warcraft or Second Life if the government insists that you have to present an old gas bill and a video rental card in order to play online. More regulation is on the way, I would think, so presumably organisations with experience of dealing with that kind of regulation (let's call them for sake of argument, "banks") would have an advantage.

Meanwhile another virtual world, Project Entropia, is about to adopt an alternative regulatory regime for banks: auction banking licences to the highest bidder. Successful bidders will be afforded the opportunity to help design and name their own virtual bank buildings, and offer banking services directly through avatars. So not only will a new money market come into existence, but the participants in that market may not be "conventional" players.

Digital money tribes [07/02/2007]

Different groups of people are interested in digital money for different reasons. Personally, I fall into the techno-determinist tribe: digital money is going to happen simply because it can be done; hence you may as well try to influence the evolution. But there are other, more idealist tribes who look to the advent of an electronic alternative to notes and coins as a means to change the money system in some way. I might (very) broadly categorise them as the euroleft and the ameright. The euroleft want digital money to become a vehicle for social or community currencies, whereas the ameright want digital money to become a vehicle for commodity currencies. But in both cases, they want to use digital money technology to carry something other than fiat currency.

What would happen if digital money meant that consumers and businesses had a real choice in which currency to use for everyday transactions? Some already do, of course. In the US, for example, where you can use pesos to pay for pizza in Dallas. But this isn't really that interesting: before the euro was introduced there were many places in Europe where you could pay in a handful of different currencies. But all of these currencies -- the euro, the dollar, the peso -- are fiat currencies. They are issued by governments, essentially, and have no intrinsic value. If we put commodity currencies to one side for the time being, are there really people out there using local currencies rather than national currencies? Actually, there are quite a few. One such currency that has been attracting attention recently is in the Bavarian region of Chiemgau, where you can exist in a euro-free zone with a population of half a million people. Restaurants, bakeries, hairdressers and a network of supermarkets all accept the local currency: the Chiemgauer. Notes are exchanged freely like legal tender. You can even use a debit card. The Chiemgauer is one of 16 regional currencies that have sprung into existence across Germany and Austria since the launch of the euro five years ago and another 49 regions are in the pipeline. They are outside the control of the political authorities, mostly run by activists, farmers, eco-enthusiasts, anti-globalists, and citizen committees. This is really rather interesting, and a subject that we have touched on before at the Digital Money Forum with experts such as Bernard Lietaer, Michael Linton and Dr. Margrit Kennedy.

The e-selfish gene [03/05/2007]

It looks like more of our attitude to money may be down to DNA than we might think. I rather enjoyed the story in many of the papers yesterday concerning the discovery that the experience of losing money is processed by the brain in a similar fashion to pain and fear, which may well explain the reasonably well-known phenomenon that people dread financial misfortune more deeply than they value gains. Perhaps it's time to add a new category to the blog, "neuroscience".

Sometimes the findings of research into the relationship between mind, body and money are more obvious. When scientists reported that the mere thought of money makes people selfish, I naturally assumed that their research findings extended into the e-money world. This explains why, for example, that everyone who wants to be part of the e-payment value chain wants all of it! One of the scientists quoted in the article says that "cooperation really goes down the drain when money is an issue." As no. 1 son would say, "duh".

Help is at hand though. Next time I go to a meeting between -- let's say -- banks and mobile operators, I intend to take an umbrella with a hidden drug injection unit in the tip. This is because it may be possible to influence decision-making around trust and investments by altering brain chemistry (please don't forward this to our finance director). It turns out that a group of economists at the University of Zurich have demonstrated that this is feasible through a "trust game", in which one player gives some money to another player, who invests it on his behalf and then decides how much to return to him and how much to keep. The more the first player invests, the more he stands to gain, but the more he has to trust the second player. If the players trust each other, both will do well. If they don't, neither will end up with much money. Here's the fun part: the experimenters divided students into two groups and one group were dosed with oxytocin, a hormone that the brain produces during breast-feeding, sexual intercourse, and other intimate types of social bonding, while the others got a placebo. Of the twenty-nine students who were given oxytocin, thirteen invested the maximum money allowed, compared with just six out of twenty-nine in the control group. Wow. I'm not wasting time on PowerPoint or Excel ever again: it's oxytocin nasal spray all the way from now on.

Ten more years of technology [15/05/2007]

I was asked to write something about the next ten years of technology in retail e-payments, so I thought it might be a good idea to begin by looking at how things have changed over the last decade. Thinking about it, the answer is not much. All of the technologies that the payment card industry are focusing on today were already in use ten years ago (with one exception, and that is NFC). Ten years ago, we (the payment card industry) had already started to plan for EMV migration, which it has to be said went remarkably smoothly in the first country to move, the UK. Ten years ago there was a biometric ATM installed (in Swindon, my home town and the payment city of tomorrow). Ten years ago we had already started using credit cards on the Internet. Ten years ago we were already talking about mobile payments and the strength of the customer proposition around the GSM handset: many people thought that would be the next big thing, remember? Well, the EMV roll out is continuing and in many countries the members are now moving their plans on to the next phase of smart card evolution, the development of chip-based value-added services for customers and for merchants. We might have liked to see things move faster with respect to chip migration, but on the whole it is proceeding well. By comparison, I think payment cards have performed poorly with respect to the Internet. Back in 1997, cards supported almost all e-commerce. Next year, they will account for less than half of all online purchases (despite increasing their share of total consumer spend). The false start with Secure Electronic Transactions (SET) and the slow take-up of 3D Secure have led us to the point where, in the UK at least, CNP fraud is now as big as total card fraud was when we began the EMV journey. Clearly this is going to change, and change soon.

It seems to me that both the post-EMV evolution of the business at point-of-sale and realistic mass-market solutions to both the general problem of online security and the specific issue of CNP fraud are linked to the most important (on a global scale) technology platform for consumer services: the mobile phone. In the UK, mobile web access is now almost a fifth of PC web access: 5.7 million people in the UK use the mobile web, as opposed to 30 million who access the web by PC. (The comparable statistic in the US is 30 million out 176 million, or about 17%). It looks as if the US mobile lag is shrinking. So not only do most people have phones, more and more people are happy using them to access data services.

The customer proposition around mobile phones and payments has always been strong, but the technology has not fulfilled its promise, at least in developed countries. But there is now an "X factor" in payment technology: contactless. We all understand the proposition around contactless: speed and convenience. We all understand the proposition around mobile: ubiquity and connectivity. Put the two things together, in the form of near-field communication (NFC) handsets and you have something special. These factors mean that new technology will have a much bigger impact on the card business over the next ten years than it did over the last ten. Over the coming decade, the mobile phone will shift from being a network end-point to being a pivot between local and global environments, an indispensable and personal security token that bridges physical and virtual commerce.

First and last money [30/05/2007]

The first money appears to have been shells coloured with red ochre. These appear 100,000 years ago in Africa. Are we now in the days of the last (physical) money? APACS report that in 2004 cards overtook cash by value and that in 2014 they will overtake them in volume. That's if anyone is still using cards by then: I'll be using my phone to buy packs of gum.

The annual APACS report on the Way We Pay has just been released and it shows that we're using more cash than ever in the UK. The proportion of cash demands met by cash machines has nearly doubled over the last ten years from a third to two-thirds (which means a lot of people must still be going to the bank to withdraw cash, something I can't remember doing) with the total amount withdrawn more than doubling from £80 billion to £180 billion. The figures show that other card-based cash withdrawals (e.g., cashback at retailers) are now 12 per cent of personal cash needs in 2006 (up from 8 per cent in 1996). But the acquisition of cash through non-bank channels (such as wages and state benefits) and via cheque and passbook withdrawals from accounts has diminished significantly from almost two-thirds of all cash acquired ten years go to under a quarter today.

Sandra Quinn, director of communications at APACS, says:

"During 2006 we spent £274.3 billion in cash; it is interesting to look at the methods we use to acquire this cash and how our preferences have changed over the years... Demographic trends have also shaped the pattern of cash acquisition; in 2006 for the first time, more than half of over 65s are regular users of cash machines."

The report goes on to forecast that cash machines will dispense an increasing proportion of all personal cash acquired, reaching 81 per cent in 2016, with £220 billion expected to be paid out. I'm not sure about this prediction, because I am convinced that the use of cash will fall much further by then. Sandra says that

"Cash currently accounts for 63 per cent of all the payments we make, however looking forward, the total demand for cash in value terms is projected to see a very modest decline over the next ten years due to the increasing popularity of non-cash payments, in particular developments like contactless cards."

It's not contactless cards, I think, that are the key technology in terms of non-cash payments, its mobile phones. And having been playing around with the combination of contactless cards and NFC phones for a variety of clients, I'm more that cash is on the way out quicker than APACS predict.

If we're looking forward to 2014, though, I think you should pay more attention to what young persons think rather than what people like me think. I came across some interesting comments from young persons in an article from *NorthJersey.com*. Alex Miller (19) uses a debit card for purchases instead of taking money out at a cash machine because it's easy and it avoids ATM fees. Susanna Goulert (21) uses a debit card because she's worried about taking on debt. The article refers to them as Generation P, but I've no idea what this means. I've only ever heard of Generation X (which I think I used to be) and Generation XXL (which I am now). Anyway, it says that Generation P think it's easier to spend more with plastic than with old-fashioned dollar bills, which may well be true but I like to hear some other opinions. The Dell computer kiosk where Alex Miller (19) works doesn't even accept cash, forcing customers to trade cash for gift cards at the mall's customer service counter. He figures that's the rule because cash can be stolen. Not only that, but an employee would have to count the cash and take it to the bank and goes on to say that

"It saves money in the end not to have money."

The coffee shop where Katie Sterner (19) works abandoned their minimum transaction size and now customers regularly put payments of less than $5 on cards. I don't know what this does for tipping, or if the tips are automatically added (unless the customer presses some kind of "decline service charge" button or something). Seven out of 10 consumers in Generation P use payment cards for small payments. Susanna Goulert (21) charges cans of drink to her card and Alex Miller (19) once charged a pack of gum. Neither would be surprised if one day paper dollars and metal cents go away, and nor would I. But talking about cans of drink reminded about the complex relationship between P and XXL: it transpires that Coca-Cola have discovered that customers spend a third more at vending machines that take cards, which is why I am so confident in my prediction that in the short term it will be unattended channels that are most revolutionised by contactless and mobile payments.

When Monopoly money was real [12/06/2007]

We think about money as a law of nature, as a kind of constant, but the way that money works today is not only just one of many ways in which it could work, it's a relatively recent invention in the great scheme of things. It wasn't that long ago that the developed world was on a commodity standard (i.e., gold) and there was no national fiat currency. Seventy five years ago, in America, there wasn't even a circulating medium of exchange. At the height of the Great Depression, 1932 and 1933, when the interest rate on US Treasury bills was negative, unemployment was 25 percent and bank runs and closings were common, Americans reverted to barter.

It's hard to imagine now, but this is a time when the USA literally ran out of money. In his first week in office in 1933, FDR passed legislation to enforce bank holidays, end the convertibility of gold and to force the population to sell their gold to the Federal government. It's surprising, I think, to Europeans to realise just how much passion these events still stir today: there are no end of books, magazines, pamphlets and websites that still refer to FDR's actions then as if they were yesterday, and not all of them come from guys living on the top of mountains in West Virginia (i.e., the guys who think that the Federal Reserve is a Jewish conspiracy).

Anyway, the point is this. Because there was no cash -- no Federal Reserve notes -- available, people began to print their own money. This is known as "scrip" and it is by no means limited to this single historical case: it's a common phenomenon. An often-used example closer to home comes from the Irish bank strike in 1966, when people in Ireland wrote personal cheques to each other and these were then passed on to form a cash substitute. British Postal Orders circulate on the Indian subcontinent performing a similar function.

The "depression scrip" issued around America took many forms (there is a vibrant collectors' market for this: just search on eBay) and was issued by communities, companies and individuals.

As Forum friend Bernard Lietaer points out in his 1990 article, Dean Acheson, then Assistant Secretary of the Treasury, had been approached by Professor Irving Fisher with the idea of scrip with a high "negative interest" rate (2% per week) and was calculated so that the face value would be amortised over one year, and the currency withdrawn at that point. Acheson decided to have it checked by his economic advisor, Professor Russell Sprague at Harvard. The answer was that it would work, but that it had some implications for decentralised decision making which Acheson should verify in Washington. By this time, the "stamp scrip movement" as it became known, had created interest by no less than 450 cities around the United States. For example the City of St. Louis, Missouri, had decided to issue $100,000 worth of stamp money. Similarly, Oregon was planning to launch a $75 million stamp scrip issue. A federal law had been introduced in Congress by Congressman Pettengil, Indiana, to issue $ 1 billion of stamped currency. Fisher published a little handbook entitled "Stamp Scrip" for practical management of this currency by communities, and described the actual experience of 75 American communities with it. It looked as if the US might adopt a decentralised money system, but on 4th March 1933 Roosevelt announced the New Deal and, in addition to closing the banks, prohibited the issue of "emergency currencies". The experiment was over.

What's the point of this post? Well, I happened to be reading "Monopoly: The World's Most Famous Game and How It Got That Way" by Philip Orbanes and it mentions in passing that in 1933, Parker Brothers used their printing presses to print scrip that was accepted in their home town of Salem, Mass. Games to the rescue! I wonder if next time the banks fail, it will be World of Warcraft gold, not Monopoly money, that stands in for fiat currency!

Export and controls [20/07/2007]

Well, its summer (I can tell that because of the traditional concurrent English flood warning and hosepipe ban) and time to think about my forthcoming holiday. Better get my spending money ready. As it happens, under European Union regulations, if you attempt to leave the EU with more than 10,000 euros in cash (but not prepaid cards, phone top-up balances, wampum belts or any other instrument) then you must report yourself to the tax authorities, in my case Her Majesties Revenue and Customs. Now, as a matter of policy this blog is not for political comments, but I am moved to say that I don't believe this will make the slightest difference to terrorists or drug dealers, but will probably result in some holidaying pensioners going straight to chokey. Accountants likened the law to a stealthy re-introduction of exchange controls which Margaret Thatcher's administration abolished in 1979. We've explained before, for younger readers, what exchange controls were[22].

The best bit of the recent coverage of the EU story was the revelation that British national treasure Cilla Black and her husband, may he rest in peace, Bobby were international currency smugglers. It transpires that while living in the misery of Harold Wilson's Britain and labouring under the £50 limit for foreign exchange (about 1,000 euros in new money) -- and at a time when travellers had their passports marked with the amount of foreign currency they had bought at the bank -- Cilla was struggling to pay the final £1,000 for a Spanish villa because of the controls. Her husband Bobby, a former baker, came up with a successful plan to hide the money in a hollowed-out loaf of

---

22

http://digitaldebateblogs.typepad.com/digital_money/2006/11/all_you_need_is.html

bread. The maid at their villa was said to be intrigued to discover the couple eating toast with a hole in the middle.

Presumably the statute of limitations prevents an amusing and entertaining trial of the Scouse songstress for conspiracy to evade exchange controls.

Cash is a stealth tax [03/08/2007]

If you have a look at the Bank of England's annual report for the year to 28th February 2007, you'll find a section called Issue Department. Last year, they had an income of £1.7 billion and costs of £57 million. What a business! The most profitable nationalised industry in history, they didn't get to spend the profits themselves. Under the various Bank Acts in the United Kingdom, since 1844 they have had to hand over the lot to Her Majesty's Treasury, a whopping £1.65 billion straight into the Chancellor's pockets. If I'm doing the maths right (I may not be) that's the equivalent of 2p on the standard rate of income tax. Banknotes are, in effect, a stealth tax: each British banknote you have in your pocket is an interest-free loan to the Bank of England, and the interest they get on the money (they use it to buy government bonds) goes to the government.

There's no need for the new Chancellor (I'll update this with his/her name when I look up who it is) to panic and start hunting around for something else to tax to get a couple of billion quid. The seigniorage will keep coming in for a while. A Gallup survey in the UK nearly a decade ago -- *Bull survey predicts cashless future* in the *Financial Times Virtual Finance Report.* **3**(3): p. 2 (March 1998) -- found that two–thirds of people in the UK thought that notes and coins will not be needed in the future and almost half thought that notes and coins would disappear within a decade (one–fifth thought they would see the end of physical cash within five years). More surprisingly, four–fifths said they thought e-cash would be more convenient than physical cash even though none of them could possibly have used it. Yet a decade on, more cash than ever is in circulation (up from about £22 billion at the time of that survey to about £38 billion now) and the take from the stealth tax continues to rise (I don't resent the money: after all, it's not as if the government just wastes it).

Its easy running money, isn't it [20/08/2007]

Running a retail payment system is pretty easy, which is why new entrants are attracted to it despite the thin margins, as we've discussed before. But it isn't easy when things go wrong. Take a look at what's been going on in Hong Kong, where there are currently 15 million Octopus cards in circulation and the company handles 10 million transactions totalling more than HK$78 million (about five million quid) every day. Octopus has been found to have taken an average of HK$240 from six cardholders every day for the past seven years (amounting to HK$3.7 million) because of faulty transactions. Octopus are, of course, going to refund the money to the 15,270 people affected going back to 2000. There are no records before 2000, so the additional HK$300K overcharged during that period is going to be donated to charity. The fault meant that about six in every 10,000 top-ups went wrong: the money was deducted from the cardholder's bank account but not credited to their Octopus account. Octopus Holdings chief executive Prudence Chan Bik-wah said the main cause of the failed transactions was a malfunction of an electronic funds transfer (EFT) module in the add-value machines at transit stations and that all top-up transactions from the machines will remain suspended until the problem is completely fixed. She also pointed out that since 90% of the customers are anonymous; it's complicated to sort out refunds so customers are being encouraged to use personalised cards free of charge for the next 12 months.

The problem came to light some time ago when Octopus admitted that its investigations failed to discover why money was deducted from the accounts of more than 500 card users without topping up their cards with the appropriate amounts. The Hong Kong Monetary Authority (HKMA) ordered an enquiry at the end of last year. Although it was originally believed that problems began with the upgrade of the EPS add-value system at the beginning of December, the inquiry revealed a limited number of failed add-value transactions arising before that date with refunds outstanding. Although the problem appeared to be restricted to a limited number of EPS add-value transactions, it had been decided to call for an independent review and they appointed Professor Andrew Chan Chi-fai of the Faculty of Business Administration of the Chinese University of Hong Kong and the Chairman of the Hong Kong Deposit Protection Board to advise the management of Octopus Cards Limited (OCL). The HKMA has also served notice to OCL under Section 59(2) of the

Banking Ordinance, requiring the company to submit to the Professor an independent auditor's report on the operation of add-value services through EPS as well as OCL's operational risk control environment. It's this report that is the heart of the news story above. It's taken them a few months to work through it all, but they seem to have got to the bottom of it.

The saga raises a few points for non-bank organisations looking to move into the payments business:

It's really hard to test payment system properly because of their operational scale; therefore it's best to assume that something will go wrong. Having detailed specifications and semi-automated testing driven from those specification (not from the design) is critical, but someone somewhere is still going to implement something incorrectly.

It's best not to jump to conclusions about what has gone wrong. Given the complexity, you may be looking at misleading symptoms.

Have a good procedure in place for when it does go wrong. Don't panic. Turn off the component that doesn't work -- any well-designed system has fallbacks (i.e., if POS top-up doesn't work, consumers can use mobiles instead) -- and set about finding the problem. People are naturally sensitive about money, so it's important to get it fixed.

Finally, if something goes wrong then turn the big guns on it, don't try and sweep it under the carpet or hope it can be fixed in the back room. Octopus has kept public confidence by being open about the investigation, the results and their actions.

A useful case study for anyone going into this business.

Not a lot of people know that, no. 94 [09/10/2007]

I don't normally read Paul Johnson's Spectator articles, in fact I don't normally read *The Spectator* (although I am reading "A City Spectator: Bulls, Bears, Booms and Boondoggles", the collection of Christopher Fildes' superb Spectator columns on the City), but I happened on his recent piece on gold. It includes the story of the guinea, which I'm ashamed to say I didn't know. In 1663, under Charles II, a new gold coin was minted in England. It became known as the guinea, because the gold had come from the West African coast. It was originally worth one pound Sterling, but by 1694 it had risen to thirty shillings (note to non-British readers or British readers under the age of 40 or so: there were twenty shillings in one pound) because of inflation. Remember that England's currency was a bit of a mess at the time, which is why the cleverest man who ever lived, Sir Isaac Newton (who, as an aside, invented the cat flap as well as universal theory of gravitation), was put in charge of the mint. The value of the pure gold guinea rose against the debased coinage of the realm. Under the currency reform of William III, it was pegged at 21 shillings and six pence (note for younger viewers: there were twelve pence in a shilling). In 1717, it was fixed at 21 shillings, which is why to this day in merry England (and other parts of the United Kingdom) a guinea is one pound and one shilling, or one pound and five pence in new money. From the eighteenth century onwards, the professional classes -- as distinct from the working classes -- dealt in guineas rather than pounds: I'm pretty sure that horses are still priced in guineas today although bills from gardeners and such like no longer have this charm.

Meanwhile, Forum friend Chris Leather points me to a cute publicity stunt by Travelex, the National Space Centre and the University Of Leicester: "coins" for use in space. The Quasi Universal Intergalactic Denomination - or Quid for short - is the world's first currency that can be used in space. Quids -- plastic disks with pictures of the planets -- are supposedly safe for use in zero-gravity. So guineas may not boldly go where no coin has been before, but quids will!

Nine is a magic number [23/10/2007]

I'm going to have to stop using the time-worn vernacular "as bent as a nine-bob note". Up until decimalisation in 1973, the British shilling of twelve pennies was known as the "bob". Hence the ten shilling note was the ten bob note. For some odd reason, and I really can't remember why, I never saw the replacement 5p piece as a bob, nor have I ever referred to a 10p piece as two bob, but for a long time I called a 50p piece a "ten bob piece" (in fact I can distinctly remember once asking my younger brother for ten bob and being genuinely surprised when he had no idea what I was talking about). So ten bob was a sizable amount of coin of the realm whereas nine bob meant something that was clearly fraudulent (as in "the Enron P&L statement was as bent as nine bob note"). But it now transpires that there was in fact at least one nine bob note: the Irish "Newports Bank" issued a nine shilling note in 1799, and a specimen has just been sold at auction in the UK for three thousand euros. So what is to be our post-cash alternative: as bent as a... what? As bent as a card with a magnetic stripe on it... no, wait... as bent as an IBAN with an invalid check digit... as bent as an SDA clone with an invalid digital signature... they don't seem to have the ring to them, do they?

Our children will surely miss the rich language of cash once it evaporates into cyberspace. No more greenbacks or dimes, no more fivers or farthings. No appropriate slang term has yet arisen to mean -- specifically -- electronic cash. We need to put our thinking caps on: what is the 21st century addition to beans, bread, bucks, cabbage, chips, dough, lucre, loot, mazuma, moolah, wad or spondoolicks that will make its way into the thesaurus? I've always liked wonga, so I was thinking "vonga" (constructed from virtual wonga) or perhaps "wenga" (I don't know why, I just like the "e" in there).

Glossary

2FA (Two Factor Authentication) – Authentication that uses two different mechanisms to verify identity for security purposes. An example of 2FA might require both a password and a smart card thus determining both what the user knows and what the user has.

3D Secure (Three Domain Security) – A protocol developed by MasterCard (SecureCode) and Visa (Verified by Visa) to authenticate cardholders during electronic payment transactions.

ACH (Automated Clearing House) – A network that clears and settles interbank credit and debit transfers.

AML (Anti-Money Laundering legislation) – Legal controls that financial institutions must obey, which includes monitoring suspicious money transfers, then investigating and if necessary reporting them to the country's central bank.

APACS (Association for Payment Clearing Services) – The payments trade association in the UK.

ATM (Automated Teller Machine) – An electronic device that allows consumers with accounts to perform financial transactions including the withdrawal of cash; generally known as a "hole in the wall" in the U.K.

CA (Certificate Authority) – The organisation, in a PKI, that produces certificates containing digitally-signed public keys bound together with other information. These certificates can then be used to identify transaction parties.

CAP (Chip Authentication Program) - A MasterCard product which authenticates transactions in online and telephone banking. CAP is a MasterCard implementation of 2FA.

CASPIAN (Consumers Against Supermarket Privacy Invasion and Numbering) – A US pressure group against supermarkets tracking consumer spends and RFID technology.

CNP (Card-Not-Present) – A transaction type performed when the card details are provided to the merchant without the merchant having physical contact with the card. Examples include telephone orders, mail orders and orders placed over the Internet.

Consumer Credit Act – UK consumer protection legislation for borrowing money; offences and appeals are handled by the Office of Fair Trading.

CRM (Customer Relationship Management) – Is a business strategy that relies on gathering information from the customers, and is focused on improving profits and customer satisfaction.

CVV (Card Verification Value) – A three or four digit security code printed on the card which is not encoded in the magnetic stripe data; its purpose is to give added protection against fraud.

DDA (Dynamic Data Authentication) – An EMV transaction authentication mechanism that uses public key cryptography for mutual authentication of card and terminal.

Debased – The lowering of the value of a currency, for example by reducing the quantity of the metal that makes up a coin.

DFID (Department for International Development) – A UK government department that manages Britain's aid to poor countries and works to get rid of extreme poverty.

DPA (Dynamic Passcode Authentication) – Visa's implementation of 2FA allowing purchases to be made using a one-time password generated from the card when entered into a pocket sized PED the customer has.

DWP (Department for Work & Pensions) – A UK government department who's goals include helping individuals into employment.

EACHA (European Automated Clearing House Association) – An association of ACHs in Europe who came together to help contribute to SEPA.

EAPS (Euro-Alliance of Payment Schemes) – An alliance between European payment schemes to develop SEPA products.

ECB (European Central Bank) – The central bank in charge of the euro, so far introduced into 15 European Union countries.

EFT (Electronic Funds Transfer) – A method of transferring money electronically direct from one bank account to another.

EMD (Electronic Money Directive) – Provides regulation on the issuance of electronic money. This is superceded by the Payment Systems Directive.

EMV (Europay, MasterCard and Visa) – A standard for Integrated Circuit Cards and their interaction with POS terminals.

ExpressPay (American Express) – An American Express credit and debit card product for contactless payments using RFID technology.

FDCF (Financial Deepening Challenge Fund) – Works to improve access to financial products and services by low-income customers.

FDR (Franklin D Roosevelt) – American President between 1933 and 1945.

Fed (Federal Reserve) – The central banking system of the United States set up based on the Federal Reserve Act.

FPS (Faster Payments Service) – UK initiative backed by APACS to perform transfers at near real time rather than at the current three to seven working days.

FSA (Financial Services Authority) – An independent body regulating the financial services industry in the UK.

GDP (Gross Domestic Product) – A measure of the size of the economy in a specific country. It is the total market value of goods and services produced by a country each year.

Gresham's Law – The theory that "bad" money (possibly debased or in some other way less appealing) is used more than "good" money as the participants in a transaction would rather keep the "good" money for themselves.

GSM (Global System for Mobile communications) – A popular standard for mobile phones, it allows consumers to use their mobiles in foreign countries.

HKMA (Hong Kong Monetary Authority) – It is Hong Kong's central banking institution which ensures the stability of Hong Kong's currency and its banking system.

IBAN (International Bank Account Number) – A standard used internationally to identify bank account numbers in foreign countries.

ICVV (Integrated Card Verification Value) – A card security code to give added protection from fraud specifically for Integrated Circuit Cards. (see CVV)

IM (Instant Messaging) – A computer based real-time communication between two or more people.

IOTP (Internet Open Trading Protocol) – A payment system independent framework designed for business to consumer electronic commerce on the Internet.

IPO (Initial Public Offering) – The first share sales of a company which is being made public.

KYC (Know Your Customer) – Requirements in the form of due diligence and banking regulation applicable to companies dealing with financial transactions. The goal is for them to identify their customer correctly in order to help prevent identity theft fraud, money laundering and terrorist financing.

Law Reform Commission – A commission in Ireland set up under the Law Reform Commission Act 1975 which reviews the law and makes recommendations about its reform.

M0 – The amount of physical money in circulation.

M2 – A broader look at the amount of money in circulation including checking accounts and saving deposits.

MFI (Micro-Finance Institution) – A financial institution that aims to provide sustainable financial services to poor people.

MFS (Mobile Financial Services) – Common Financial services offered through a mobile phone, including P2P money transfers and contactless payment options.

MMORG / MMORPG (Massively Multiplayer Online Role-Playing Game) – A computer role-playing game, based in an online virtual world where large numbers of players can 'meet' and interact with each other to play out scenarios in the game.

Moore's Law – An observation by Gordon E. Moore (Intel co-founder) that the number of transistors in a chip will approximately double every two years.

M-PESA – Safaricom's mobile payment system, used by more than 1.6 million people in Kenya.

MSC (Merchant Service Charge) – The charge paid by merchants to their acquiring bank for using a particular payment mechanism (e.g. Credit Cards)

MVNO (Mobile Virtual Network Operator) – A company providing mobile services without having its own spectrum (radio frequencies).

NFC (Near-Field Communication) – Wireless communication technology which allows data to be exchanged between two devices within a certain proximity to each other.

NYCE Payments Network – US electronic payments network connecting financial institutions with ATMs and POS.

OFT (Office of Fair Trading) – A UK government department that enforces consumer protection and competition law, it is in effect the UK's economic regulator.

Octopus card – A widely used contactless payment card system originally for public transport in Hong Kong which has now grown to include shops, fast-food restaurants and various POS stations.

Oyster card – A contactless payment card used singularly for train and bus tickets in the Greater London area of the UK.

P&L (Profit and Loss) – Statement summarising revenue, costs and expenses usually for a financial year.

P2P (Person-to-Person) – A financial transaction occurring directly between two people.

PAN (Primary Account Number) – A unique number that a card has that identifies the cardholder and the type of financial account the card is connected to.

PASMO – Japanese transport card for use on buses and trains. It is a rechargeable ticket.

PayPass (MasterCard) – The MasterCard brand for the contactless interface to their payment products.

PayWave (Visa) – The Visa brand for the contactless interface to their payment products.

PCI-DSS (Payment Card Industry – Data Security Standards) – A set of standards designed to help organisations protect customer account data.

PED (PIN Entry Device) – A device that requires the user to enter a valid PIN before performing its main function; it is usually a device meant for financial transactions either an ATM or a POS terminal, where the PIN would be part of the authorization process.

PIN (Personal Identification Number) – Usually a four digit number chosen by the user for authorization purposes when they try to access their account. The PIN is known only to the user and the system to allow a way for a machine to identify a valid account/card holder.

PKI (Public Key Infrastructure) – A particular architecture for using asymmetric cryptography in a mass market, allowing counterparties to communicate securely without prior trust.

POS (Point-of-sale or Point-of-service) – It can refer to a variety of definitions including the location of the retail establishment, or the specific counter, however it also could mean the hardware and software of the device used for the money transfer or (most often in this book) the terminal where the transaction occurred.

PSD (Payment Services Directive) – Provides the legal standards for a single payment area in Europe where individuals and businesses can make cross-border payments easily. A critical part of the plans for SEPA to be successful.

QSR (Quick-Serve Retail) – Refers to retail establishments like newsagents, transport ticket booths, fast-food restaurants and parking meters where the possibility for a faster payment process between the vendor and the customer is available. Usually these are locations where the contactless payment market is developing.

REAL ID – Refers to the US REAL ID Act of 2005, where valid documents for identification must be presented; the identification must have met specific security and authentication standards to be valid. The Act requires people who enter federal buildings, board planes or opens bank accounts to provide a valid ID.

RFID (Radio Frequency Identification) – Usually in the form of a tag which can be imbedded into products, the tag contains a microchip and an antenna. The chip stores information which can be retrieved when a reader device is waved over the antenna of the tag.

RMT (Real Money Trade) – Is the trade of virtual money and assets in virtual worlds, which can then be transferred into the real world as real money. The virtual worlds are mostly for recreation, however due to the RMT some players purposely create businesses in the online worlds as a way to make money.

ROI (Return-on-investment) – Is an equation for the profits returned from an investment made after the costs have been subtracted. The calculation can also be used to find the efficiency of the investment.

Sarbanes-Oxley Act 2002 – A US law which introduced improvements to existing legislation as well as new legislation into financial practices and corporate governance.

SCT (SEPA Credit Transfer) – A payment scheme which works between SEPA countries in which payment is made within three working days.

SDA (Static Data Authentication) – An EMV transaction authentication mechanism that uses symmetric cryptography for mutual authentication of card and online terminals.

SEC (US Securities and Exchange Commission) – Administers federal securities laws in the US.

Seigniorage – The money gained from the issuing of currency; the cost of producing, distributing and retrieving the coin/note subtracted from the actual worth of the coin/note. An important form of income for many central banks.

SEK – currency code for the Swedish Krona.

SEPA (Single European Payment Area) – A self-regulatory harmonisation project being introduced across the European payments market by banks with support from the European Commission (EC) and the European Central Bank (ECB). The SEPA initiative will encompass new, standard business and technical frameworks to make cross-border payments with the eurozone the same as domestic payments. The SEPA Credit Transfer went live in January 2008.

SET (Secure Electronic Transactions) – Created jointly by MasterCard and Visa, it is a standard for protecting the privacy, and authenticity of electronic transactions so that vendors and consumers can ensure that online financial transactions are authentic with privacy guaranteed.

SIM (Subscriber Identity Module) – Is part of a removable integrated circuit card for mobile phones, the SIM cards securely store the keys necessary to identify the subscriber.

SMS (Short Message Service) – A text based communication protocol between two mobile phones. The key issue for this communication type is that only short messages can be sent, it therefore more commonly known as a 'text message'.

SSL (Secure Socket Layer) – An encrypted connection made between two computers used in particular for secure interactions with web servers over the Internet. Requires the server (and optionally the client) to have a certificate issued by a trusted Certificate Authority. (see PKI)

Tube – Alternative name for the London Underground Rail Network.

WoW (World of Warcraft) – A MMORG created by Blizzard Entertainment, where players interact with each other in a fantasy virtual world called Azeroth.

Index

2
2FA, 31, 57, 106

3
3D Secure, 56, 57, 154, 155, 156, 175, 194

A
ACH, 30, 31, 50, 88, 89, 175
Adam Laurie, 188
Adam Smith, 83
Adil Moussa, 123
Akio Shiibashi, 15
Alex Salmond, 78
Alfredo Padilla, 68
alternative payments, 108, 153
American Express, 36, 40, 41, 55, 76, 123, 188, 189
  ExpressPay, 36, 188
AML, 65, 161, 162, 163
Aneace Haddad, 69, 85, 91, 109, 128, 176
Angela Knight, 142
anonymity, 33, 149
Anthony Pickup, 177, 179, 181
anti-fraud, 154, 173, 187
anti-money laundering. *See* AML
APACS, 90, 121, 147, 187, 189, 195, 196
Apple, 144, 184
ATM, 34, 51, 53, 60, 66, 73, 75, 82, 133, 134, 135, 141, 142, 150, 179, 185, 186, 195, 196

authentication, 16, 17, 23, 31, 39, 52, 53, 57, 63, 88, 106, 156, 176, 179, 182
authorise, 51, 77, 89
automated clearing house. *See* ACH
automated teller machine. *See* ATM
Avivah Litan, 183

B
BancoPosta, 65
Bank Machine Limited, 34, 39, 60
banking
  future of, 98
banks
  acts, 200
  Alliance & Leicester, 61
  bank account, 61, 64, 65, 69, 75, 80, 88, 97, 110, 111, 113, 171, 186
  Bank of America, 87, 141, 166
  Bank of England, 77, 78, 79, 83, 139, 142, 159, 181, 200
  Bank of Finland, 72
  Bank of Japan, 97, 129, 149
  Bank of Mozambique, 137
  Bank of Scotland, 79
  Bank of Sweden, 137
  banking licences, 98, 192
  Banking Ordinance, 202
  banknotes, 77, 78, 79, 83, 150, 173, 181
  Barclays, 21, 23, 27, 28, 40, 43, 53, 57, 66, 106, 133, 141, 166, 167, 176, 179, 185
  Belgian Central bank, 158
  central bank, 56, 77, 97, 135, 136, 139, 157
  Chinese central bank, 119

Chongqing Commercial Bank, 20
Citibank, 41, 51, 52, 119, 166, 182
Comerica Bank, 80
Commerzbank, 90
cost of, 162
Deutsche Bank, 90, 164
Dresdner Bank, 90
Dutch Central Bank, 134, 158
European Central Bank, 144, 158, 159, 160, 161, 162
Federal Reserve Bank, 150
Garanti Bank, 21, 22
HSBC, 123
ICICI Bank, 71
ING, 90
Lloyds TSB, 66, 165
MBNA, 123
Mitsubishi-Tokyo-UFJ Bank, 115
National Irish Bank, 144, 145
Newports Bank, 203
Northern Rock, 78, 105, 142, 169
Norwegian Central Bank, 160
Rabobank, 90
Reserve Bank of India, 111
Reserve Bank of New Zealand, 183
Royal Bank of Scotland, 21, 23, 25, 27, 28, 60, 78, 79, 123, 168, 176, 182
Société Générale, 90
Standard Chartered Bank, 115
State Bank of India, 111
Swedish Central Bank, 43, 135
The British Linen Bank, 79
The World Bank, 118
Unicredito, 90
Barclaycard, 14, 36, 40, 57, 61, 122, 166, 189
Basel II, 169
BBC, 9, 38, 40, 50, 83, 132, 133, 184, 189, 191
Ben Steil, 120

Bernard Lietaer, 193, 198
Bill Gates, 100
Bill Me Later, 84
biometric, 50, 51, 52, 53, 54, 89, 108, 109, 194
bitWallet, 15, 128, 129
Blackhawk Network, 61
Bluetooth, 27, 55
Bob Egan, 16
Bouygues, 17
BRC, 82, 147, 148
Brian Aldiss, 56
British Pound, 39, 66, 135, 202, 203
British Retail Consortium. *See* BRC
Britney Spears, 49
Bruce Cundiff, 89
BT, 25, 80, 113
business models, 24, 25, 27, 28, 82, 84, 101, 108, 110
Business Week, 70

C

Capital One, 30, 90, 158
car parking, 146
Card Authentication Programme. *See* MasterCard:*CAP*
Card Technology, 14, 15, 20
card verification value. *See* CVV
card verification value for integrated circuit cards. *See* ICVV
CardForum.com, 76
card-not-present. *See* CNP
Carl Belgrove, 165
Carol Coye Benson, 30
cash
    cashback, 82, 83, 110, 153, 196
    cost of, 46, 72, 87, 130, 160

machine. *See* ATM
usage, 147, 150, 160
CASPIAN, 32
Cathleen Conforti, 146
CCTV, 17, 186
Center for Financial Services Innovation, 80
Centre for European Reform, 167
Centre for the Study of Financial Innovation. *See* CSFI
c-*gold*, 119, 120
Charles Bronson, 42
check. *See* cheque
cheque, 52, 73, 74, 80, 97, 120, 121, 136, 143, 144, 175, 178
   cost of, 74
   pension, 143
chip and PIN, 36, 112, 132, 153, 172, 173, 177, 178, 179, 185, 189
Chipknip, 91, 92
Chris Black, 23
Chris Leather, 203
Chris Pickles, 135
Chris Skinner, 105, 149, 154, 161
Christine Farnish, 170
Christopher Fildes, 202
Cilla Black, 199
Clay Shirky, 101
Clayton Christensen, 39, 84, 110
CNET News.com, 188
CNP, 54, 109, 154, 155, 175, 183, 185, 194, 195
Congressman Pettengil, 198
Consult Hyperion, 9, 28, 69, 122, 180
Consumer Credit Act, 91, 164
contactless
   interface, 15, 41, 42, 48, 63, 127, 129, 181, 188
   payment cards, 41, 53, 108, 145, 188
   payment technology, 21, 22, 41
   payments, 21, 33, 37, 44, 91, 127, 139, 140, 145, 177
   card, 34
credit cards
   figures, 26, 45, 61, 66, 67, 73, 90, 99, 100, 104, 122, 127, 136, 147, 174, 183
   future of, 40, 55
CRM, 13, 53
cross-border, 135, 160, 168, 169
   money transfers, 93
   transactions, 90, 155
cryptography, 58, 89, 187
CSFI, 9, 113, 124
Customer Relationship Management. *See* CRM
CVV, 42, 103, 177, 189
   ICVV, 190
CyberCash, 101
Cybercoins, 104

D

Daily Mail, 62, 63
Dan Schatt, 81
Dan Speed, 99
Datamonitor, 34, 147
David Boyle, 124
David Edgerton, 50
David Grooms, 36
David Nordell, 153
David Sarnoff, 26
David Shirreff, 167
DCMX, 18, 127, 128
   DCMX GOLD, 15
DDA, 187
Dean Acheson, 198
debased, 203

debit cards
  figures, 34, 61, 66, 90, 136, 148, 159, 175
Deloitte, 24, 25, 26, 27, 46, 84
Denzil Lawson, 86
Department for International Development, 64
Department for Work & Pensions, 143
Deutsche Bahn, 16
Dexit, 20
DGC, 119, 138
DigiCash, 101, 104
digital identity, 23, 182
Digital Identity Forum, 51, 54, 176
digital money, 23, 26, 33, 35, 48, 82, 96, 110, 112, 118, 119, 127, 133, 143, 157, 174, 191, 192
Digital Money Forum, 101, 111, 112, 122, 125, 168, 183, 193
Digital Transactions, 154
Digital Transactions News, 45
digital wallets, 28
Direct Express, 80
Discover, 16, 123
DoCoMo, 14, 15, 18, 46, 57, 81, 82, 84, 127, 128, 129
Docutel, 134
Dollar. *See* US Dollar
Dominic Peachey, 163
Don Wetzel, 134
Douglas Jackson, 112
Douglas Roberts, 121
Duncan Martin, 22
dynamic data authentication. *See* DDA
Dynamic Passcode Authentication. *See* Visa:*DPA*

E

e-
  e-barter, 35
  e-bill, 73, 103, 143, 166
  e-card, 49
  e-cash, 14, 102, 112, 128, 133, 153, 161, 174, 200
  e-cheque, 84
  e-commerce, 14, 61, 84, 100, 129, 130, 163, 194
  e-crime, 182
  e-Dinar, 119
  e-finance, 119
  e-gold, 79, 112, 119
  e-invoicing, 164
  e-mail, 13, 16, 28, 52, 97, 166, 174, 182
  e-money, 15, 16, 18, 19, 24, 96, 97, 127, 138, 144, 149, 161, 181, 193
    Japanese market, 96
  e-payment, 14, 15, 72, 80, 81, 84, 110, 112, 116, 135, 136, 139, 148, 149, 155, 157, 162, 166, 171, 174, 175, 193, 194
  e-purse, 14, 15, 20, 48, 50, 91, 127, 128, 129, 158, 161
  e-statement, 166
EACHA, 73
EAPS, 90, 163
eBay, 25, 94, 103, 115, 122, 123, 124, 138, 198
eCheck, 66
Economist.com, 78
Ed Balls, 142
Edward Castronova, 94
Edward de Bono, 124
Edy, 15, 18, 48, 96, 127, 128, 129
E-Finance & Payments Law and Policy Journal, 9
EFT, 121, 201
electronic funds transfer. *See* EFT

Electronic Money Directive, 157
Elizabeth Chambers, 36
emergency currencies, 199
EMV, 21, 34, 40, 49, 55, 58, 85, 140, 176, 181, 189, 190, 194, 195
Entropia Universe, 105
ePort, 45
Ericson Chan, 115
Eros, 140
EU Council, 155
euro, 39, 66, 124, 135, 138, 157, 161, 167, 199
Euro-Alliance of Payment Schemes. *See* EAPS
European Automated Clearing House Association. *See* EACHA
European Commission, 72, 98, 162
European Directive on Electronic Money Issuing, 95
European Parliament, 155, 162
eurozone, 159, 160, 162, 164
EVE Online, 98, 99
Evening Advertiser, 141
Evening Standard, 38, 140, 141
EverQuest II, 94
exchange controls, 199, 200

F

Facebook, 66, 67
Faithfone, 63
faster payment service. *See* FPS
Fed. *See* Federal Reserve
Federal Reserve, 19, 68, 75, 100, 120, 129, 150, 166, 183, 198
Feed Tribes, 12
FeliCa, 18, 48, 57

fiat currency, 192, 197, 199
FinanceTech, 45
Financial Deepening Challenge Fund, 64
Financial Services Authority. *See* FSA
Financial Times, 98, 102, 120, 200
Financial World, 9
FinanSer, 105, 149
Finextra, 57, 104
First Virtual Holdings, 101
Foreign Affairs, 120
foreign currency, 75, 112, 187, 199
FPS, 88
framework, 73, 122
  legal, 160
  regulatory, 162, 168, 169
Franklin D. Roosevelt, 197
FSA, 104, 163
FT.com, 105

G

GBP. *See* British Pound
G-Cash, 122
GDP, 118, 158, 159
George Chastain, 134
Gertrude Tumpel-Gugerell, 160
Get Safe Online, 154
Glenbrook Partners, 30, 33
Google, 66, 84, 124, 130
Google AdWords, 84
Google Checkout, 66, 84
Gordon Brown, 105
Gottlieb Daimler, 24
Gresham's Law, 35
GSM, 153, 194
GSMA, 22, 25, 62, 110, 122, 153

H

Hannes van Rensburg, 13
Harry Leinonen, 72
Harvard Business Review, 110
Heat magazine, 50
Her Majesties Revenue and Customs, 199
Hideo Kumano, 97
HKMA, 201
home banking, 49, 52, 57, 188
Home Office, 177
Hong Kong Monetary Authority, 201, *See* HKMA
House of Commons Justice Committee, 184

I

IBAN, 178, 204
ICVV, 189, *See also* CVV
iD, 15, 18
IDATE, 156
identity, 17, 31, 53, 106, 161
   identity card, 31, 84, 89
   identity theft, 32, 41, 150, 154, 178
IM, 15, 119
ING, 105
innovation, 24, 40, 49, 53, 70, 77, 78, 79, 84, 85, 87, 88, 91, 100, 104, 110, 118, 169
instant messaging. *See* IM
interchange fees, 44, 83
international bank account number. *See* IBAN
Internet, 13, 83, 89, 101, 109, 153, 155
   access, 13, 51, 67
   banking, 13, 70, 116, 117, 143, 176
   Internet Open Trading Protocol, 88, 167
   payments, 73

purchasing, 48, 56, 62, 88, 129, 156, 175, 194
surfing, 16
interoperability, 21, 73, 127, 167
iPhone, 144, 184
IPO, 99
iTunes, 65, 101

J

James Gardeners, 70
James Goodfellow, 134
Jason Schripsema, 99
JCB, 15, 18, 52
Jérôme Sion, 167
Joanna Weston, 97
John Chaplin, 87
John Galt Games, 99
John Maynard Keynes, 132
John Philip Coghlan, 16
John Shepherd-Baron, 133
John Smedley, 95, 106
Journal of Internet, 9

K

Kevin Duffey, 14
Kevin Gallen, 144
Kevin Hawkins, 147
know your customer. *See* KYC
KushCash, 13
KYC, 65, 161

L

Law Reform Commission, 145
Lawrence White, 79
legal tender, 145, 183, 184, 193
Lego, 70, 118
Leo van Hove, 48, 144, 156
Linkdump on Payments, 92, 130, 135, 161
Liz McIntyre, 32

Lord Hope, 165
Louise Brett, 24
low-value, 21, 34, 35, 46, 91, 140, 148, 164
loyalty scheme, 31, 50, 89, 109, 110, 131, 166

M

m-. *See* mobile
M0, 139, 150
M2, 139
Maestro, 62, 76, 91, 160
Marco Behrmann, 105
Marina O'Rourke, 19
MasterCard, 15, 16, 23, 34, 36, 38, 41, 45, 52, 56, 57, 61, 65, 69, 75, 82, 83, 86, 90, 98, 99, 103, 111, 116, 123, 146, 153, 156, 167, 176
   CAP, 57, 176
   MasterCard SecureCode, 156
   PayPass, 21, 34, 36, 38, 40, 45, 65, 146
McDonald's, 36, 39, 81
Mehmet Seazgin, 22
Merchant Payments Coalition, 83
merchant service charge. *See* MSC
Mervyn King, 139, 142
Michael Linton, 193
Micro Tag, 40
microfinance, 51, 113, 122
micropayments, 101
MicroPlace, 122
Microsoft, 70, 100, 118
Mike Bond, 187
Mister Cash, 91
MMORG, 93
mobile
   banking, 13, 23, 64, 113, 115, 116, 117

mobile financial service, 113, 114
operators, 16, 22, 23, 25, 27, 28, 53, 111, 115, 122, 128, 140, 167, 193
payments, 12, 16, 18, 19, 23, 28, 36, 44, 54, 73, 81, 109, 113, 117, 122, 123, 133, 145, 149, 174, 194, 197
mobile virtual network operator. *See* MVNO
Mondex, 14, 24, 43, 48, 69, 141
MoneyCard, 68, 76, 98
MoneyPak, 103
MoniLink, 14
Monopoly, 197, 199
Monster Raving Loony Party, 39, 64, 135
Moore's Law, 132, 148
Motley Fool, 128
M-PESA, 28, 64, 111, 117, 121, 122, 149
Mr Jamieson, 152
MSC, 30, 33, 82, 92, 133, 141, 165
MVNO, 14, 116
MySpace, 182

N

nanaco, 15, 18, 128
Nationwide Building Society, 57, 179, 190
near-field communication. *See* NFC
Neil McEvoy, 120
Netbanker, 116
New York Times, 41, 55
NFC, 14, 16, 17, 19, 20, 21, 22, 23, 25, 26, 36, 45, 108, 110, 116, 121, 167
Niall Ferguson, 79
Nick Holland, 29, 45
Nick Hughes, 117

Nick McBride, 183
Nick Mourant, 82
Nick Szabo, 190
NorthJersey.com, 196
NYCE Payments Network, 146

O

O2, 23, 29
Octopus, 141, 149, 201, 202
Office of Fair Trading. *See* OFT
OFT, 74, 148
Oliver Steeley, 38
OnePulse, 21, 36, 40, 43, 46, 53, 57, 141
Oyster, 27, 36, 37, 40, 141

P

P&L, 168, 169, 203
P2P, 27, 55
   payments, 74, 121
   transfers, 28, 36, 114, 117, 153
Paleo Future, 55
Pam Zuercher, 16
PAN, 41, 42, 177, 181, 188, 189
pan-European, 72, 88, 90, 164, 168, 169
Parliamentary IT Review, 9
PASMO, 18, 128
passport, 61, 64, 65, 66, 163, 199
Paul Geedes, 27
Paul Johnson, 202
PavingWays, 29
Pay By Touch, 50, 51, 53, 54
Pay-Buy Mobile, 22
Payez Mobile, 167
Payforit, 28, 91

Payment Card Industry Data Security Standards. *See* PCI-DSS
Payment developments, 72
Payment Services Directive, 155, *See* PSD
Payment Systems Europe. *See* PSE
payments
   card, 25, 60, 86, 103, 153, 157, 185, 194, 197
   card industry, 84, 154, 194
   cash alternatives, 103
   cost of, 98, 135
   fraud, 175, 176
   future of, 55, 56, 92, 135
   industry, 82, 84, 162
   instruments, 44, 56, 85, 89, 130, 136, 137, 155, 157, 158, 159, 160, 163, 164
   processing, 84, 157
Payments News, 30, 66, 81, 108, 113, 140
Payout Service, 97
PayPal, 25, 52, 66, 84, 103, 114, 121, 123, 125, 173
PCI-DSS, 183
PED, 58
Peerflix, 35
PEP, 162
Peppercoin, 101
personal identification number. *See* PIN
person-to-person. *See* P2P
Peter Ayliffe, 82
Peter Jones, 163
Philip Orbanes, 199
phishing, 106, 156, 173, 176, 182
Pierre Boces, 163
PIN, 12, 36, 39, 50, 58, 63, 134, 153, 172, 173, 178, 187, 189
PIN entry device. *See* PED

PKI, 23
PlayNoEvil, 94, 118
PlayStation 3, 48, 129
Poh Mui Hoon, 91
point-of-sale. *See* POS
Politically Exposed Person. *See* PEP
POS, 12, 24, 28, 30, 44, 45, 52, 63, 85, 88, 91, 110, 141, 190
Post Office, 26, 66, 75, 97, 98, 173
Pound Sterling. *See* British Pound
Pragati, 51
prepaid, 61, 65, 68, 69, 74, 75, 76, 80, 98, 105, 114, 131, 148, 152, 163, 199
Prezzy Card, 152, 153
primary account number. *See* PAN
Privredna Banka Zagreb, 176
profit and loss. *See* P&L
Project Entropia, 98, 105, 192
Prospect, 9
Prudence Chan Bik-wah, 201
PSD, 88, 155, 157, 169
PSE, 163
public key infrastructure. *See* PKI

Q

QQ, 118, 119, 123, 124
quick-serve retail, 37
QUICPay, 15, 19

R

Rachel Ehrenfeld, 153
radio-frequency identification. *See* RFID
REAL ID, 31, 89, 98
real-money trades. *See* RMT

Remote Check Deposit, 52
retail banking
 future of, 167
retail payments, 54, 71, 72, 74, 81, 82, 84, 88, 92, 128, 148, 155, 157
return-on-investments. *See* ROI
rewards, 83, 109, 110
RFID, 41, 42, 54, 57, 177
Richard Allen, 75, 179, 180
risk analysis, 32, 37, 169, 171, 187
risk management, 169
RMT, 94, 118, 119
Rob Balgley, 33
Robert J. Samuelson, 150
ROI, 24, 27, 145, 147
Ron Delnevo, 35, 39
Ronnie O'Toole, 145

S

S! Town, 96
Sandra Quinn, 189, 196
Sarbanes-Oxley, 98
scrip, 198, 199
SCT, 56, 124
SDA, 187, 204
Second Life, 104, 105, 192
Second Sight, 9
Secure Electronic Transactions. *See* SET
secure sockets layer. *See* SSL
security, 32, 37, 38, 41, 153, 156, 172, 173, 174, 176, 178, 182, 184, 187, 188, 189, 195
seigniorage, 78, 140, 159, 200
SEK, 137
Senator Carl Levin, 67
SEPA, 30, 72, 88, 124, 135, 137, 155, 157, 161, 163, 169

SEPA Credit Transfer. *See*
    SCT
SET, 104, 194
Shakira, 50
short message service. *See* SMS
SIM, 14, 16, 17, 22, 28, 55,
    110, 111, 116, 122
Simpay, 26
single currency, 119, 135
Single European Payments
    Area. *See* SEPA
Sir William Preece, 26
smart card, 18, 19, 49, 51, 57,
    104, 112, 176, 188, 194
Smartplus, 19
SMS, 12, 13, 29, 77, 108
Snap Cafe, 183
social cost, 44, 87, 149, 157,
    158, 160
Softbank, 129
Sony, 18, 48, 57, 94, 95, 106
Spectator, 202
SPEED, 9, 72
SSL, 50, 156
static data authentication. *See*
    SDA
Steve Mott, 41, 153
Steve Rathgaber, 146
Steve Verdier, 76
sub-prime, 56, 68, 69
subscriber identity module. *See*
    SIM
Suica, 15, 18, 96, 128, 129
Sun, 40, 75, 76
Sunil Bharti Mittal, 111

T

Techdirt, 35, 184
TechRadar.com, 57
telco, 14, 17, 20, 82
Telegraph, 142, 171, 178
Terror Finance Blog, 153, 174

Tesco, 60, 82, 98, 124
The Boston Globe, 150
The Economist, 77, 117, 167,
    173
The Guardian, 9, 60, 185, 191
The Payments Council, 74
ticket, 16, 23, 28, 57, 87, 121,
    127, 132
TIME magazine, 25
Times, 28, 101
Tom Alexander, 14
Tom Barnes, 134
Touch & Travel, 16
transaction costs, 33, 60, 98,
    111, 147, 149, 161
transaction fees, 26, 29, 44, 71,
    84, 111, 117, 136, 137
Transport for London, 23, 141
Treasury, 74, 78, 80, 142, 159,
    184, 197, 198, 200
Trevor Pavey, 145
Trey Ratcliff, 99
Tube, 37, 46
two-factor authentication. *See*
    2FA

U

UKP. *See* British Pound
universal serial bus. *See* USB
University
    Chinese University of Hong
        Kong, 201
    University Of Leicester, 203
    University of Massachusetts,
        177
    University of Zurich, 193
US Dollar, 105, 138
US Securities and Exchange
    Commission, 98
USB, 17, 48, 57
USD. *See* US Dollar

V

Victor Miguel, 137
virtual
   assets, 94, 96, 118
   banking, 104, 107
   currencies, 95, 105, 106, 119, 123
   economy, 93, 96
   environments, 60, 105
   identity, 23
   payments, 104, 123
   transactions, 63
   worlds, 60, 93, 94, 96, 97, 98, 105, 106, 107, 118, 191, 192
Visa, 15, 16, 24, 52, 53, 57, 61, 65, 68, 69, 76, 82, 83, 85, 87, 90, 98, 99, 103, 123, 128, 133, 148, 152, 156, 167, 176
   DPA, 57, 176
   Verified by Visa, 156
   Visa Electron, 65
   Visa PayWave, 57, 140
   Visa ReadyLink, 61
   Visa Swap, 166
   Visa Touch, 19
   VisaCash, 14, 43, 104
VocaLink, 58, 72, 142, 155
Vodafone, 16, 28, 29, 111, 116, 117, 122

W

Wall Street Journal, 32, 42, 80, 119, 162
wallet phone, 16, 17, 127, 128
Wal-Mart, 67, 68, 76, 84, 98, 103, 113
washingtonpost.com, 150
WebMoney Transfer, 138
Wells Fargo, 19, 166
What Japan Thinks, 19
Wired magazine, 24
Wise Marketer, 109
World of Warcraft, 52, 106, 153, 192, 199
World Online Gambling Law, 162

Y

Yiping Huang, 119
YouGov, 34

Z

ZigBee, 54, 55